# Strategies for Teaching Self-Discipline in the Middle Grades

# Strategies for Teaching Self-Discipline in the Middle Grades

Charles H. Wolfgang
*Florida State University*

Betty J. Bennett
*University of North Florida*

Judith L. Irvin
*Florida State University*

**Allyn and Bacon**

**Boston London Toronto Sydney Tokyo Singapore**

*Vice president and editor-in-chief:* Sean W. Wakely
*Series editorial assistant:* Jessica Barnard

**Library of Congress Cataloging-in-Publication Data**

Wolfgang, Charles H.
    Strategies for teaching self-discipline in the middle grades /
Charles H. Wolfgang, Betty J. Bennett, Judith L. Irvin.
       p.  cm.
    Includes bibliographical references (p.  ) and index.
    ISBN 0-205-27329-7
    1. Classroom management.   2. Junior high school students--
Discipline.   3. Self-control--Study and teaching (Middle school)
I. Bennett, Betty J.   II. Irvin, Judith L.   III. Title.
LB3013.W65   1999
371.5--dc21
                                  98-30674
                                    CIP

Printed in the United States of America
10  9  8  7  6  5  4  3  2  1    03  02  01  00  99

# Contents

## SECTION IV
## The Incentive System    161

## SECTION V
## The Encouragement System    185

## SECTION VI
## The Management System    217

# Preface

*Strategies for Teaching Self-Discipline in the Middle Grades* is for teachers, administrators, and parents who work with middle grade students in a classroom setting.* Becoming self-disciplined is an important developmental task of early adolescence. Ideally, discipline is taught within the context of a loving and supportive home. As educators, it is our responsibility to provide a structured and nurturing environment. The purpose of this book is to help educators implement a system of classroom management and discipline that will ultimately help students become self-disciplined.

The *Three Faces of Discipline* construct helps teachers analyze their own philosophy of discipline and understand how to create and maintain an orderly, predictable, and caring climate for young adolescents. The Teacher Behavior Continuum illustrates the degree of power necessary to orchestrate effective discipline practices in a middle-level school. This book was written with a thorough understanding of the discipline theory within a context of the developmental tasks of early adolescence. It is our hope that *Strategies for Teaching Self-Discipline in the Middle Grades* will serve as a guide to those educators interested in creating a developmentally appropriate environment that maximizes learning for young adolescents.

*For those interested in kindergarten or preschool age, please read *The Three Faces of Discipline for Young Children* and *School for Young Children,* both written by Charles H. Wolfgang and Mary E. Wolfgang and published by Allyn and Bacon.

# Strategies for
# Teaching Self-Discipline
# in the Middle Grades

# Introduction

In the first few days of the new school year, you quickly learn that one of the students in your class (let's call him or her Pat) is going to challenge your skills as a teacher and as a disciplinarian. To put it more bluntly, if less professionally, you sense that this student is going to drive you nuts this year. When fellow teachers see your class roster, they quickly exclaim, "Oh, no, you got Pat! Better you than me! Good luck!" This student destroys others' property, fights, uses profanity to the extent that parents and classmates complain, and engages in a host of other misbehaviors that require you to deal with him repeatedly, sapping your energy. The bus driver, cafeteria workers, janitor, and other teachers begin a barrage of complaints about Pat, and they expect you to do something about him. Many lessons are routinely disrupted by Pat, and you begin to get the terrible feeling that Pat is out to get you. It is as if this difficult student deliberately sets "fires" that you are forced to put out, taking up far too much of your teaching time and ruining the pacing and continuity of the school day.

Other students are stimulated by Pat's misbehavior as they watch his actions, and they are beginning to attempt similar activities to see if they can get away with it, in a disruptive game of "monkey see, monkey do." Sending Pat to the principal's office does not seem to help. Although the principal tries to put the "fear of God" into him by figuratively talking his ears off, three minutes after returning from the office, Pat is up to his old tricks. In fact, he seems to look forward to those "discipline" trips.

You feel all alone in your classroom. Fellow teachers and school administrators are busy with their own tasks. You seem to be locked in your "classroom-cave" with 25 to 40 students who are beginning to challenge your authority, with Pat leading the charge by throwing "hand grenades" into your daily classroom routine. You also begin to have the feeling that you are no longer in control of your classroom; depression and a feeling of "battle fatigue" are quickly setting in, and you are becoming concerned that your professional evaluations might suffer. September is not even over yet, and you are already thinking about the end of the school year. You have no idea how to regain control of your classroom and deal effectively with Pat.

## DISCIPLINE MODELS

Many discipline approaches, or models, are available for teachers to use with misbehaving students such as Pat. Few proposed discipline methods or models, however, deal specifically with the unique needs of young adolescents, even though most teachers who work with students of middle school age usually feel that, in reference to classroom discipline, this particular age group is the most difficult group. Perhaps this lack of a specific middle school model is partially due to the fact that there is no single model of the "all-American young adolescent" because of the vast physical, emotional, social, and cognitive differences among them. It is important for the middle school educator to be knowledgeable about these differences so that he or she can consider them when deciding on a method of discipline intervention.

Most of the existing models (among them T.E.T., Value Clarification, Magic Circle, Reality Therapy, Control Theory, Behavior Analysis, Positive Discipline, and Assertive Discipline) claim to have the "right" way to discipline. They seem to be saying, "Follow my system and I will lead you to the blissful Promised Land of educational heaven, a world of perfectly disciplined classrooms populated by happy, cooperative students." All models provide some good ideas, most of them based to varying degrees on psychological theory. Each has a fairly narrow and differing view of what motivates children and their misbehavior, and each prescribes various techniques for dealing with a misbehaving student. Some models rely on very light requests of the student, while others make clear demands to stop misbehavior; some use strong controlling actions to extinguish the misbehavior, while others suggest methods of dealing with violent-assaultive acts directed at the teacher.

These models progress along a continuum from minimum to maximum use of teacher power. The continuum of misbehavior can be placed side by side with the continuum or pathway of discipline models with regard to the power these techniques give teachers and administrators. Some models may be effective with some students, but totally ineffective with the very difficult Pats of this world. The *Three Faces of Discipline* position is that no one model can work successfully for all students at all times, nor will the same model always succeed for the same student as he or she experiences different stimuli and exhibits different kinds of misbehavior. In fact, most teachers do not use the same techniques with all students. Some students who are "out of line" need only to be looked at; an eye-to-eye signal is enough to stop their misbehavior. With others, more confrontation is necessary, along with some discussion of how they can get "back in line." With still others, such as Pat, very strong intervention actions become necessary, using various forms of encouragement or punishment. Based on a host of variables, teachers change their "face."

In the real world of Monday morning in the classroom with Pat, teachers are rarely discipline purists—one who uses Assertive Discipline and only Assertive Discipline, or Glasser's Reality Therapy and only Glasser. More likely, teachers use many of the techniques from generally one model, but with his or her own "spin" on the techniques. Teachers add other techniques previously learned and tested—techniques individual teachers determine are successful for them.

All of the various discipline models in vogue have some strengths and some limitations. As authors of this book, our approach is to take the best from each of these models and present a system based on a continuum of power and control. The teacher must be the judge of which technique is most appropriate for the situation.

Understanding of the term *discipline* is an essential beginning. *Discipline* is the required action by a teacher or school official toward a student (or group of students) after his or her (or their) behavior disrupts the ongoing educational activity or breaks a preestablished rule or law created by the teacher, the school administration, or general society. The educator's actions may fall into three broad categories of response:

- Relationship-Listening (a therapeutic process)

- Confronting-Contracting (an educational and counseling process)

- Rules and Consequences (a controlling process)

These three processes combine to constitute the *Three Faces of Discipline* and may be placed on a power continuum from minimum to maximum use of a pathway of power. The continuum reflects the level of autonomy and control given to the student to change his or her own behavior or the aversive actions used by the teacher or school officials to get the desired change in student behavior and reestablish order and safety in the educational setting. Following is a list, based on a continuum of power, of classic discipline models. These models—based on varying degrees of psychological theory and, to a lesser extent, research-supported knowledge—serve as the knowledge base of practical techniques and skills needed to handle the wide variety of discipline situations the educators will face in today's schools.

In Chapter 1, a quick and minor discipline incident is presented and how the teacher escalates his or her use of power across a continuum use of power is demonstrated. The general categories of behavior used by the teacher are placed along a power continuum, called the Teacher Behavior Continuum. This continuum, or TBC, provides a construct that can be used to demonstrate the power inherent in the teacher techniques and actions eclectically drawn from the models listed in the chart. In essence, the TBC is a "power pathway" on which all of the techniques from various discipline models are arranged so the teacher can clearly see the specific and concrete steps suggested by each model as he or she faces another Monday morning with Pat. Using the Three Faces of Discipline, the teacher will learn how to develop a path-

| Classic Discipline Models | | |
|---|---|---|
| ← | **TEACHER'S POWER** | → |
| **MINIMUM POWER** | | **MAXIMUM POWER** |
| **RELATIONSHIP-LISTENING FACE** | **CONFRONTING-CONTRACTING FACE** | **RULES AND CONSEQUENCES FACE** |
| • *T.E.T.: Teacher Effectiveness Training* (Gordon, 1974)<br>• *Teaching Children Self-Discipline: At Home and at School* (Gordon, 1989)<br>• *I'm OK—You're OK: A Practical Guide to Transactional Analysis* (Harris, 1969)<br>• *Values and Teaching* (Raths, Harmin, & Simon, 1966)<br>• *Human Development Program* (The Magic Circle) (Bessell, 1976)<br>• *Grounds for Growth: The Human Development Program's Comprehensive Theory* (Palomares & Ball, 1980) | • *Discipline Without Tears* (Dreikurs & Cassel, 1972)<br>• *A Teacher's Guide to Cooperative Discipline: How to Manage Your Classroom and Promote Self-Esteem* (Albert, 1989)<br>• *Control Theory in the Classroom* (Glasser, 1985)<br>• *Schools Without Failure* (Glasser, 1969)<br>• *The Quality School: Managing Students Without Coercion* (Glasser, 1992) | • *Teaching Discipline: A Positive Approach for Educational Development* (Madsen & Madsen, 1981)<br>• *Applied Behavior Analysis for Teachers* (Alberto & Troutman, 1990)<br>• *Dare to Discipline* (Dobson, 1970)<br>• *Assertive Discipline: Positive Behavior Management for Today's Classroom* (Canter & Canter, 1992)<br>• *Succeeding with Difficult Students* (Canter & Canter, 1993)<br>• *Your Perfect Right: A Guide to Assertive Living* (Alberti, 1982)<br>• *Stand Up, Speak Out, Talk Back* (Alberti & Emmons, 1975)<br>• *Positive Classroom Discipline* (Jones, 1987)<br>• *Nonviolent Crisis Intervention* (National Crisis Prevention Institute, n.d.) |

way of techniques based on escalation and deescalation of his or her own power in working with a very difficult child who is disrupting the classroom, and, at the same time help students to develop strategies of self-discipline and responsibility.

# REFERENCES

Albert, L. (1989). *A Teacher's Guide to Cooperative Discipline: How to Manage Your Classroom and Promote Self-Esteem*. Circle Pines, MN: American Guidance Service.

Alberti, R. E. (1982). *Your Perfect Right: A Guide to Assertive Living*. San Luis Obispo, CA: Impact Publishers.

Alberti, R. E., & Emmons, M. L. (1975). *Stand Up, Speak Out, Talk Back*. New York: Pocket Books.

Alberto, P. A., & Troutman, A. C. (1990). *Applied Behavior Analysis for Teachers* (3rd ed.). New York: Maxwell Macmillian International Publishing Group.

Bessell, H. (1976). *Human Development Program*. La Mesa, CA: Human Development Training Institute.

Canter, L., & Canter, M. (1992). *Assertive Discipline: Positive Behavior Management for Today's Classroom*. Santa Monica, CA: Lee Canter & Associates.

Canter, L., & Canter, M. (1993). *Succeeding with Difficult Students*. Santa Monica, CA: Lee Canter & Associates.

Dobson, J. (1970). *Dare to Discipline*. Wheaton, IL: Tyndale House.

Dreikurs, R., & Cassel, P. (1972). *Discipline Without Tears*. New York: Hawthorn.

Glasser, W. (1969). *Schools Without Failure*. New York: Harper & Row.

Glasser, W. (1985). *Control Theory in the Classroom*. New York: Harper & Row.

Glasser, W. (1992). *The Quality School: Managing Students Without Coercion* (2nd ed.). New York: Harper Perennial.

Gordon, T. (1974). *T.E.T.: Teacher Effectiveness Training*. New York: David McKay.

Gordon, T. (1989). *Teaching Children Self-Discipline: At Home and at School*. New York: Times Books.

Harris, T. A. (1969). *I'm OK—You're OK: A Practical Guide to Transactional Analysis*. New York: Harper & Row.

Jones, F. H. (1987). *Positive Classroom Discipline*. New York: McGraw-Hill.

Madsen, C. H., & Madsen, C. K. (1981). *Teaching Discipline: A Positive Approach for Educational Development*. Raleigh, NC: Contemporary Publishing.

National Crisis Prevention Institute. (n.d.). *Nonviolent Crisis Intervention*. Brookfield, WI: Author.

Palomares, U., & Ball, G. (1980). *Grounds for Growth: The Human Development Program's Comprehensive Theory*. Spring Valley, CA: Palomares and Associates.

Raths, L. E., Harmin, M., & Simon, S. B. (1966). *Values and Teaching*. Columbus, OH: Merrill.

# 1

# Teacher Behavior, Misbehavior, and Discipline

Mr. McDaniel's seventh-grade math class is divided into five groups. Because the class contains 39 students, the groups are larger than desirable; however, the students are working quietly on their group activities. Suddenly, Sean, a normally quiet student, springs from his seat with a loud, "Hey, what was that?" The students around his group begin to laugh as Mr. McDaniel makes his way to the area. Mr. McDaniel moves to Sean and asks quietly, "What's the matter, Sean?" Sean replies, "Someone just spit on the back of my chair or something! Look, it's wet." Carla, who sits next to Sean, says, "It was Mark. He's got a squirt gun and has been squirting it all day!" Mark yells, "Man, I don't have a squirt gun!" Carla disagrees, "Yes, you do and you just squirted Sean's chair with it."

Mr. McDaniel moves next to Mark and makes eye contact. (Step 1: Looking)

The teacher says, "When you use something that you should not have here at school, like a squirt gun, and disturb another student by squirting it, you also disrupt the rest of the class so that everyone stops their work. We then lose valuable time, and I find that quite annoying." (Step 2: Naming) Mr. McDaniel backs out of Mark's "personal space" and gives him several moments to respond. Mark takes a squirt gun from his backpack, squirts it up into the air, and then puts it back into his backpack with a grin on his face.

"What is the rule regarding toys at school?" the teacher asks. "What are you going to do to solve this problem, Mark, so that we may all get back to our work?" (Step 3: Questioning) Mr. McDaniel is still speaking softly so only the students near Sean and Mark can hear him. Mark does not respond.

Mr. McDaniel states, "Mark, take the squirt gun out of your backpack and hand it to me." (Step 4: Commanding) Mark still does not respond; he just sits with the smile on his face. So the teacher adds, "If you cannot quickly take the squirt *gun out of your backpack and give it to me now, I will call the front office and have Mr. Carlson, the assistant principal, come and remove you from the classroom to his office."* (Promise a Consequence) *"Give me the squirt gun now!"* (Commanding) *The students sitting around Mark turn to look at Mark, and slowly he removes the squirt gun from his backpack and hands it to Mr. McDaniel. If Mark had not responded, Mr. McDaniel would have followed through on his stated intent to remove the student.* (Step 5: Acting [Physical Intervention])

For purposes of this example, the incident ended successfully; the squirt gun was secured with limited disruption to most of the other students and to ongoing classroom activity. However, the experienced teacher realizes that more likely this squirt gun incident may have degenerated into a situation requiring the teacher to remove Mark (physical intervention), to restrain Sean (who might angrily strike out), or to take some other action to get the students back to their classroom work activity. Later, methods and constructs for dealing with raw aggression and removal will be provided, but first it is important to understand the dynamics of the preceding incident through the use of the construct of the *Teacher Behavior Continuum (TBC)* (Wolfgang & Glickman, 1986), which describes the teacher's *escalation* from minimum to maximum use of power (see Figure 1.1).

---

### ESCALATION/DEESCALATION OF POWER

The gradual movement up and down the TBC through the use of stronger or more demanding teacher behaviors (escalation of power) or a retreat back through this continuum with less intrusive behaviors (deescalation).

---

**FIGURE 1.1   Teacher Behavior Continuum (TBC)**

Minimum Power ◄───────────────────► Maximum Power

Step 1:   Looking

    Step 2:   Naming

        Step 3:   Questioning

           Step 4:   Commanding
               (Promise a Consequence)

               Step 5:   Acting
                   (Physical Intervention)

When a student acts in an inappropriate manner in the classroom, it is logical to ask, "What should be done to stop this behavior?" The natural tendency, especially for a beginning teacher, is to rush toward the misbehaving student, state in a loud and forceful manner *(high-profile desist)* what the student must not do ("Don't do that, Mark. Stop clowning around!") and then, if compliance is not obtained, begin a classroom search for the squirt gun or physically remove Mark. Once the situation becomes "high profile" in the audience of peers, a personal power struggle is likely to ensue for a number of reasons.

Students at this age have a need for peer acceptance and are naturally concerned about what others think of them. Approval and acceptance by peers is a dominating need for a young adolescent (Brown, 1990; Clasen & Brown, 1987; Eccles & Wigfield, 1997; Lipka, 1997). This need is apparent in the formation of "tightly constructed cliques or groups, each one concerned about who may or may not be accepted, and consisting of individuals who are happy to be in and willing to do generally whatever is required to retain membership" (Beane & Lipka, 1986, p. 21). Any confrontation, especially in a context where peers are onlookers, places pressure on these students to save face, to avoid being seen as foolish, or to sense a challenge to their power, requiring them to demonstrate "macho" responses. This pressure can cloud a student's logical thinking on how to respond to the teacher's demand. Thus, a so-called high-profile response from the teacher in front of the class can make a student confused and he or she will more likely respond in an aggressive or foolish and destructive manner toward the teacher. The behavior of the teacher is reflected in the behavior of their students (Bennett & Irvin, 1996).

In addition to young adolescents' strong need for peer acceptance, the extremes in emotion that they encounter, probably caused by hormonal activity, can cause radical fluctuations in their behavior. A teacher may observe the same student sad and tearful one moment, happy the next, and angry a few moments later. This emotional variance is "heightened by the young adolescents' feelings of confusion about the changes within themselves and about their place within the social group" (Irvin, 1998, p. 21). Permitting the student to take a few minutes of personal space, perhaps using a time-out method, may allow for a shift in emotions that may facilitate a solution to the problem. This time-out period will also serve to take the student out of the spotlight of his or her peers.

A final difficulty with the high-profile response used in the previous example is that young adolescents are in a sort of "holding pattern" in which they are expected to act like adults yet not enjoy any adult privileges (Beane & Lipka, 1986; Lipka, 1997). This ambiguous status of young adolescents, being treated like children one minute and adults another, can cause them frustration that sometimes leads to their lashing out at adults. Their disagreement with adults, both at school and at home, can be interpreted as a sign of rejection. This rejection is a manifestation of the young adolescents' need for autonomy. Although some degree of autonomy from parents and teachers should be granted, this is not an appropriate time for adults to alienate themselves completely (Irvin, 1998; Steinberg, 1990). The goal in using and understanding the Teacher Behavior Continuum is to grant students maximum power to change their own behavior by beginning with a low-profile desist command and giving them time for the change. When the teacher is unsuccessful in gaining compliance, the teacher should then gradually escalate the power until the student responds by acting appropriately.

Adults have traditionally viewed early adolescence as a time of "storm and stress" and a time for turbulence and disruption (Hill, 1980). Recent information, however (Brazee, 1997; Brooks-Gunn & Reiter, 1990; Hauser & Bowlds, 1990; Ofer, Ostrov, & Howard, 1989; Scales, 1991; Steinberg, 1990), clearly indicates that only a small percentage of students (less than 20 percent) exhibit signs of serious disturbance. Although the changes experienced are stressful for students, teachers, and parents, Dorman and Lipsitz (1981) argue that adults should "distinguish between behavior that is distressful (annoying to others) and behavior that is disturbed (harmful to the young person exhibiting the behavior)" (p. 4). Often, when adults expect irresponsible behavior, they may, indeed, exacerbate the occurrence.

Other factors such as relevant curriculum, effective and engaging teaching strategies employed, and a positive and supportive school climate play a part in the motivation and discipline of students. Although these factors can reduce the severity and frequency of student disruption and misbehavior, they will not be directly addressed in this book. (For further reading, see recommended readings at the end of this chapter.) The remainder of this book will address student misbehavior and suggest appropriate teacher response.

## THE SEVERITY CLAUSE AND "STOP" STATEMENTS

For every rule there is an exception. When a student performs some act that is life threatening, is likely to produce injury, or will destroy expensive or irreplaceable property, the *severity clause* applies. In such a case, a teacher states firmly or even shouts a "No, Stop!" statement to attempt to get the student to desist immediately. If a high-profile type of response is saved for situations that truly warrant it, an emergency "No, Stop!" statement is more likely to be obeyed immediately.

---

### SEVERITY CLAUSE

If the student's actions threaten to endanger himself or herself or destroy significant property, you are justified in escalating up the continuum to the most intrusive or demanding teacher behaviors of *Acting (Physical Intervention)*.

---

## THE TEACHER BEHAVIOR CONTINUUM: THE TBC

The confrontation between Mark and Mr. McDaniel over the illegal squirt gun and refusing to surrender the squirt gun at the teacher's request contains examples of those myriad small desist requests—which may be called *teachable moments*—that a classroom teacher faces daily in working with students. The incident is dealt with in a matter of minutes, and the teacher escalates up the TBC power continuum as he or she intervenes, modifying his or her approach as he receives—or fails to receive—certain responses. With some students, especially physically and verbally aggressive students, these teachable moments may arise five or six times in an hour and occur daily. Understanding the Teacher Behavior Continuum and the many techniques found in the following chapters can be of great help to you in your daily interactions with students.

The steps and general categories of behavior on the TBC suggest a power continuum of teacher action moving from the minimum use of power at *Step 1: Looking* (or *Modality Cueing*) to the maximum use of power at *Step 5: Acting (Physical Intervention)*. This escalation to more powerful techniques on the TBC also reflects a very real attitudinal change on the part of the intervening teacher. This attitude change may be characterized as the *Three Faces of Discipline:* Relationship-Listening, Confronting-Contracting, and Rules and Consequences.

---

### TEACHER BEHAVIOR CONTINUUM

A systematic process that you may use daily to intervene with the kinds of misbehavior normally seen in most students in classroom settings. The TBC contains a group of five general teacher behaviors *(Looking, Naming, Questioning, Commanding,* and *Acting)* placed on a continuum, suggesting that actions may move from minimum teacher intrusion or power to maximum teacher control.

---

The *Relationship-Listening Face* involves the use of minimum power. This "face" reflects a view that the student has the capability to change his or her own behavior, and that if the student is misbehaving, it is usually because of inner emotional turmoil. The goal is to signal or make the student aware of his or her actions and get the student to talk out his or her emotional concern. This "talking it out" by the student generally leads him or her to more purposeful behavior, and the misbehavior stops. The "face" of the Relationship-Listening teacher would rely only on such minimal intervention techniques as Looking and Naming (see Figure 1.2).

The teacher's "face" when escalating to a *Confronting-Contracting* method of intervention is one of "I am the adult. I know misbehavior when I see it and will confront the student to stop this behavior. I will

FIGURE 1.2   The Three Faces of Discipline

grant the student the power to decide how he or she will change, and encourage and contract with the student to live up to a mutual agreement for behavioral change." The Confronting-Contracting position primarily involves the use of Questioning techniques found on the TBC (see Figure 1.2).

The most powerful intervention technique is a teacher attitude of the *Rules and Consequences Face,* which communicates an attitude of "This is the rule and behavior that I want and I will set out assertively to get this action. I will teach and reward new positive behaviors acquired by the student." Drawing from the TBC, the "face" of the Rules and Consequences teacher will use the powerful techniques of Commanding and Acting (Physical Intervention) (see Figure 1.2).

---

### "FACES" OR TEACHER ATTITUDES

A metaphor for the concept that a teacher may act toward a misbehaving student in a number of conscious, predetermined ways, and that the teacher's attitude and methods can change (take on a new "face") to match circumstances.

---

The Teacher Behavior Continuum and the escalation and change among these attitudes or faces of discipline may be used in two ways to help a young adolescent's behavior move to a more mature level:

- First, for the student who is simply having a rare misbehavior, it would be appropriate to escalate across the TBC within a few minutes. This was demonstrated in the example of Mark and the squirt gun incident.

## THE THREE FACES OF DISCIPLINE

### Relationship-Listening
This face is the least intrusive of the three discipline faces. It views students as inherently good, and if they are misbehaving, it is because they are suffering the blockage of some inner emotional need. The teacher's role is to establish a nonjudgmental relationship and encourage the student to "talk out" the problem while the teacher listens; this talking helps empower the student to solve his or her own problems and needs. *These methods are based on Rogerian theory (Rogers, 1969).*

### Confronting-Contracting
This face maintains an adult relationship with a misbehaving student, by requesting the student to stop and change. The solution for how the student will change remains in the student's hands. *These methods are based on Glasser's Reality Therapy (Glasser, 1969) and Adlerian theory as defined by Rudolf Dreikurs (Dreikurs & Cassel, 1972).*

### Rules and Consequences
The most power or controlling face, with philosophy and methodology that clearly states rules for behavior and assertively takes actions through reward to get the positive behavior sought by the teacher. *These methods are based on theories of assertiveness training (Canter & Canter, 1976) and behavior modification (Alberto & Troutman, 1982).*

- Second, for the attention-getting, power-seeking, and revengeful student whose life-stance position is one of a day-in, day-out series of classroom disruptions, a teacher may stay with a single face of discipline—with its accompanying techniques—for many weeks. The face may gradually change to increase your power if these techniques are unsuccessful, or to decrease your power to less intrusive techniques if the student's behavior begins to change and becomes more purposeful and guided.

## LIFE-STANCE POSITION

When a student (or adult) becomes so overwhelmed by a world of frustration and accompanying inner emotional turmoil, he or she may defensively take a passive or aggressive stance, 24 hours a day, toward life experiences and toward classmates and teachers.

## THE THREE FACES OF DISCIPLINE: A CONCEPT, NOT A RECIPE

The purpose of the Three Faces of Discipline, with the use of the TBC and its accompanying teacher behaviors, is not to give the teacher a clear-cut recipe for responding to misbehavior. One example of a recipe is suggested in *Assertive Discipline* (Canter & Canter, 1976), which calls for the teacher to place a student's name on the board as a warning of misbehavior, followed by a check mark for each new act of misbehavior; after three checks, the student suffers some form of punishment. This approach takes the ability to decide away from the teacher by assuming that this recipe will be effective with all students and in all situations. The Teacher Behavior Continuum and the concept of the Three Faces of Discipline simply provide an orderly arrangement of teacher techniques that may be used as they relate to degrees of power. This concept permits the teacher to use his or her ability to decide how much power is needed for which student under what type of circumstances.

For example, with a certain misbehaving student, a teacher may choose to ask, "Carol, what are you doing? This may not go on!" (Confronting-Contracting Face). The student, without any undue stress, realizes what she must do to comply, and the discipline incident is over. With another student who is getting out of hand, you may simply need to make eye contact (Relationship-Listening Face) for the student to become aware of what he or she is doing wrong and how to stop doing it. Still other students require you to assertively state the rules and to demand immediate compliance (Rules and Consequences Face) before they stop their inappropriate behavior. Based on past experiences with these students and an intimate knowledge of them, a decision is made as to how much power and which techniques would be most effective with each individual student. The Three Faces of Discipline concept would go one step further in that with those students requiring the strong intervention of Rules and Consequences (and to a lesser extent Confronting-Contracting), over many weeks you would gradually teach or lead the students to respond by using techniques of less and less power, until the students can effectively control themselves. As a result, at the end of this process, only the Relationship-Listening techniques are necessary, or none at all.

Subsequent chapters contain a more detailed explanation of the teacher behaviors found on the Teacher Behavior Continuum, with many new subbehavioral techniques defined and presented under each of these larger behavioral categories. Recall that in the squirt gun incident, the teacher used the behavioral category of *Commanding* and then progressed to a subcommand under this category called *Promise a Consequence*. Other behaviors on the TBC will also contain subbehaviors and techniques under these broader categories. The TBC becomes a "construct" or a visual display related to degrees of power, and each of the techniques is taken from various discipline models (i.e., T.E.T., Glasser, and Assertive Discipline). The TBC is presented in the following chapters, with the use of the continuum, to display the concrete techniques that are available to the teacher when dealing with a discipline incident and using one of the three faces of discipline.

---

### TEACHER BEHAVIOR CONTINUUM (TBC)

**Step 1: Looking**
In the first (minimum power) behavior on the TBC, the teacher uses a modality of looking, touch, or sound to signal the student to become aware of his or her own actions.

**Step 2: Naming**
In the second behavior on the TBC, the teacher uses words to describe the feelings, problem, or situation the student is facing regarding some episode (e.g., difficulty with another person or objects and materials).

**Step 3: Questioning**
In the third teacher behavior on the TBC, the student is called on to reflect on the situation and to think of new ideas to solve the situation; alternatively, questioning could be the teacher's offer to provide assistance.

**Step 4: Commanding**
In the fourth behavior on the TBC, the teacher makes a powerful direct statement, telling the student what to do. *Promise a Consequence* is a subbehavior under the larger category of *Commanding*. Once the teacher has told the student what to do and sees that the student is not complying, the teacher verbally gives a promise of a consequence—a promise to follow up with a strong action (physical intervention) if the student does not quickly comply.

**Step 5: Acting (Physical Intervention)**
In this strongest and most intrusive behavior on the TBC, the teacher physically takes the student by the hand or restricts his or her body to stop an action that is occurring.

---

## TEACHER PERSONALITY TYPE

Many teachers do not escalate or deescalate their power along a continuum, but instead wear one "face," generally performing two to five discipline actions consistently with most students. These teachers tend to have a set philosophy or orientation.

All teachers have a deep memory of the child within themselves. This memory is an accumulation of how parents, teachers, and other significant adults disciplined them when they were young. Consequently, the tendency is to parent the way you were parented, or teach the way you were taught. When a teacher sets limits with students, he or she is projecting the degree of autonomy that he or she feels comfortable giving to the students to control their own behavior, or how much he or she needs to be in control (Bennett, 1997). Therefore, for some teachers, the Rules and Consequences techniques may be too strong a form of teacher control, or the Relationship-Listening face too "touchy-feely" in nature, or the Confronting-Contracting face too uncomfortable to bring discipline issues for group discussion. Based on their individual personalities, then, many teachers tend to use naturally—and unthinkingly—methods and techniques that cluster under one of these three schools of thought, or "faces." The question arises: Which one of these "face" philosophies best fits your personality? The Beliefs about Discipline Inventory on pages 17 through 19 is a tool that facilitates answering a series of value questions to help you identify which "face" philosophically comes more naturally—based on the child within yourself. It would be helpful to stop reading now and complete the inventory, so that after you become familiar with the methods under each of these positions, it will be possible to see if your values have changed.

## SUMMARY

The wide variety of discipline models may be considered on a continuum relative to the power the models call for to get off-task students to change their behavior. Instead of relying on just one model, any or all of the models may build a system or personal model of discipline. The Teacher Behavior Continuum provides a construct for deciding how much power to use when interacting with a student. The degree of power of control needed in a classroom may vary from time to time.

### Beliefs about Discipline Inventory

The 12 questions on this inventory will give you insights about yourself by helping you determine where your personality and the techniques you currently tend to use would cluster under the three philosophical "faces." In each numbered question you are asked to choose between two competing value statements. With some questions, you will definitely like one statement and dislike the second, and it will be easy for you to decide. With others, you will like or dislike both, leaving you with a frustrating choice—but you still must choose.

**Forced Choices**

*Instructions*: Select A or B to indicate the item you value most. You must choose between the two statements for each item. Circle item A or B.

1. a. Because students' thinking is limited, rules need to be established for them by mature adults.
   b. Each student's emotional need, rather than some preestablished rule, must be taken into consideration.

2. a. During most group time, the teacher needs to assign each student his or her own desk or table space, and all students should be taught routinely to take those spaces after transitions.
   b. Groups of young students can, through class meetings, decide what rules they need to govern themselves.

3. a. During the beginning of the class period, students should be given the opportunity to select the activity they wish to participate in, and then once chosen, they must keep to that decision for most of that period.
   b. What students must learn and the tasks to be performed must be determined by the teacher, and a specific sequence of instruction to accomplish these goals must be followed.

4. The books in the classroom library are being misused, soiled, and at times destroyed. I most likely will:
   a. Hold a class meeting, show the damaged books to the class, and ask the students how we may solve this problem, including what action should be taken toward a student misusing books.
   b. Physically remove or limit the number of books available and observe closely to see who was misusing the books. I would then tell that student how such action was affecting other students and how I felt about such loss of books.

5. Two students of equal power and abilities are in a rather loud verbal conflict over classroom materials. I would:
   a. Approach the students to keep the situation from getting out of control, telling them of the classroom rule and demanding that they desist in their actions, promising a sanction if they fail to comply.
   b. Avoid interfering in something that the students need to resolve themselves.

*(Continued)*

**Beliefs about Discipline Inventory** *(Continued)*

6. a. The student strongly requests not to work in a group today. This would be permitted based on the teacher's feeling that this student has some emotional or personal concerns related to the group experience.
   b. One student is being refused entrance into group activities; the teacher will raise this as an issue in a class meeting, requesting a discussion of reasons and solutions by the student and the group.

7. The noise level in the classroom is at such a high level that it is bothering me. I would:
   a. Flick the classroom lights to get the students' attention, ask them to become quiet, and later praise those who are talking quietly.
   b. Select the two or three students really making most of the noise, take them aside and question them to reflect (think) about their behavior and how it might affect others, and get an agreement with them to work quietly.

8. During the first few days of class, I would:
   a. Permit the students to test out getting along as a new group and make no predetermined teacher rules, until the students feel they are needed.
   b. Immediately teach the class rules and the fair sanction I will apply if the rules are broken.

9. My response when one student swears at another is:
   a. The student is frustrated by a classmate and has responded by swearing; I do not reprimand the student, but encourage him to talk out what is bothering him or her.
   b. I bring the two students together, sit them facing each other, and attempt to get them to work out this conflict while I ask questions and keep the focus on the negotiation.

10. If a student disrupts class while I am trying to teach, I would:
    a. Ignore the disruption if possible and/or remove the student to the back of the room as a consequence of his misbehavior.
    b. Express my feeling of discomfort to the student about being disrupted from my task.

11. a. Each student must realize that there are some school rules that need to be obeyed, and each student who breaks them will be punished in the same fair manner.
    b. Rules are never "written in stone" and can be renegotiated by the class; sanctions will vary with each student.

12. A student refuses to put away her work or materials after using them. I most likely would:
    a. Express to the student how "not putting away" will affect future activities in her space, and how frustrating this will be to everyone. I would then leave the materials where they are for the remainder of the day.
    b. Confront the student to reflect on her behavior, think about how her non-compliance affects others, and tell her that if she cannot follow the rules, she will lose the use of the materials in the future.

---

**Beliefs about Discipline Inventory** *(Continued)*

---

**Scoring Key and Interpretation**

Locate your responses for each numbered question on the table below and circle it.

| Table 1 | | Table 2 | | Table 3 | |
|---|---|---|---|---|---|
| 4b | 1b | 2b | 4a | 2a | 1a |
| 6a | 5b | 3a | 6b | 3b | 5a |
| 9a | 8a | 7b | 9b | 7a | 8b |
| 12a | 10b | 11b | 12b | 11a | 10a |

Total number of responses in Table 1 _____

Total number of responses in Table 2 _____

Total number of responses in Table 3 _____

The table with the highest total number of responses shows the "face" where your values tend to cluster. Table 1 represents Relationship-Listening, Table 2 is Confronting-Contracting, and Table 3 is Rules and Consequences. The table with the next highest score would be your secondary orientation, and the table with the least number may be the "face" that you value least. If your responses are equally distributed among all tables, you may be an eclectic teacher who picks and chooses from all philosophies. In Chapter 2, you will learn more about how this value position will relate to your "personality fit."

---

# REFERENCES

Alberto, P., & Troutman, A. (1982). *Applied Behavior Analysis for Teachers.* New York: Merrill.

Beane, J., & Lipka, R. (1986). *Self-Concept, Self-Esteem, and the Curriculum.* New York: Teachers College Press.

Bennett, B. (1997). Middle level discipline and young adolescents: Making the connection. In J. L. Irvin (Ed.), *What Current Research Says to the Middle Level Practitioner* (pp. 73–85). Columbus, OH: National Middle School Association.

Bennett, B., & Irvin, J. (1996). Middle school discipline: How you see is what you get. *Middle School Journal, 27* (3), 52–54.

Brazee, E. (1997). Curriculum for whom? In J. L. Irvin (Ed.), *What Current Research Says to the Middle Level Practitioner* (pp. 187–201). Columbus, OH: National Middle School Association.

Brooks-Gunn, J., & Reiter, E. O. (1990). The role of pubertal processes. In S. S. Feldman & G. R. Elliott (Eds.), *At the Threshold: The Developing Adolescent* (pp. 16–53). Cambridge, MA: Harvard University Press.

Brown, B. B. (1990). Peer groups and peer cultures. In S. S. Feldman & G. R. Elliott (Eds.), *At the Threshold: The Developing Adolescent* (pp. 171–196). Cambridge, MA: Harvard University Press.

Canter, L., & Canter, M. (1976). *Assertive Discipline: A Take Charge Approach for Today's Educator.* Seal Beach, CA: Lee Canter and Associates.

Clasen, D. R., & Brown, B. B. (1987). Understanding peer pressure in the middle school. *Middle School Journal, 19* (1), 21–23.

Dorman, G., & Lipsitz, J. (1981). Early adolescent development. In G. Dorman (Ed.), *Middle Grades Assessment Program.* Carrboro, NC: Center for Early Adolescence.

Dreikurs, R., & Cassel, P. (1972). *Discipline Without Tears.* New York: Hawthorn Books.

Eccles, J., & Wigfield, A. (1997). Young adolescent development. In J. L. Irvin (Ed.), *What Current Research Says to the Middle Level Practitioner* (pp. 15–29). Columbus, OH: National Middle School Association.

Glasser, W. (1969). *Schools Without Failure.* New York: Peter H. Wyden.

Hauser, S. T., & Bowlds, M. K. (1990). Stress, coping, and adaptation. In S. S. Feldman & G. R. Elliott (Eds.), *At the Threshold: The Developing Adolescent* (pp. 388–413). Cambridge, MA: Harvard University Press.

Hill, J. P. (1980). *Understanding Early Adolescence: A Framework.* Carrboro, NC: Center for Early Adolescence.

Irvin, J. L. (1998). *Reading and the Middle School Student: Strategies to Enhance Literacy* (2nd ed.). Boston: Allyn and Bacon.

Lipka, R. (1997). Enhancing self-concept/self-esteem in young adolescents. In J. L. Irvin (Ed.), *What Current Research Says to the Middle Level Practitioner* (pp. 31–39). Columbus, OH: National Middle School Association.

Ofer, D., Ostrov, E., & Howard, K. I. (1989). Adolescence? What is normal? *American Journal of Diseases of Children, 143,* 731–736.

Rogers, C. (1969). *Freedom to Learn.* Columbus, OH: Charles E. Merrill.

Scales, P. C. (1991). *A Portrait of Young Adolescents in the 1990s: Implications for Promoting Healthy Growth and Development.* Carrboro, NC: Center for Early Adolescence.

Steinberg, L. (1990). Autonomy, conflict, and harmony in the family relationship. In S. S. Feldman & G. R. Elliott (Eds.), *At the Threshold: The Developing Adolescent* (pp. 255–276). Cambridge, MA: Harvard University Press.

Wolfgang, C., & Glickman, C. (1986). *Solving Discipline Problems: Methods and Models for Today's Teachers.* Boston: Allyn and Bacon.

## FOR FURTHER READING

Beane, J. A. (1993). *A Middle School Curriculum: From Rhetoric to Reality* (2nd ed.). Columbus, OH: National Middle School Association.

Beane, J. A. (Ed.). (1995). *Toward a Coherent Curriculum.* Alexandria, VA: Association for Supervision and Curriculum Development.

Irvin, J. L. (Ed.). (1997). *What Current Research Says to the Middle Level Practitioner.* Columbus, OH: National Middle School Association.

Irvin, J. L. (1998). *Reading and the Middle School Student: Strategies to Enhance Literacy* (2nd ed.). Boston: Allyn and Bacon.

Muth, K. D., & Alvermann, D. E. (1992). *Teaching and Learning in the Middle Grades.* Boston: Allyn and Bacon.

Pace, G. (Ed.). (1995). *Whole Learning in the Middle School: Evolution and Transition.* Norwood, MA: Christopher-Gordon.

Siu-Runyan, Y., & Faircloth, C. V. (1995). *Beyond Separate Subjects: Integrate Learning at the Middle Level.* Norwood, MA: Christopher-Gordon.

# 2

# The Three Faces of Discipline System

A discipline situation normally requires the teacher to initiate a desist toward a student whose behavior is off task, disruptive, or in violation of a rule. This interaction typically involves a clash between the teacher and the student, such as in the squirt gun incident in Chapter 1. Historically, a teacher's desist action has been an intuitive action, possibly learned from his or her own childhood home and school experiences, acquired from the student-teaching experience, or learned through trial and error. These actions typically range from simply looking at the off-task student through the use of a visual prompt, to various forms of verbal actions (including mild verbal prompts, threats, and commands), and even to the use of physical intervention whereby the student is removed from the classroom.

*Limit setting,* through a desist action by the teacher, is the central skill in establishing positive and effective classroom discipline and classroom climate (Kounin, 1970). Teachers often have a clear and articulated procedure for how an instructional lesson is to be taught, but have little clear and overt understanding of why they act as they do when disciplining students: It is largely intuitive. What should a teacher do if a student swears or says "shut up"? To help you acquire the ability to make effective limit-setting responses, two broad categories of variables are explained in this chapter: (1) a skill and value system related to your individual personality and (2) various discipline models involving how to set limits, based on psychological theories and research.

## TEACHER SKILL AND PERSONALITY TYPE

For the last quarter of the century, responsible and well-meaning district or building administrators have observed teachers in classrooms and realized that many of these teachers could benefit by having increased training in classroom discipline. The need for discipline training has historically been a political problem, often prompted by a glaring negative incident (e.g., a high school teacher punches a tenth-grader or suffers an injury during a discipline action that results in a lawsuit) that makes the front page of the local newspaper.

District administrators and others outside the classroom know they have a problem and want an immediate solution. Therefore, they look around to see what is nationally available in discipline training, or what the district next door is using. This investigation often leads them to Teacher Effectiveness Training (T.E.T.), or Glasser, or Assertive Discipline, or the many other widely known discipline models; discipline experts are hired to conduct in-service training workshops and their books and media are purchased. The pressure placed on the teachers by the district or the school to follow the techniques of this one chosen expert ranges from a suggestion, to a strong encouragement, to a command that everyone will use this districtwide model. One superintendent was heard to declare, "We have gone Assertive Discipline," meaning he had invested considerable money and effort into having the teachers in his district trained in a particular model and he expected every teacher to use it.

When one principal heard a presentation involving the Three Faces of Discipline model with the six or more different models it uses, he was overwhelmed and stated, "You expect my teachers to do all of that, when we have been 'doing Glasser' for five years and 40 percent of my teachers are still not using it?" Often, lack of teacher ability to handle discipline problems is targeted as the source of the problem (Allen, 1988).

A return visit to teachers one year after their discipline model training often reveals that the techniques have eroded. A small minority of teachers may still use the techniques, but rarely in their pure form; most eclectically incorporate a few of the techniques into the basic discipline systems they have always used. While teachers often have difficulty changing their patterns of interactions with students, discipline is generally ranked at the top of the list for in-service training. When Glasser or Assertive Discipline models are presented at workshops, even on Saturday mornings, teachers show up for these training sessions enthusiastic, optimistic, and eager for ideas—they are generally motivated. The reason most discipline training historically has failed to have a lasting effect is that (1) the training was delivered in a verbal modality of teaching as a one-shot training with no long-term opportunity for practice and (2) the idea of one discipline orientation for all teachers was a failure of personality fit.

## Personality Fit

The concept of personality fit can best be explained through the example of two mothers, Mother 1 and Mother 2, as they feed 9-month-old infants in high chairs. Mother 1 prepares and stores all warm and cold food on a counter nearby, covers herself completely with an apron, has a moist towelet nearby, and places a bib on the infant that would cover Manhattan. Mother 1 feeds the child one spoonful at a time, making sure that all food goes into the child's mouth and "down." Mother 1 is not harsh and uses fun games such as "Open up the tunnel (child's mouth)—here comes the train (a spoon full of peas)" and uses her warm and gracious personality to get the food into the infant—no spills or mess! The infant enjoys the process. By her actions, Mother 1 needs to be in control of all actions, and by her behavior, she follows a series of rules or has a structure as to how things should be done. Mother 1 has structured for "control of error" but gives limited or no "degrees of freedom" for the child to deviate from the routine.

By contrast is Mother 2. While feeding her infant, she covers the floor under the high chair with a sheet of plastic, dresses the child in a diaper and small shirt, places the food on a serving tray with suction cups secured to the high chair's table, gives the infant a spoon, and shows him how to use it. Mother 2 allows the baby to feed himself with his hands while she carries on a "conversation" with her child as she works nearby. Mostly using his hands, the infant gets a third of the food in his mouth, a third on himself, and the other third on the floor. The child enjoys the eating experience. Mother 2 is not upset by this messiness and has observed to see that the infant has eaten an adequate amount of food. She then throws the child's shirt into the wash, kisses him warmly, gives him a bath, and hoses off the plastic sheet for the next time. Mother 2 grants the infant much autonomy, or self-control, but is not naive or permissive. She has structured for "control of error," covered the floor with plastic, dressed the child for the occasion, and organized the suction feeding bowl so the food would not get knocked from the high chair—but she also has granted the child near total "degrees of freedom" for carrying out this feeding activity. Both mothers have communicated with their children in a warm and supportive manner.

If the two mothers continue their patterns of child rearing for the next 17 years, the result would be very different adult personalities. What if the children were to become teachers and incorporate nearly the exact personality characteristics, techniques, and attitudes toward children, parenting, and teaching? Continuing in this line of thinking, what if you, as a school administrator, forced a model of Relationship-Listening on teacher-child 1, Mr. Control, whereby the students were to help establish rules and sanctions? Would there be a personality fit with this teacher? The answer is no. What if teacher-child 2, Mr. Autonomy, was required to use the obedience model of Assertive Discipline? Could there be a fit here? Most likely, the answer again would be no.

Now, what would it be like if, at a dinner party at Mr. Control's house, there was no cream on the table for the coffee? Knowing how busy the host is, and not wanting to trouble him, someone goes to his refrigerator, opens it, and retrieves the needed cream. Mr. Control may or may not say it directly, but he likely thinks that opening the refrigerator at someone else's home is too "forward" and impolite. ("How dare you? This is my home. What makes you think you can just go into my refrigerator?") Mr. Autonomy, on the other hand, most likely would not even take notice that someone opened his refrigerator, and might even consider it rather silly to be asked permission to do so.

Later, in Mr. Control's classroom, a student's pencil is broken and he needs to use the pencil sharpener. Can he just get up and use the sharpener any time he wishes? In Mr. Control's class, the answer is no—pencils may be sharpened at the beginning or end of the period, but not during class. This classroom offers minimum "degrees of freedom." Mr. Control also has a can of sharpened pencils nearby that students may borrow and then return, so they will have a pencil if theirs happens to break—this is "control of error." By contrast, Mr. Autonomy permits students to sharpen pencils any time they wish, and he does not even seem to notice when it occurs. Both Mr. (or Ms.) Control and Mr. (or Ms.) Autonomy are effective teachers who are loved by their students, but they have very different personalities and run very different discipline and classroom management programs. Observers, such as school administrators, would evaluate them both as excellent teachers.

The problem comes when Mr. (Ms.) Control and Mr. (Ms.) Autonomy are asked to be something that they are not. Most of us mother (or father) the way we were mothered (or fathered), and most likely teach the way we were taught—this is a projection of each individual's personality structure. Each of us, as teachers, has a personality core that is the child within us, reflecting the way we were raised, and we draw on this core when we interact socially with others. We have varying degrees of need for control and for formalizing rules to guide interactions between us and others. That core of personality will most likely be who we are for most of our lives, but with some minor changes as we mature.

As a teacher, establishing rules and setting limits with students in a classroom is a projection of your personality core of who you are as a person (Lunenburg, 1990). Forcing a person to practice techniques that are diametrically opposite to his or her personality core results in false, mechanical, and ineffective behavior—it simply will not work. Some of the discipline models, because of their degrees of power and the development of rules, are a mismatch to some teachers' personality cores. A lack of personality fit exists—it is not the individual's "face." So, when the principal says, "We have been 'doing Glasser' for five years and 40 percent of my teachers are still not using it!" what he or she is really saying is that Glasser was not a personality fit for two out of every five teachers in the school—that Glasser was not a "face" or philosophy that those teachers were psychologically comfortable using.

The power continuum, as part of the Three Faces of Discipline, takes the position that all of these models are of value and that teachers cannot be dictated to regarding the use of one model. Instead, they must find the model, or face, that fits their personality cores. Mr. Control would be called strict by his students, whereas Mr. Autonomy might be called a "softy" by the same students, but both of these teachers are effective and well liked by students and administrators.

It is Ms. Waffle who has the serious discipline difficulties. One time she strongly disciplines a student for breaking a rule, but the next day she says nothing when the same rule is broken. Ms. Waffle is not fair, firm, or consistent. The students will say that they can never tell "where she is coming from"—Ms. Waffle waffles. She is unpredictable and will be ineffective as a teacher and disliked by the students.

One may help Ms. Waffle by assessing her personality core, by administering the Beliefs about Discipline Inventory, by understanding her ideology of pupil control, and by training her in the one discipline model—one of the three "faces" that most fits her personality (see Chapter 1 for the Inventory). This model will permit Ms. Waffle to stop waffling, to create an orderliness to her behavior that students can understand, and thus to become predictable and no longer "scary" to the students. These models and three "faces" may also be used in other ways.

## THE FIVE SYSTEMS OF AN EFFECTIVE DISCIPLINE PROGRAM

The brief definition of discipline and the squirt gun incident in Chapter 1 explained the desist or limit-setting process. This example showed how a teacher's attitude, methods, and procedures changed in a way that became more demanding as the teacher escalated the use of power and changed his "face" of discipline. But, to have a complete discipline program in a classroom or school, one must go beyond limit setting by adding the aspect of classroom management. Putting together discipline and classroom management, including schoolwide management, will involve the following five subsystems, each of which will be described in detail in subsequent chapters:

1. Limit-Setting System (stops misbehavior)

2. Professional-Administrative Backup System (enlists the help of students, colleagues, parents, and other professionals)

3. Incentive System (maintains, increases, and speeds up desired behaviors)

4. Encouragement System (encourages positive behavior)

5. Classroom Management System (organizes objects and students to support and maintain desired behavior)

These subsystems are interdependent. For this process to be effective, each of the five systems must be fully implemented—no single subsystem (such as limit setting) can stand alone.

### Limit-Setting System

Limit setting and its process of desist is the system for taking actions, in the privacy of your own classroom or hall, toward one or more students, who, by their actions, are preventing teaching and learning, or who are failing to follow required procedures and rules. Simply put, it is a request to the student to "Stop what you are doing, and do what I want you to do." Limit setting will start with the day-in, day-out small off-task behaviors that can explode to conflict management and blow up as outward defiance in the form of an assault against the teacher. To be effective at discipline, one must know how to set limits. Each action carries with it an inherent degree of power; the crucial skill of limit setting is knowing how much power is appropriate to use in a given situation. Employing too much power would be like using a sledgehammer to drive in a tack, whereas too little power may communicate to the students that you are afraid of them or do not mean business (Jones, 1978).

## Professional-Administrative Backup System

When all the limit-setting methods and techniques have been used and the student's behavior is still disrupting the classroom learning climate, perhaps this student's actions and behavior are beyond a teacher's skills and abilities at that moment. Professional help from others outside the classroom is then appropriate, which makes the discipline action public. Such professional help might involve the other teachers, school counselor, school psychologist, and various mental health organizations, or—in the most extreme cases—even institutionalized care for the student. The actions of the student could also involve criminal acts, which would necessitate the involvement of the administration, school board, police, juvenile authorities, and the court system.

The professional-administrative backup system requires two parts (see Figure 2.1). The first entails a *professional sphere,* with clearly delineated steps and procedures designed to permit the teacher, as the primary deliverer of educational services, to gain professional consultation, through staffing, from colleagues. The objective is to enable teachers to increase their skill and become more effective with a very difficult student.

The second part uses an *administrative-legal sphere* involving a yielding of primary responsibility for the management and restraint of the student's behavior. This situation would occur because of the severity of the student's actions, which may be criminal or at the least threaten the safety and well-being of teachers, students, or even the disruptive student. Understandable and clearly defined steps and procedures must be established to dictate when such crisis students should be referred to the administrative authorities or legal system.

## Incentive System

While the limit-setting system provides techniques for getting students to stop their misbehavior so teaching is not disrupted, the incentive system is a classroom process of motivating students to increase their work and positive behaviors, or to acquire new behaviors not already in their repertoire. Examples would include getting students to do their homework or to care for school property.

## Encouragement System

A teacher may have a very difficult student for whom the incentive system may not work—in fact, this student, by his or her behavior, may actually destroy the incentive system. The teacher is now required to use an encouragement system especially designed to deal with the more

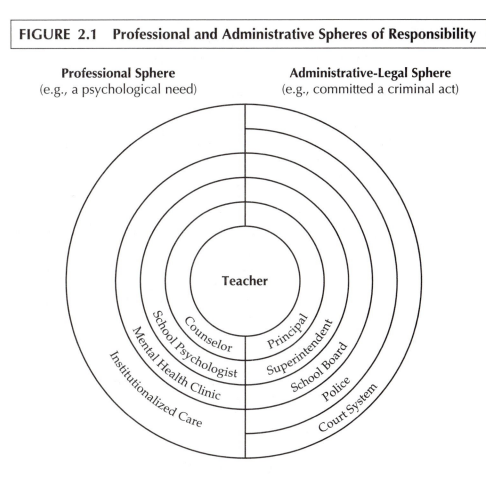

**FIGURE 2.1    Professional and Administrative Spheres of Responsibility**

difficult student and to work tangentially—in something of a piggyback approach—with the incentive system. The encouragement system is an individualized, targeted system to deal with the very discouraged and difficult student.

## Classroom (and School) Management System

The key method of eliminating many discipline problems is the skillful management of, or the understanding and use of the technology of management of (1) the design of classroom objects, furniture, and materials; (2) the arrangement of students in large groups, small groups, and one-to-one relationships; (3) the teaching and creation of rules; and (4) the collective and accepted procedures of the schoolwide staff and administration regarding the open field management of the total school environment (e.g., hallways, cafeteria, playground, and similar areas).

The Three Faces of Discipline and the five systems demonstrate that each of the systems draws on techniques from existing discipline models, placing them into the three categories of Relationship-Listening, Confronting-Contracting, and Rules and Consequences. Techniques for managing violent and assaultive student behavior are also included.

## SUMMARY

For the experienced teacher who already has had some training in previous discipline models, such as Glasser or Assertive Discipline, the advantage of this new Three Faces of Discipline model is that you do not need to learn a totally new model, but can continue to use past practices while adding many more techniques and systems to create a complete, effective discipline program. This new, more inclusive model wraps around the experienced teacher's present techniques by adding to and expanding teaching skills. Teachers can select and design a power pathway of techniques (the three "faces" or degrees of power) to fit their individual teaching style. The Beliefs about Discipline Inventory (see Chapter 1) helps determine which techniques are most comfortable. One model is not forced on every teacher in the school, so each teacher can find and employ techniques that fit well with his or her values and style of interaction. This model is not a simplistic recipe.

Thus, obtaining good discipline in the classroom, using the Three Faces model, involves five systems:

1. Limit-setting system

2. Professional-administrative backup system

3. Incentive system

4. Encouragement system

5. Classroom management system

The Three Faces of Discipline enables teachers to help learn rules gaining control of their classroom; gradually, the students will then be taught to be self-disciplined. The daily incentive system allows a teacher to relate to the students in positive ways; the encouragement system enables a teacher to deal with one particularly discouraged student. Also, the Three Faces of Discipline model gives the principal or administrator a positive role as part of the backup system. Finally, the model is not limited to the close confines of the classroom, because it provides techniques for managing schoolwide student behavior in such open field settings as the hallways, playground, cafeteria, and buses.

## REFERENCES

Allen, R. (1988). *Common Sense Discipline: What to Say and Do When Kids Need Help.* Tyler, TX: Common Sense Publications.

Jones, F. (1978). *Positive Discipline.* New York: McGraw Hill.

Kounin, J. (1970). *Discipline and Group Management in Classrooms.* New York: Holt, Rinehart and Winston.

Lunenburg, F. (1990). *Educators' Pupil-Control Ideology as a Predictor of Educators' Reactions to Pupil Disruptive Behavior.* Paper presented at the Annual Meeting of the American Educational Research Association, Boston, MA (ERIC Document Reproduction Service No. ED 321 361).

# The Limit-Setting System

## Using the Pathway of Power of the Teacher Behavior Continuum

Ultimately, all meaningful classroom discipline must begin with setting limits. However, discipline cannot survive on limit setting alone and a teacher cannot expect students to exhibit appropriate behavior if he or she has not identified the boundaries that define that behavior. Limit setting, with its process of desist, enables the teacher to take steps to minimize the disruption caused by one or more students whose actions are preventing the teacher from instruction and the other students from learning. The limit-setting system can be used effectively within the individual classroom or in open field settings such as hallways, the playground, or the cafeteria. In its simplest terms, it is a tool for the teacher to tell the misbehaving student to stop what he or she is doing and begin doing what the teacher wants done.

To be effective at discipline, a teacher must know how to set limits. The crucial skill for using the limit-setting system is knowing how much power is appropriate to use with a given student in a given situation. Too much power can cause the misbehaving student to rebel even more, whereas too little power can signal the student that the teacher is hesitant and does not mean business.

# 3

# Looking
## The Relationship-Listening Face

Minimum Power ◄─────────────────────────────► Maximum Power

*Relationship-Listening Face*　　　*Confronting-Contracting Face*　　　*Rules and Consequences Face*

| LOOKING | NAMING | QUESTIONING | COMMANDING | ACTING |
|---|---|---|---|---|
| 1. Square off<br>　• slow down<br>　• shoulders to<br>　　shoulders<br>　• broad foot<br>　　stance<br>　• unbroken eye<br>　　contact<br>2. Relaxing breaths<br>3. Close space<br>　• far<br>　• near<br>　• intimate | | | | |

The following is a classroom discipline incident involving the teacher's use of limit setting and the first step on the Teacher Behavior Continuum—*looking* (sometimes called *modality cueing*) (see Figure 3.1). The nonitalicized words in these vignettes highlight the techniques or processes being used and will be defined throughout this chapter.

> *Ms. Sanders's seventh-grade math class is quietly working in their groups on a geometry unit. Ms. Sanders is standing by a group near the rear of the classroom. While working with the group, she hears whispers and giggles coming from a group at the front of the classroom. She* looks up *(check it out) to see Jamie quickly look down at her desk and pick up the shapes that she is pasting into her shape definition booklet. A moment later, there are whispers again, and Ms. Sanders sees Jamie playfully talking and giggling with her neighbor, Cindy, while trying to take the scissors from Cindy's hands. Jamie is clearly*

*Note:* Many of the techniques in this chapter can be found in the Positive Discipline Model created by F. Jones, *Positive Discipline* (New York: McGraw-Hill, 1987).

*off task, as well as distracting other students, requiring Ms. Sanders to take some action to get Jamie to use this time constructively and get back to work.*

---

### CHECK IT OUT

You periodically scan the classroom for off-task behavior while at the same time continue to work with students.

---

*Ms. Sanders (1) slowly stands fully erect, (2) turns her body and feet so that she is squared off with Jamie, (3) takes two controlled relaxing breaths, and (4) attempts to make eye contact with Jamie, who is not looking in her direction. Ms. Sanders remains squared off and maintains an unbroken gaze at Jamie. The other class members see Ms. Sanders's cues and signal Jamie to look in the teacher's direction. Jamie now makes eye contact with Ms. Sanders and sees the teacher looking straight at her. She picks up one of the shapes from her desk and pretends to be busy placing it on her paper in a precise spot (pseudo-compliance). She looks again to see Ms. Sanders still holding the same unwavering eye contact. Jamie meets Ms. Sanders's eye contact directly and smiles at her with an open-mouth-and-teeth smile, with a slight cock of her head and raised eyebrows ("smiley face"). The endearing smile is one that would encourage anyone to smile back automatically or reflexively, but Ms. Sanders holds her same upright posture. She maintains the eye-to-eye visual lock with Jamie and returns Jamie's smiling overture with a flat facial expression that clearly communicates "I am not amused!" At the same time, the teacher takes two more relaxing breaths. It is a look worthy of England's unsmiling Queen Victoria, notorious for her icy stare.*

---

### "SMILEY FACE"

A misbehaving student's attempt to be "innocent" and appeal to the confronting teacher by showing an open-mouth-and-teeth grin (typically the student's eyebrows lift in the middle and the head is cocked to one side).

---

### EYE CONTACT

You establish eye contact with a misbehaving student and maintain it unwaveringly until the student returns to work.

*Jamie drops her eyes to her paper and begins to take actions (pseudo-compliance) as if she is busy working with her shapes and glue. Ms. Sanders stands staring at Jamie for another minute, and then moves to a nearby student to inspect his work; however, in bending over the student's desk, she places herself so that she is still facing Jamie. Again, whispers and giggles are heard from Jamie's direction. With her body still bent over the student's desk, Ms. Sanders takes two more relaxing breaths and cranes her neck to scan the classroom, where she discovers that Jamie is off task again. Staying down, the teacher (1) excuses herself from the student she has been helping, (2) takes two more relaxing breaths, and (3) stands at a deliberate pace, slightly faster than slow motion, to an upright position. For the second time, she takes on the "I am not amused" facial expression. She then (4) stares directly at Jamie across the room while (5) placing her hands behind her back (body telegraphing).*

---

## BODY TELEGRAPHING

Through nonverbal body actions *(kinesics),* you communicate to the observing students your disapproval, or that you "mean business."

---

*Jamie sees Ms. Sanders and quickly returns to her gluing, pretending to do some form of work as a form of pseudo-compliance. Ms. Sanders takes two more relaxing breaths and waits. Seconds, or more likely minutes, click by, with Jamie being aware of receiving visual "heat" from Ms. Sanders. Like a boiling pot, she becomes active in an array of actions—she picks up the scissors from Cindy's desk, picks up a piece of construction paper, and appears to be studying the piece of paper to decide where to begin cutting (pseudo-compliance), all for the purpose of convincing Ms. Sanders that she is now working and that the teacher can turn off the visual heat.*

---

## PSEUDO-COMPLIANCE

When you signal a student to get back to work, the student performs a series of behaviors designed to convince you that the student is complying when in reality he or she is not.

---

*This time, Ms. Sanders is not fooled. She takes two more of her controlled breaths and then—still holding her visual stare—begins to walk slowly across the room, directly toward Jamie. She moves with a deliberate gait, straight out of the movie* High Noon. *She stops and squares off, just inches in front of Jamie's desk, again assuming the posture, with her hands behind her back and her face in the flat Queen Victoria "I am not amused" expression. Finally, her eyes are fixed, looking directly down at Jamie. Ms. Sanders takes her two relaxing breaths and waits.*

*Jamie responds, "Wha-a-t?" Ms. Sanders again takes two controlled breaths and maintains her fixed stare at Jamie. Seconds or even minutes pass. Jamie whines, "I wasn't doing anything. What? (back talk: denial). I needed the scissors and Cindy had them" (back talk: blaming). Ms. Sanders maintains her posture and stares. Jamie drops her eyes and becomes passive. Ms. Sanders reaches out with her right hand, moves the guide for making an octagon onto Jamie's construction paper, and points to it (prompt). She then returns to the upright Queen Victoria stare. Jamie now puts down the scissors, picks up her pencil, and begins tracing the shape onto her paper. Seeing that Ms. Sanders is still looking, Jamie whines for a second time, "I can't see the shape once I trace it to cut it out" (back talk: helplessness). Still, Queen Victoria waits before her subject (camping out in front). Again, Jamie attempts another defensive ploy: "These scissors are so old that they aren't sharp enough to cut this heavy paper. You need to get us better supplies if you want us to do stuff like this" (back talk: accusing the teacher of professional incompetence). Queen Victoria Sanders takes two more controlled breaths, holds her position, and stares. Jamie finishes tracing the shape onto her paper, picks up the scissors, and slowly cuts out the shape (giving the teacher "part of the loaf"). She now looks up at Queen Sanders with her second "smiley face"—open-mouth-and-teeth smile, raised eyebrows, and slight cock of the head. Except for two more controlled breaths, Ms. Sanders maintains her royal pose.*

---

### CAMPING OUT IN FRONT

A limit-setting technique through which you place your palms on the misbehaving student's desk, indicating that you will stay until the student's behavior changes.

---

*Jamie puts down the scissors and again appears to be contemplating where to cut out her next shape. Jamie's position seems to say to the teacher, "I'll return to my talking and playing once I get you out of my face." Jamie now appears passive and fails to continue. Ms. Sanders leans forward or eases over in a slow controlled manner and places the palms (palms) of her two hands flat on the far side of Jamie's desk and seatwork, and takes two relaxing breaths.*

*The teacher remains palms-down on Jamie's desk and watches, maintaining unwavering eye contact with Jamie* (camping out in front). *Ms. Sanders is still looking when Jamie again whines, "I'm too tired. I can't cut out any more"* (back talk: helplessness). *Queen Victoria Sanders waits before her subject* (camping out in front). *Again, Jamie retries her defensive ploy, "You need to plan ahead better so we have decent scissors. These scissors made my hands sore. I can't cut out any more shapes"* (back talk: accusing the teacher of professional incompetence). *"Cindy was hogging the scissors, I was only getting them from her"* (back talk: blaming).

*Cindy, the neighbor, now joins Jamie's power team and attempts to gang up on Ms. Sanders, stating, "Yeah, we were just sharing because there aren't enough. Get out of her face. Are you gay or something? F--- off!!"* (back talk: profanity).

*Ms. Sanders takes two more relaxing breaths and then, in a slow and controlled manner, stands erect, does her Queen Victoria imitation, takes two breaths, and slowly moves behind and between the two girls. Ms. Sanders eases between the girls and places her elbow on Jamie's desk. She then leans over and meets Jamie in a face-to-face, eyeball-to-eyeball fixed stare, with her back to Cindy* (camping out from behind). *She creates a wall between Jamie and Cindy, thus splitting up this gang of two. The teacher has divided up the problem.*

---

### CAMPING OUT FROM BEHIND

A limit-setting technique through which you move behind the off-task student and place an elbow on the student's desk, putting up a wall that blocks out a second misbehaving student, all the while using limit-setting teacher behaviors.

---

*Jamie picks up three more shape guides, traces each onto her construction paper, and then begins to cut one of the shapes out while Ms. Sanders is "camped out." When Jamie is finished cutting out the first of these shapes, Ms. Sanders speaks to her for the first time: "Thank you, Jamie." The teacher smiles, then picks up her elbow and turns around to face Cindy. She places her other elbow and her weight on Cindy's desk. Cindy does not look up and is obviously working like an eager beaver on her own geometric shapes. Ms. Sanders smiles and says, "Thank you, Cindy."*

*Queen Victoria Sanders begins to ease out from this confrontation; she slowly stands (moving out), breathes, turns, and walks to the front of Cindy's desk. She takes two relaxing breaths, assumes the royal pose, and looks directly at Cindy. Ms. Sanders slowly walks away from the girls (moving out), but first takes five or six steps, stops, turns, takes two relaxing breaths, and looks at Jamie and then Cindy. Both girls are too busy to look up.*

*Ms. Sanders walks back to the group that she was originally working with, but before bending over to help, she again takes a Queen Victoria look at Jamie and Cindy. After finally being reassured, she takes two more relaxing breaths and bends over to observe the work done by one of the students in the group, placing herself beside the student but again in direct view of Jamie and Cindy, as well as the rest of the class.*

*Once she has finished working with the group, Ms. Sanders slowly walks among the students' groups, traversing an interior circle around the classroom as she passes among the working students. She checks on various students' work, and passes again before Jamie and Cindy.*

*While walking about, she stops, looks, checks, and in a voice soft enough that a neighbor cannot hear, makes comments about a particular student's work before moving on (working the crowd). In all, she speaks to six or seven students. When she comes to Cindy, three minutes before the bell is to ring, she appears to stop, look, check, and comment in a similar fashion. But this time, she whispers a different nonacademic statement: "Cindy, after the bell rings I would like you to stay behind—we need to talk" (camouflage).*

---

### WORKING THE CROWD

While instructing, you walk around the room to make eye contact and be physically close to each student (proxemics) to retain control and compliance.

---

### CAMOUFLAGE

You stop and whisper to several students about their work, but when you whisper to a misbehaving student, you deliver a limit-setting statement, thus disguising the confronting behavior from the other students.

---

*Minutes later, the bell rings and the students depart, passing Ms. Sanders as she stands at the door. When Cindy arrives, the teacher signals her to move to a nearby desk, then closes the door to the now empty classroom* (private meeting). *It is time for Ms. Sanders to deal with Cindy regarding her use of profanity* (don't go public!). *Ms. Sanders has not forgotten Cindy's words, "Get out of her face. Are you gay or something? F--- off!!"*

## LIMIT SETTING: THE TBC'S *LOOKING*

The objective for all limit setting is to calm the students and get them back on task, as Ms. Sanders did with Jamie. Jones (1987), author of *Positive Classroom Discipline,* documented that 80 percent of all discipline problems involve the off-task behavior of students talking to others when they should be working. The second most common form is goofing off or out-of-seat behaviors (15 percent), followed by such misbehaviors as note passing, playing with items smuggled into class, and tying shoelaces. When most people think of discipline problems, however, they usually think of the "big ticket" items of physical aggression, overt defiance, and destruction of property. Using time as a central variable, one can justify and think out the value of a teacher's actions, asking, "How much does this teacher technique cost in time?" Discipline procedures may be employed, but if they use so much of class time that none is left for instruction, the techniques are of no value.

Big-ticket discipline actions—assault and clear defiance of the teacher's authority—are normally rare occurrences. These incidents take five minutes or less, and generally are seen by teachers no more than five times in a school year. By simply multiplying the five incidents by five minutes, one may spend a great deal of time worrying about big-ticket discipline incidents that might actually consume 25 minutes or less of one's teaching time in an entire school year. What is more important is to watch the "nickel-and-dime" actions of talking and out-of-seat behavior, which, when combined, could eat up one-third or more of the total class time. For all the concern about big-ticket incidents, it is these nickel-and-dime misbehaviors that consume most of a teacher's energies and eventually wear him or her down. Jamie and Cindy's talking may be seen as a minor incident at first, but it did cause the teacher to stop her instruction. Multiply that by 8 to 10 such incidents in a relatively short span, and they will add up, wear teachers out, and cut deeply into "time on task," which is necessary for academic achievement.

The Jamies and Cindys of the classroom play a power game and participate in penny-ante gambling. When these girls face Ms. Sanders for the first time, they may wonder, "Does she really mean what she says? Do we have to work in this classroom or can we play?" Jamie, as a *low roller,* or gambler, has an advanced degree in the "Teacher Game" to see who will hold the power in this classroom—to see how far she can go, to test this teacher, to see if this woman means business. Jamie has learned a host of pseudo-compliance behaviors to sidetrack the teacher during power plays.

---

## LOW ROLLER

A student who attempts to play power games with you in subtle ways that do not involve much risk of detection.

---

If Jamie can get the teacher to buy into these behaviors when the teacher asks her to stop playing and get to work, the teacher will lose the game and control will shift to Jamie's game playing. Although these behaviors look different and take various forms and can be negative or positive, the techniques are all labeled as *back talk*. When confronted for compliance, Jamie and Cindy began a conscious and unconscious series of back talk maneuvers to take Ms. Sanders down a blind alley toward powerlessness and defeat. This back talk took the following forms in the scenario just witnessed:

- *Helplessness:* "I can't see the shape once I trace it to cut it out."

- *Denial:* "I wasn't doing anything. What?"

- *Blaming:* "I needed the scissors and Cindy had them."

- *Accusing the teacher of professional incompetence:* "You need to plan ahead better so we have decent scissors."

- *Excusing the teacher to leave:* "Yeah, get out of her face."

- *Insult:* "Are you gay or something?"

- *Profanity:* "F--- off!!"

Other forms of back talk that do not appear as such to most teachers include:

- *Crying:* The student attempts to get the teacher's sympathy.

- *Compliments:* The student makes flattering statements to the teacher.

- *Tangential statements:* The student asks a question about a topic not under discussion.

- *Pushing you aside:* When the teacher puts her hands on the desk, palms down, the student pushes them aside and off the desk.

- *Romance:* The student actually kisses the teacher's hand or makes a sexual overture.

Every student knows the power game that is proceeding, with the ultimate prize being to see the teacher lose her cool, signaling victory for the students and a total lack of control of the classroom.

## Fight-or-Flight Response

Suppose that you were driving your car and stopped at a red light. The light changed and you slowly pulled into the intersection, but another driver ran the light and barreled through the intersection at excessive speed. If you had not suddenly jammed on your brakes and turned your steering wheel quickly, you would have had a very serious accident. The adrenaline pumped through your body, your heart was in your throat, your face was warm, and your teeth were clenched. For a moment, you felt as if you might throw up, and as you got out of your car 15 minutes later, your legs were still wobbly. You were experiencing the results of a *fight-or-flight* response.

---

### FIGHT OR FLIGHT

A primal, unthinking reflex action either to dig in for a fight or to run away, all triggered by frightening or confrontational behavior.

---

As another example, suppose a 2- or 3-year-old child has broken from mother's hand and run into a busy street, or pushed over the white-hot charcoal grill, or released the parking brake on dad's car, or some similar action that clearly could be life-threatening for the child or others. Moments later, the parent may be nose-to-nose with the child, screaming at the child never to do that again. The parent's emotional state and inside feelings are similar to the near automobile accident. For all intents and purposes, the parent—quite understandably—is hysterical and out of control, and the child will be lucky to avoid being hit or shaken harshly. Teachers in schools and classrooms, of course, cannot deal with students in the same manner as the parent deals with the misbehaving child.

In situations such as these, the body experiences an *adrenaline dump* triggered by an external stimulus that causes a reflex body action. Like the parent, one usually goes out of control in this hyper-alert state, meaning that for a short period, one loses the use of rational reasoning and functions as an automatic defensive being. Rational thinking is too slow for sudden emergencies, and the body has a built-in survival process that shuts down higher-order thinking so the defensive reflexes can act to save themselves. When animals are cornered, their lack of language abilities and rational thinking leaves them with only two choices—they can fight or they can flee. Humans experience a similar response when events push them out of rational thinking. This fight-or-flight response exacts a high price in the level of stress and burned-up energy.

---

### ADRENALINE DUMP

An emotional state, triggered by some action, causing a fight-or-flight state with a huge rush of adrenaline into the blood stream, resulting in extremely high and sudden levels of tension or stress.

---

Theoreticians suggest that humans have what may be thought of as three brains. This *triune brain* contains (1) a reptilian brain located at the base of the brain stem; (2) a paleocortex, or an ancient cortex; and (3) a neocortex, or a new cortex of higher intelligence. The Triune Brain Theory (see Figure 3.1) suggests that each of these three brains has its own functions, but under stress, a person's thought processes downshift to lower primal brain centers for purposes of survival. Under moderate arousal, the management of behavior shifts from the neocortex to the paleocortex. Under extreme arousal, the management of behavior shifts from the paleocortex to the reptilian brain. This means that when a person is angry, frightened, or upset, he or she becomes a noncortical, animal-like being, and higher thinking from the neocortex is unavailable until he or she calms down. The downshift occurs in two forms: an *adrenaline dump* or a *slow "bleeding"* of adrenaline into the body system, which maintains a constant defensive state of stress.

In the automobile near-miss and the parent reprimanding the child for a dangerous action, a full regression or downshifting occurs to either the reptilian brain or the paleocortex as a result of a full adrenaline dump. In the classroom, discipline incidents may occur that are extremely confrontational toward the teacher, as seen in Jamie's

---

**FIGURE 3.1   Triune Brain Functioning**

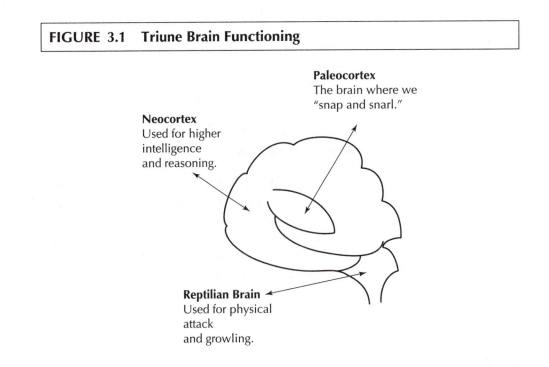

**Paleocortex**
The brain where we "snap and snarl."

**Neocortex**
Used for higher intelligence and reasoning.

**Reptilian Brain**
Used for physical attack and growling.

implicit verbal aggression of "I'll return to my talking once I get you out of my face, so buzz off!" Other examples, admittedly less frequent, may include a student who has a weapon, who is spiteful and hurtful to others, or who exhibits a willful destruction of school property. More likely for most teachers are in the day-in, day-out moderate arousals that cause the *slow bleeding* of adrenaline into their systems. The constancy of small "nickel-and-dime" discipline incidents, such as Jamie's chatting and off-task behavior, can cause an educator to teach and function continually at a moderate arousal level. For the teacher partially in a fight-or-flight stance with its accompanying stress, classroom life may be compared with the soldier who begins to suffer battle fatigue—a constant draining of energy.

---

### ADRENALINE "BLEED"

A state of hyper-alertness where the body is in a partial fight-or-flight state, continually producing adrenaline and causing constant tension.

---

The "slow bleed" phenomenon is caused by stress; clear and practical actions to control this stress can maintain the teacher's classroom power and effectiveness. In the student power game, the ultimate way of winning control of the classroom is for the teacher to regress to a state where he has "lost his cool," meaning the teacher is so emotional that he is reflexively acting from his reptilian brain and his higher-order thinking is unavailable. A high probability exists that this teacher, in the absence of cortex thinking, will do something dumb. When the teacher has regressed *(gone brain stemmed),* it is "show time" for the students. The teacher is now out of control and the students are in control, and the teacher's behavior tends to be quite amusing to the students as he struggles in an attempt to regain control of his classroom.

---

### "GOING BRAIN STEMMED"

In a heated conflict, the brain downshifts to the reflexive, noncognitive reptilian brain. When this occurs, it suggests that you are out of control and are instead controlled by emotions.

---

Another example of a high-stress situation is a baseball umpire. It's the last of the ninth inning and the home team is down by two runs with two outs and the bases loaded. The batter hits a single to right field. The runner on third base scores, and the runner on second base rounds third and heads for home as the tying run. The right fielder makes a powerful, accurate throw to home plate. It's a close play, and as the dust clears, 50,000 spectators, millions watching on television, and the players—their multimillion-dollar contracts depending on the outcome of games such as this—are all waiting for this one individual, the umpire, to call the play. The umpire looks (see it), points his thumb to the heavens, shouts, "You're out!" (sell it), and prepares himself as all hell breaks loose (must live it). The home team's players and manager pour from the dugout and descend on the umpire—a lone man in a stressful situation who now needs to live with his decision. A power game begins with the manager shouting in the umpire's face. The manager's power game is to see if the umpire "means business" or if he can get the umpire to back down.

Note what the umpire does. He removes his face mask, plants his feet firmly on the ground, and squares off to the manager, who is screaming in his face as the TV cameras zoom in for a close-up. The umpire puts his hands behind his back and crosses them, while he maintains unwavering eye contact with the hostile manager. He takes on a facial expression that says, "I am bored. I wonder what I'll have for dinner tonight," and appears to mentally leave the ball park. If he is skilled, he says nothing and stands his ground, maintaining unwavering eye contact with everyone who is back talking to him. He simply stands there and breathes deeply, waiting for the manager and players to wear themselves out with insults, blame, and questions of his professional competence (back talk).

Doing nothing is the umpire's act of power and control. If he cannot control the adrenaline rush moving through his body, he will *go brain stemmed,* or lose his "cool," and begin to talk back to the manager and players. If this happens, he is doomed to lose control, and real violence may erupt. This would cause the most dangerous of situations among the players and fans. A very important lesson for the classroom teacher can be learned from the baseball umpire's behavior. As a teacher, you will find yourself in confrontational situations with students involving heated and stressful interaction and back talk, but, like the umpire, you must control your behavior and maintain power. "Calm is strength. Upset is weakness" (Jones, 1993, p. 32).

The behavior of a teacher who has "gone brain stemmed" or *"gone chemical"* (meaning physically full of adrenaline and overcome by fight or flight posture) clearly leads to ineffective discipline.

---

### "GONE CHEMICAL"

During a confrontational limit-setting process, you become so emotional that adrenaline is heavily released into the body, making you so tense that you cannot think correctly.

---

*In a harsh voice one step short of actually shouting, Ms. Hopkins says, "If I have told you once, Wanda and Marie, I have told you a hundred times." (The teacher stands with her left hand on her left hip, balancing on her left leg and tapping her right foot, as she points and shakes her finger across the room at the girls in a threatening action.) "This is work time. I don't want to see you two talking, and I don't want to have to come over there! This is valuable class time and you, young ladies, are losing it. I am sick and tired of having to stop my work because of you two girls!"*

This teacher is a nagging person who is under stress and has regressed to a fight-or-flight position, probably with only her paleocortex in gear. Like an animal, the teacher "snaps and snarls" and does silly talk; the words she says mean nothing and are even poor examples of threats. The hand pointing and similar physical actions are nonverbal territorial actions, used in the animal kingdom by creatures to intimidate and scare off rivals. The screaming baseball manager is a good example of silly talk as he gestures and shouts, but these are a part of the manager's powerlessness and game playing. The fans, however, are entertained because it is show time. Students see these behaviors in teachers and are not fearful, but are entertained by the sight of a teacher who is so weak that the students can "push her button" and get such an entertaining action from an adult who is supposed to be mature and in charge: "It's show time, classmates."

## Eye Contact and Proxemics

In animal species and also among humans, contact with another individual is done by reading nonverbal body messages, and the eyes are the most expressive source of nonverbal communication. An unswerving eye lock with an individual is the most powerful confrontational stance involving real power and subservience. Eye contact with another individual is a direct challenge or exercise of power, and when the other individual breaks the visual lock, it is read as capitulation and subservience ("I don't wish to fight; I yield to your power"). One person literally stares the other down. The dominant person looks and the other person smiles back as a signal of capitulation, or "I wish to be your friend." If the dominant person smiles back, the offer of friendship is accepted. If the dominant person does not smile back or break the heat of looking, there is a direct power challenge.

*Jamie meets Ms. Sanders's eye contact directly and smiles at her with an open-mouth-and-teeth smile, with a slight cock of her head and raised eyebrows ("smiley face"). The endearing smile is one that would encourage anyone to smile back automatically or reflexively, but Ms. Sanders holds her same upright posture. She maintains the eye-to-eye visual lock with Jamie and returns Jamie's smiling overture with a flat facial expression that clearly communicates "I am not amused!" At the same time, the teacher takes two more relaxing breaths.*

The "heat" that the other person will feel from being visually confronted will depend on the spatial distance between the two people, as indicated by the concept of proxemics. Across the classroom, the challenge may be very strong but can be fended off by many game-playing students. However, when the teacher moves to the edge of the student's desk and leans over it, the visual heat is turned up dramatically and the student's inner kettle of emotions begins to bubble—fueled by the output of adrenaline and stress within the student. The student is now in a fight-or-flight confrontation with the teacher.

Most people have personal space around them—an invisible three-foot "bubble" in which they feel safe. When this space is invaded by others, the person becomes emotionally uncomfortable and feels potentially threatened. When you touch students, place your hands on what they touch, or place your face inches from theirs, you burst their bubble and the protective safety of their personal space. You force them to resist or back down (fight or flight).

When visually confronting a misbehaving student, space distances can be classified as *proximity-far* when the teacher is across the room, *proximity-near* when within three feet or at the edge of the student's comfort bubble, and *proximity-intimate* when mere inches from the student's face. As the teacher, you actually use these three distances as a technique of signaling the student to desist and return to work, and escalate the intrusion by doing a slow walk. You begin a process of *closing space* and start to turn up the heat in the confrontational process. The slow movement of walking and all other easing movements are for the purpose of giving the student time to recognize and understand the challenge, and to allow you to maintain and body-telegraph a calm message of "I am in charge" and "I mean business."

---

### COMFORT BUBBLE

An invisible three-foot circle around the student, in which the student is secure and feels threatened if someone invades this space.

---

### CLOSING SPACE

In limit setting, you escalate the confrontation by moving toward the student and "accepting" the student's challenge.

---

## Limit Setting on the Wing

"Proximity is accountability. Distance is safety" (Jones, 1987, p. 57). The teacher who has been trained in the Three Faces of Discipline will not be found lecturing from behind her desk, seated on top of his desk, or seated in a chair. The Three Faces of Discipline style of teaching requires the teacher to be on his or her feet slowly walking and working the crowd, moving among the students who are seated at desks or tables. When walking, or "on the wing," the teacher is aware of and uses eye contact and proximity to maintain the attentiveness or work activity of each and every student. The combination of walking and looking creates a conscious ballet of movement that will bring the teacher in proximity-far (as far as 10 feet) and proximity-near (at the edge of the 3-foot "comfort bubble" of each student). Periodically, when bending over to help one student for a few moments, the teacher is in proximity-intimate. Throughout the entire class period, students will always feel the teacher's presence, whether the teacher is instructing or the students are doing independent seatwork.

For the teacher to perform this walking ballet and to work the crowd, it is critical to have well-designed staging of the students' desks, chairs, and tables. Classrooms traditionally are thought of as six rows of five or more chairs each, with the teacher's desk before a chalkboard at the front of the classroom. In such a room arrangement, however, the desks act as a defensive wall, placing distance between the teacher and the students and always maintaining the teacher at the proximity-far. Instead, the students' desks should be arranged with an interior loop as a pathway for the teacher to walk through (see Figure 3.2).

**FIGURE 3.2    Classroom Arrangement**

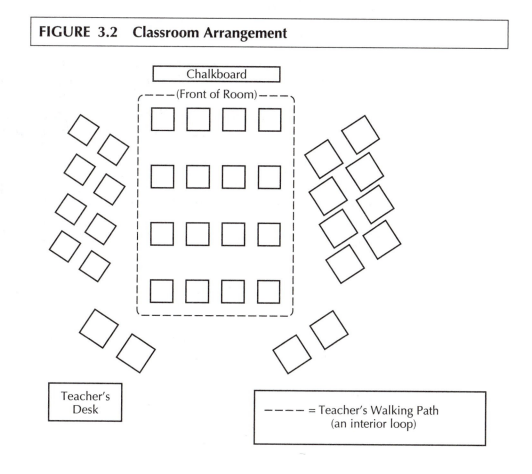

The use of an interior loop of free floor space, where the teacher can walk without obstruction, permits easy teacher movement and excellent supervision through the use of proximity and eye contact. The effective arrangement of furniture, space, and objects will be discussed in detail in Section VI, but it is important to point out that space and its arrangement are critical for the use of proximity constructing and the TBC's *Looking*.

## *LOOKING* AND THE THREE FACES CONCEPT

The practical applications of these techniques can be explained using the same students from the earlier example but with two entirely different teacher approaches.

> *It is Monday morning and the class is working in groups. The quiet working atmosphere is somewhat disrupted by giggles from the far side of the room. Two students' heads bob up to look, and then return to their talking. The teacher sees Jamie and Cindy's heads together and hears them giggling, and it is apparent that they are off task.*

Now lets observe two entirely different teachers—Ms. HIGH Profile and Ms. LOW Profile—as they attempt to get Jamie and Cindy to stop their off-task behavior.

### Ms. HIGH Profile

> *In an angry voice from across the classroom, Ms. HIGH Profile says, "That is enough! Stop it, and stop it right now!" She points and wags her finger at the girls. "I have had enough of your behavior, and I am sick and tired of it. Get back to work immediately!" (This is the paleocortex brain speaking.)*

As a result of Ms. HIGH Profile's strong verbal broadcasting across the room, all the students in the class—who previously were working—are now looking and, like spectators at a tennis match, have their heads bouncing from the teacher to the girls, back to the teacher, and again back to the girls. Their concentration on their seatwork has been disrupted and most have experienced a mild form of fight-or-flight response as they initially wondered if the teacher was reprimanding them. The students then recognized that the teacher's outburst was directed at Jamie and Cindy, and they now wish to see if a confrontation will develop between Ms. HIGH Profile and the girls. They wonder to themselves, "Is this show time?"

Only a few of the classmates will now be able to focus and return their concentration to their work. The rest begin to wiggle in their chairs, check their watches, and begin mentally "gathering wool." Meanwhile, Jamie and Cindy make pseudo-compliance behaviors (Jones, 1987) and pass a victory smile between themselves.

### Ms. LOW Profile

*Walking about the classroom, Ms. LOW Profile notices the off-task girls. She stops, slowly takes two relaxing breaths, stands upright with her hands clasped behind her back, and looks directly at the girls. They look up and see her looking directly at them. Ms. LOW Profile takes two more relaxing breaths and broadcasts the nonverbal facial expression of "I am not amused." Jamie puts down the scissors that she was in the process of taking from Cindy's desk and turns her attention to the shapes and paper on her own desk. Cindy picks up her pencil and pretends to be tracing a shape on her paper (pencil posturing). Ms. LOW Profile takes another two relaxing breaths and maintains unwavering eye contact. She walks slowly across the room and stops at the edge of the girls' desks and takes two relaxing breaths. The girls now shift their legs under their desks and away from each other and begin to do real work. Ms. LOW Profile maintains her eye contact for another two minutes, then returns to her previous task. No one else in the class was even aware of this interaction.*

Kounin's (1970) classic study in classroom management demonstrated that classroom teachers who used high-profile desists had poor classroom discipline and fewer academic gains than teachers using low-profile correction. It is this "nickel-and-dime" day-in, day-out limit setting, which Kounin labels *desists,* that makes or breaks a teacher's discipline and classroom management practices. The high-profile teacher in the example caused a greater disruption than the off-task girls she was disciplining. In reality, the teacher was the person who most disrupted the learning in that classroom.

Middle grade students' learning about appropriate social interactions and peer approval is of paramount importance. When adults model ineffective interactions and "attack" students, the other students are naturally inclined to defend their peers (Chernow & Chernow, 1989).

Getting students to desist, or stop, requires a technique of skills and teaching abilities if these desists are to be skillful and effective. Two general problems may arise when a desist is ineffective: (1) the teacher can overpower or "slam dunk" the off-task student(s), as Ms. HIGH Profile did, or (2) the teacher can use behaviors that do not have enough power, and students view the teacher as not meaning business. The teacher can use appropriate desist techniques but the misbehaving student may escalate the power game from minimum pseudo-compliance to defiant back talk, or may fully escalate to the point of assaulting the teacher. The teacher, therefore, needs a range of techniques and teacher behaviors to deal with such varying degrees of student challenges to the teacher's authority.

The Three Faces of Discipline position with the use of the Teacher Behavior Continuum, then, is an array of techniques for teacher responses ranging from minimum to maximum use of power and intrusion by the teacher. It will be the well-trained and skilled teacher who will know how to use this power and varying degrees of techniques effectively. The result will be compliance and cooperation from the off-task student while still maintaining the teacher-student relationship and avoiding alienation.

Limit setting is the process of taking actions toward one or more students who, by their actions, are preventing the teacher from teaching or other classmates from learning, or are failing to follow required procedures and rules. Simply put, it is a request that says to the student, "Stop what you are doing and do what I, the teacher, want you to do." Limit setting will start with the day-in, day-out small off-task behaviors, but can also expand to conflict management and blow up to outward defiance by the student in the form of an assault against the teacher. To be effective at discipline, a teacher must know how to set limits. The crucial skill in limit setting is knowing how much power, inherent in your action, is appropriate. Too much power is like using a sledgehammer to drive in a tack, whereas too little power may communicate to the students that you are afraid of them and do not mean business (Jones, 1993).

## Private versus Public Desist

Beginning in the elementary school years and blossoming in middle childhood, students begin to assert their own autonomy in relating to adults, while at the same time they wish to find social acceptance among peers. Peer pressure and loyalty can be much stronger than teacher and adult pressure (Milgram, 1992). When the teacher gives a high-profile desist (e.g., confronting Jamie or Cindy with the entire class as an audience), the student feels she must stand up to the teacher to gain or maintain status in her peers' eyes. Therefore, an informed and skilled teacher will heed the cardinal rules of limit setting, as part of the Three Faces of Discipline, and attempt to keep any desist actions private and always low profile between the teacher and misbehaving student. If necessary, the teacher may escalate to more controlling semi-private actions, where only the misbehaving student knows what is being said but the peers are aware that something is afoot. Public actions are high profile for all to see, and may include involvement of the school principal, a counselor, parents, and even law enforcement or mental health authorities.

---

### CARDINAL RULE 1

Make a desist as private as possible.

---

The second cardinal rule of limit setting, within the Three Faces desist process, is to use as little power as necessary to get the desired change in student behavior—beginning with nonintrusive Relation-ship-Listening techniques and, if necessary, readily escalating to the more powerful techniques found in Confronting-Contracting, and, finally, Rules and Consequences. The construct applies both of these variables, power and privacy, through the use of the Teacher Behavior Continuum.

---

### CARDINAL RULE 2

Use as little power as necessary to get positive change in the misbehaving student's behavior.

---

## Limit Setting as a Desist

The Jamie and Cindy vignette shows nonverbal limit setting only while the students are doing seatwork. But other situations will also arise that demand a response, such as (1) during direct instruction; (2) while the teacher is working with a small group of students at one side of the room and a desist is needed for a student across the room; and (3) in an open field situation such as hallways, playgrounds, and the cafeteria.

## Desist during Direct Instruction

While presenting information or explaining a concept, a teacher may wish the entire class to give their total attention "up front," and students (such as Cindy) who are acting out and not paying attention begin to rival the teacher for attention. A redirect, a low-profile desist may be most appropriate at first. If that does not work, escalating to stop in midsentence and begin the first step of eye contact may be appropriate. Finally, a sidestep of the confrontation may be necessary.

> *Ms. Sanders is near the end of a lesson on geometry when Cindy giggles and draws glances of 20 percent of her classmates. The class is gradually being drawn away from its focus on Ms. Sanders, with that focus shifting toward Cindy. Ms. Sanders states, "Class, when you are trying to find the surface area of a three-dimensional shape, it might help you to try to visualize an everyday object that has the same shape. For instance, Cindy, you will notice that..." Ms. Sanders pauses for a split second, makes solid eye contact as she says Cindy's name, and then prompts by using her writing hand to sweep across the students with a pointing gesture. She checks for eye contact with all students, and stops this pointing and hand sweep in Cindy's direction. She again makes eye contact and then moves her hand in a gesture that seems to say "follow me" back to a focal point on the chalkboard. Once the chalk hits the board, Ms. Sanders again makes eye contact with Cindy and continues the lesson. "This rectangular prism looks very much*

*like a box that holds tissues and you can see clearly that it has
six sides."*

The entire sequence is a *low-profile correction* as a redirection. The
teacher said Cindy's name, made eye contact, and used a prompting gesture in a matter of seconds, and did it generally unnoticed by classmates. The rest of the class continued to be mentally and perceptually
focused on the point that Ms. Sanders was making, and the pacing of the
lesson was maintained. At the same time, Ms. Sanders gave repeated
visual prompts to Cindy to signal her to desist and comply. This is an
example of low-profile correction during instruction.

What if Cindy did not get the message or wants to play a power
game? Middle school students are especially aware of their relationships
with others. A persistent question for them in their relationships with
their peers is that of "Who do you think I am?" In addition, the movement into adolescence is one toward a greater need for freedom from
total authority of adults, including teachers (Steinberg, 1990). These
factors can influence a middle school student's desire to engage in a
power game with a teacher. In this case, we would now view Cindy as
playing the transactional analysis game of "I am the boss in this classroom and I will steal your power as the teacher." There will be some
teachers who would say, "Well, I would stop and tell Cindy to go to a
classroom time-out area, or use exclusionary time out and send her out
of the room. I would not let her get away with it."

That high-profile action is dangerous if Cindy is a student motivated by a desire for power or revenge (Dreikurs, 1964). The power/
revengeful Cindy will do a counter-escalation in her behavior, possibly
responding with "Make me!" challenges. If this occurs, Cindy has won
and the teacher and other students have lost because the lesson time
will now be eaten up by a confrontation. If Cindy cannot be the best
"good kid," she will attempt to be the best "bad kid." Because the teacher
has "gone high profile," Cindy has won and is now in control of the classroom through her behavior—Cindy is stealing time!

Handling the power/revengeful student who disrupts a lesson
requires that the student be deprived of an audience. A teacher can
either have the student move away from the class—a dangerous and
expensive risk in using time out—or have the class move away from the
student.

*Ms. Sanders states, "Class, I know that I have not quite fin-
ished my point on surface area, but I am going to stop right
here and give you time to get started on your homework. Turn
to page 24, and I want you all to do the first two problems (terminate instruction for purposes of discipline [Jones, 1987]). I
will come around in 10 minutes to see if you have done them
correctly." The teacher has now controlled classmates' reinforcement of Cindy by diverting them from looking at her misbehavior, and has sidestepped the power struggle with Cindy.
The teacher now moves about the class, stopping to whisper to*

*various students* (camouflage) *until she comes to Cindy. She now takes two relaxing breaths and gives the girl an* ear warning *using* verbal desist.

## Desist in Midsentence

One more technique, slightly more high profile in nature, can be used with a student who is disrupting during direct instruction—stop in midsentence. A student is disrupting; the teacher stops very suddenly and abruptly in midsentence and turns and *squares off* toward the student, makes eye contact, and waits while taking two relaxing breaths. The teacher waits until the student has stopped and turned around in his seat so that it is obvious his attention is back. The teacher takes two relaxing breaths and returns to the lesson.

---

### SQUARE OFF

When confronting a misbehaving student, you place your feet parallel so they face the student.

---

When a teacher holds a visual burn on a student, the class will join in by also contributing a visual burn toward their classmate. However, the student cannot hold this position for very long. Continue to wait until the class is totally quiet and inactive, joining in the visual burn. The moment any student giggles, the power ball is now in your court. You must drop the visual desist and move to sidestepping, as previously described. Get the class busy, work the crowd and do camouflage, and then end up in front of the misbehaving student to do ear warnings as a form of verbal desist or limit setting. You would only want to use a midsentence desist after first attempting a number of low-profile corrections as redirects.

## Desist across the Room

When working with a small group, it is best to locate the group meeting at the side of the room. In this way, a teacher can face each student in the small group face to face, while at the same time look over their heads to get a panoramic view of the entire classroom and the students working independently. Meeting at the front or back of the room is less preferable because it forces one to scan by making repeated head movements to the left and right.

It is also important to begin independent work with students before sectioning yourself off with a small group.

> *1. The independent workers have begun their seatwork first, before the teacher moves to the group.*

*2. The teacher has worked the crowd of seatworkers and knows that all seatworkers have completed the first problem.*

*3. A list of at least three activities is listed on the Assignment Board, located on one side of the chalkboard, that tells the students what to do if they finish this seatwork. (The last item is a catch-all general activity such as "read a book or magazine").*

*Ms. Sanders is now busy working with one of the groups and sees good old Cindy, the disrupter, off task and disturbing others. Ms. Sanders takes a greeting-card envelope from her lesson plan book and quickly gives it to a student who is seated at the end of her small group but closest to Cindy. She instructs this student to take the note, which is a desist letter, to Cindy. Ms. Sanders then returns to the small group lesson, hardly missing a beat. Cindy now has this note before her on her desk. She opens it and reads, "Stop! Get back to work!" (The teacher will collect this desist letter and envelope at the end of the period and return it to her lesson plan book, where it is always available.)*

*If this low-profile desist message is not effective with Cindy (her disruptions continue), Ms. Sanders takes two relaxing breaths and terminates the lesson with the small group ("discipline before instruction" [Jones, 1987]). She excuses herself: "Excuse me, group. Hold on just one minute, please!" Ms. Sanders takes another two relaxing breaths, and then turns, stands, looks, and says Cindy's first name. She takes another two relaxing breaths and then waits. If Cindy's misbehavior does not stop, the teacher sidesteps by putting her small group to work. She then continues to move up the limit-setting steps, beginning by walking to the desk, and then progressing to prompting the off-task student and camping out from behind. If all these nonverbal limit-setting steps fail, Ms. Sanders will abandon the limit setting of Looking and go to verbal limit setting* (explained in later chapters).

"Discipline comes before instruction" (Jones, 1987). The teacher is instructing one student at his seat and is just getting to the point of closure on her mini-lesson when a discipline situation surfaces. The teacher may think, "I will just ignore Cindy for another minute until I finish this instruction with Mark, and then I will go and take care of the problem." While instruction is, of course, the first priority of any classroom, students cannot give learning their full attention if student misbehavior is allowed to continue. But if students learn that classroom disruptions will be tolerated while instruction is occurring, they will take every opportunity for nickel-and-dime misbehaviors; they will gamble that they can get away with it, and the teacher will get little instruction done in the future. "Pay now with small change, or pay later with big dollars to remediate the problem" (Jones, 1987). Terminating instruction requires the teacher to apologize to the first student in a way that says she is about to escalate her use of power by dealing with the misbehavior.

---

### CARDINAL RULE 3

Discipline comes before instruction.

---

Some teachers may argue that Cindy has gotten away with disrupting the small group lesson. But an important principle of visual limit setting is that discipline must come before instruction, or pay pennies now and save dollars later in remediation if you discipline. If Ms. Sanders would have "gone high profile," there would have been a disruption of all learning in the classroom, with a likelihood that other students would begin to act up. The procedure just described allowed the small group to continue learning, avoided a disruption of the learning of the other students, and permitted the teacher to deal with Cindy. Ms. Sanders spent the time ("currency") to deal with Cindy in the short term, knowing that it will pay off in the long run.

A summary of the teacher techniques used in a classroom desist includes: During direct instruction or when actively involved with a small group, handle the desist first with a redirect (low-profile desist). If that does not work, escalate to stopping in midsentence and using eye contact. Finally, if need be, sidestep the confrontation. The overriding principle in such actions is to maintain control of your classroom and not permit the power/revengeful student to take over and determine the classroom agenda, yet, at the same time, stay private and use power on your own terms.

## Desist in an Open Field

Supervising the cafeteria, school yard or playground, hallways, lavatories, and other open field areas are generally part of a teacher's responsibility that place demands on limit-setting skills. All the general principles developed so far still hold true for these settings. The minimum amount of power possible should be used and a private process should be maintained. This means that the TBC's *Looking* as a nonverbal desist will dominate actions.

Making a desist in an open field setting can present a number of difficulties. The biggest of these is that many times you will not know the student you are confronting and have not built a relationship of good will with that student. To make such open field limit setting work, it is critical that the structures of the motor rules of behavior be taught to students through a schoolwide training program (described in Section VI) and that all teaching staff accept the philosophy that outside of the individual classroom, "every student is the teacher's student" (Jones, 1993).

Another potential problem is that since open field settings are so dynamic, with many students moving about, the teacher will not take adequate time to use *Looking* with eye contact and proximity, but too quickly will overpower the situation by moving to a verbal desist of naming, questioning, or commanding. When a student is acting out in the cafeteria or the hallway, a teacher should follow the nonverbal limit setting of *Looking,* as previously outlined.

1. *Work the crowd.* Talking with a colleague or student and not walking around and looking is not supervision. You must be working the crowd to use proximity as an effective tool. When misbehavior does occur, you are then in the best position to intervene.

2. *Terminate whatever you are doing.*

3. *Turn (you should be standing), look, and catch the student's attention—nonverbally cue the student.* Most students who disrupt are motivated by attention getting (Dreikurs, 1964), and since these students are an annoying and a repeated problem, your natural tendency is to move away from them. However, this is just the opposite of what is needed. If you do not know the attention-getting student's name and it is apparent that he is going to repeatedly challenge you in this supervision situation, find out his name and learn it. Personalize yourself with the student before any difficulty occurs again by chatting with him to establish good will and a solid relationship.

4. *Walk to the student.* Most likely, you will not be able to catch a student's eye, especially in an active cafeteria, from a level of proximity-far. As a result, you will be required to close space by walking to the edge of the student's "comfort bubble" (proximity-near).

5. *Prompt.* Prompting normally will be the highest step you will need to use. For example, a student departs from the cafeteria table, leaving his trash behind. You intercept him as he is about to leave the cafeteria, make eye contact, square off, take two relaxing breaths, and simply point (prompt) to the table from which he came. If he still does not understand, point to the waste cans and then back to the table. Suppress the desire to lecture, threaten, or make any remarks.

6. *Camp out in front.* If need be, you must be willing to give the time to camp out.

7. *Camp out from behind.* If two or more students are involved, attempt to put a wall between them so you can deal with one student at a time.

If the student escalates his behavior and the TBC's step of *Looking* fails, move to Step 2: *Naming,* as a verbal desist. When using a verbal desist in open field settings, obey the cardinal rule of "keep it private." Speak to the misbehaving student softly so classmates will not hear, or ask the student to walk with you (getting him or her out of the earshot of fellow classmates before delivering verbal limit setting). Unless it is a safety-threatening situation or one that could cause significant property damage, never verbally confront the student with an audience of peers in the fairly open, unstructured context of an open field setting. This nonclassroom and less formal setting will encourage the student to escalate a confrontation when he or she might never consider doing so in the classroom environment.

Effective teachers have "with-it-ness," meaning that at all times they are perceptually and cognitively aware of what is occurring in their classrooms or the open field areas such as the cafeteria. They repeatedly check out what students are doing. To be effective in doing this, consideration as to where to "park the body" is particularly important. If Ms. Sanders is helping one student and is bent over with her head down and her back to 80 percent of the classroom, she will not hear Luis tearing out a piece of notebook paper to make spitballs, or see Stan creep among the desks to snatch Harold's cap from his back pocket, or notice Angelica abandoning her math problems to snap open her purse to brush her hair for the thousandth time.

---

### WITH-IT-NESS

Your ability to be perceptually aware of what is going on in the classroom.

---

As a "with-it" teacher, park your body with your back to the closest wall so that peripheral vision will allow viewing as much of the classroom as possible. A good classroom arrangement will facilitate effective body positioning. Additionally, never get "lost" perceptually in the one student you are helping. If one student is standing before you, step back, take her by the shoulder, and turn her around, allowing full view of her and the class. Bending down to look at a student's paper necessitates heightening hearing awareness to take over for the loss of vision. Periodically bobbing a head up like radar to make a 270-degree scan of the classroom allows a teacher to make quick eye contact with any student who is giving some thought to gambling on an off-task behavior. If the classroom furniture, especially the desks, have been arranged properly, and if the teacher's' body is parked with the back to the wall and facing students, this is the best position to see what is happening in the classroom. The term *check it out* means simply that a teacher needs to keep broad perceptions running, even when focused on one student or activity, and "surfacing" regularly to visually scan and check things out.

## Facial Expression

The smiling exchange between two individuals speaks volumes. If one person makes eye contact and the second smiles, this smile is seen through an animal kingdom perspective as a submission response signaling capitulation and "I want to be a friend." The dominant individual smiles back and the communication is "Yes, I wish to return your friendship." When a smile does not occur, a power confrontation between two individuals occurs. Using the TBC's *Looking* will communicate that the classroom is your territory, that you mean business and are in control, and that you will use the eye signal to establish this dominance.

In confronting Cindy, Ms. Sanders is struggling to control the fight-or-flight response, which causes her eyes to widen and her teeth to clench, producing a fight-or-flight "face." To stop this from occurring, it is suggested that you allow your face to relax and unclench your teeth by becoming slack-jawed. While standing and staring, take your tongue and curl it back in your mouth until you can touch the beginning of the soft tissue at the back of the mouth. This opens up the jaw and creates the slack jaw effect, ensuring that in a confrontation you will not grit your teeth as a result of the fight-or-flight reflex.

Now, the student, under the heat of eye contact, will do a "silly" smile, described as an open-mouth-and-teeth smile with a slight cock of the head and raised eyebrows, much like a baby might smile at his parents. The smiley face communicates to the adult from the child, "Look at me, aren't I cute and adorable and don't you just love me!" The teacher is to return the silly smile with a flat facial expression to send a message: "I am not amused" or "I am bored and will wait right here until you comply." At the same time, the teacher maintains eye contact to provide the visual heat.

## Additional Body Cues

When using *Looking,* every part of the body communicates and telegraphs, and it is difficult to hide internal tension. Take a wide foot stance and place your hands, which are normally a give-away for tension, behind your body, clasping them together, simply standing as relaxed as possible. You should resemble a baseball umpire at this point!

Ms. Sanders now has the Queen Victoria stance established. She stands, turns, squares off, goes slack-jawed, and says nothing. What is critical is that all of these actions are taken at a speed just slightly faster than slow motion. A teacher who wants to "rip Jamie's face off" would march in sudden, quick, and intense actions, which are not actions that communicate confidence and control. "Slower is better. Calmness is strength and communicates power" (Jones, 1987, p. 83).

## Relaxing Breaths

Any instruction in how to self-master tension and control your emotional and physical actions—such as relaxation therapy, stress management, and prepared childbirth training—involves learning to breathe properly during a stressful situation. This is done by taking two controlled slow, shallow breaths, filling about 20 percent of your lung capacity and letting it out slowly, then resting for a few seconds and repeating the sequence. The slow exhaling is critical, relaxing the body and mind and slowing down the pace of all actions.

The uninitiated may have little appreciation for the value of controlled breathing, or may even find it humorous: "What, I need to be taught to breathe? Ha!" But controlled breathing is the anchor and central technique on which is based all control in a stressful confrontational discipline situation.

The reader who wishes to put relaxing breathing techniques into practice would be advised to find a person who has had prepared childbirth training and have that person explain, model, and coach you through the process until you feel comfortable and in command of these techniques. The vignette with Ms. Sanders and Jamie shows how the teacher needs to punctuate every new action by first taking two relaxing breaths before moving in a slow, controlled manner.

## SUMMARY

When first beginning a limit-setting action, the minimum teacher action from the TBC, *Looking,* is the first step. Under this category of behavior, the teacher—in order to confront the off-task or misbehaving student—first "squares off." This means the teacher dramatically slows down his or her responses, attempting not to "go chemical"—instead getting under control. The teacher moves so her body is square-shouldered to the student. She establishes unbroken eye contact with the misbehaving student to prompt the student into an awareness that the teacher wants compliance. In this squared stance, the teacher places her hands behind her back and moves to a wider solid foot stance. The teacher body-telegraphs "I mean business," but not in a scolding or hostile manner.

To maintain self-control, the teacher takes repeated relaxing breaths before initiating any overt teacher behavior. Finally, if need be, the teacher will move from proximity-far, closing space to proximity-near, and then, in some demanding situations, to proximity-intimate. A few helpful hints follow:

- Move slowly (slightly faster than slow motion).

- Take two relaxing breaths before and after each action.

- Maintain unwavering eye contact.

- Escalate your power by closing space but be prepared to stop when compliance is established.

- Do not respond to back talk.

- Prompt if necessary.

- Be prepared to use as much time as needed.

- If you must deal with more than one student, put up a wall and deal with one at a time.

- Exit or move out in a slow, predetermined manner.

- If you expect an assault, drop *Limit Setting* and begin the *Backup System* (see Chapter 8).

The limit-setting process of *Looking* uses the least form of power and conserves the teacher's energies. Ideally, simple *Looking* would be the most preferred form of getting a desist from a misbehaving student. Most of the misbehavior of middle grade students can be corrected and controlled by *Looking*. Once a teacher masters and consistently applies *Looking,* many of the more serious misbehaviors are prevented from occurring.

# REFERENCES

Chernow, C., & Chernow, F. (1989). *Classroom Discipline Survival Guide for Middle School/Junior High Teachers*. West Nyack, NY: The Center for Applied Research in Education.

Dreikurs, R. (1964). *Children: The Challenge*. New York: PLUME.

Jones, F. (1987). *Positive Classroom Discipline*. New York: McGraw-Hill.

Jones, F. (1993). *Positive Classroom Discipline: Trainee Manual*. Santa Cruz, CA: Fred Jones and Associates.

Kounin, J. (1970). *Discipline and Group Man-agement in Classrooms*. New York: Holt, Rinehart and Winston.

Milgram, J. (1992). A portrait of diversity: The middle level student. In J. L. Irvin (Ed.), *Transforming Middle Level Education: Perspectives and Possibilities* (pp. 16–27). Boston: Allyn and Bacon.

Steinberg, L. (1990). Autonomy, conflict, and harmony in the family. In S. S. Feldman & G. R. Elliott (Eds.), *At the Threshold: The Developing Adolescent* (pp. 255–276). Cambridge, MA: Harvard University Press.

# 4

# Naming
## The Relationship-Listening Face

Minimum Power ⟵————————————————⟶ Maximum Power

*Relationship-Listening Face*      *Confronting-Contracting Face*      *Rules and Consequences Face*

| LOOKING | NAMING | QUESTIONING | COMMANDING | ACTING |
|---|---|---|---|---|
| 1. Square off<br> • slow down<br> • shoulders to shoulders<br> • broad foot stance<br> • unbroken eye contact<br>2. Relaxing breaths<br>3. Close space<br> • far<br> • near<br> • intimate | 1. Limit setting<br> • I-message<br>  – student behavior<br>  – teacher feeling<br>  – effect of student behavior<br> • Door openers<br> • Active listening<br> • Acknowledgments | | | |

If limit setting is unsuccessful with the use of *Looking* (Step 1 on the Teacher Behavior Continuum) and its subbehaviors of *closing space, proximity,* and various *visual prompts,* then it may be necessary to escalate power by moving up the TBC to *Step 2: Naming,* which involves the feelings of the student. The Relationship-Listening Face and attitude is assumed.

## VERBAL ENCODING

Verbal encoding could be used by the teacher in the example of Cindy's use of profanity:

> *Cindy, the neighbor, now joins Jamie in the confrontation and attempts to gang up on Ms. Sanders, stating, "Get out of her face. Are you gay or something? F--- off!!"* (back talk: profanity).

*Note:* Many of the techniques found in this chapter can be found in T. Gordon, *T.E.T.: Teacher Effectiveness Training* (New York: David McKay, 1974).

*Ms. Sanders replies, "Cindy, those words are telling me that you are angry and there is something very wrong (verbal encoding), and that we need to talk. I need you to return to your math work, and we will meet after lunch to talk more about this."*

Some may see verbal encoding as a very "soft," or minimal power, technique. It has the sole purpose of bringing the child to a conscious awareness of his or her action, the feelings of the student and others, and the action's effect on others.

---

### VERBAL ENCODING

Labeling the student's emotions and feelings, both positive and negative, through the use of your words.

---

## RELATIONSHIP-LISTENING FACE

The Relationship-Listening position is to view the misbehaving student as a person who has internal emotional turmoil. This inner tension shows itself as acting out or misbehavior. The role of the teacher who is wearing the Relationship-Listening Face is not to view this misbehavior (such as Cindy's verbal aggression in the form of profanity) as a personal affront, but rather as an attempt to communicate and signal that a student is unhappy and needs a nonjudgmental supportive relationship and response. Punishing the student for swearing, for example, would simply increase that anger or inner tension and make the teacher-student relationship even worse.

Using the construct of the triune brain (previously described in Chapter 3), for whatever reason, Cindy has regressed. Because of an inner fight-or-flight response, she has moved from the rational thinking of the neocortex to the paleocortex by her "snapping and snarling" actions of swearing at the teacher. Students under great tension can also regress to the reptilian brain (going brain stemmed) and become either noncommunicative and passive, or physically aggressive and assaultive.

The objective of the Relationship-Listening Face is to take supportive, empathetic actions that maintain the positive relationship with the student to help him or her become more rational and self-directed through the vehicle of language and communication. What separates humans from fight-or-flight animals is that we have language and higher order of reasoning—we can rationally and collectively solve our problems.

When we wish to communicate, we must translate and encode our inner thoughts to express them to another person in such a manner that real communication occurs. However, when the student is angry and flooded with adrenaline and has regressed to the paleocortex brain, this encoding and first attempt of communication simply comes out as verbal aggression. "Shut up, get out of my face!" or "I hate you and I hate this school!" may be the student's first attempts to encode inner thoughts and feelings and to signal the teacher that something is really upsetting this student emotionally. The central Relationship-Listening technique is the use of *Naming,* which encourages the student to ventilate by "talking it out" while the teacher (attempting to understand the student's communication) uses *active listening* or verbal encoding to reflect back, or mirror, what she thinks she is hearing the student say and feel. The more the student talks, even though it is aggressive, hostile, or negative in tone, the more he is able to ventilate and externalize his inner feelings. After a period of time, he will relax sufficiently for the rational brain (neocortex) to again come into use. At this point, real student and teacher problem solving can begin. One application of the Relationship-Listening Face to Cindy and Ms. Sanders is given here:

> *The class is busy working on group assignments. Ms. Sanders is able to pull a chair close to Cindy and speak to her in such a manner that her classmates cannot hear.*
>
> **Ms. Sanders:** *"When I am told to 'shut up' and called such names* (behavior), *it makes me angry* (feelings), *and I lose respect from the other students* (effect) *and I lose a lot of valuable teaching time"* (I-message).
>
> **Cindy:** *"I hate this school!"*
>
> **Ms. Sanders:** *"School is making you unhappy"* (active listening).
>
> **Cindy:** *"Well, uh, I want to go back to where I lived before."*
>
> **Ms. Sanders:** *"You were happy where you lived before you came here"* (active listening).
>
> **Cindy:** *"Yeah, the other kids here are damn snobs" (now sits passively and appears to be thinking deeply).*
>
> **Ms. Sanders:** *"Would you like to tell me more?"* (door opener).
>
> **Cindy:** *"They're just not friendly—they act like I'm from another planet just because I didn't go here last year."*
>
> **Ms. Sanders:** *(says nothing, but maintains eye contact and nods in such a manner to indicate to Cindy that she is still listening)* (acknowledgment).
>
> **Cindy:** *"The kids here are not like the ones I knew back home."*
>
> **Ms. Sanders:** *"You had some good friends where you used to live"* (active listening).
>
> **Cindy:** *"Yeah. Really good friends . . . and my best friend, Rose.*

> **Ms. Sanders:** *"You miss the friends that you used to be with, especially Rose"* (active listening).
>
> **Cindy:** *"Yeah, I've been friends with Rose since we were 5 years old. She was never a snob and we did lots of things together."*

In this brief exchange, the teacher opened communication with the student with the use of an *I-message* (described next) but did not warn, threaten, or lecture the student about her behavior. This would have erected *road-blocks to communication.* Instead, the teacher permitted and encouraged Cindy to make attempts at communicating and to talk out her feelings. Cindy's first attempts to encode what was bothering her came out as "snapping and snarling," reflective of the paleocortex brain. The teacher simply listened nonjudgmentally and attempted to hear what Cindy was trying to say *(empathetic listening).* Her statements were partial thoughts full of bitterness and aggressive language, but the more Cindy externalized, the more it became clear what was really bothering her: She missed her old friends and was having trouble making new ones.

To understand if she was hearing Cindy correctly, Ms. Sanders played back (mirrored) a summary of what she was hearing through a process of *active listening.* She also used *door openers* in the form of questions ("Would you like to tell me more?") to encourage more externalizing and she gave periodic nonverbal *acknowledgments* to show that she was still in tune with Cindy. The more Cindy talked, the more the inner tensions were expelled and the rational brain came into play. Later, the teacher begins to help Cindy do some problem solving to deal with her anger. As noted, the teacher did not use *roadblocks to communication* by lecturing Cindy that she should at least give it some time, that it is only the beginning of the school year, and that she'd make new friends, in time. While Cindy is flooded and using the paleocortex brain, she is not ready for such rational information or facts, and may feel that the teacher "just doesn't understand and doesn't like her, just like the other kids." The teacher's position in using the Relationship-Listening techniques is to be fully available to the student in a nonjudgmental relationship, and to encourage and permit the student to verbalize while the teacher listens (thus the label Relationship-Listening). Let's see other techniques available to the teacher when using *Naming* with this Relationship-Listening Face.

## The I-Message (Behavior-Effect-Feeling)

An *I-message* is a subbehavior for the teacher under the general category of *Naming* on the Teacher Behavior Continuum. When a student such as Cindy, with her profanity and verbal aggression, is acting in such a manner that it disrupts the class and is having a tangible effect on the teacher, the I-message is the least guilt-inducing method (after the TBC's first teacher behavior of *Looking* has failed) to express verbally to the student how her actions are affecting the teacher and the entire classroom. Here is an example of an I-message:

*When I am told to "shut up" and called such names* (behavior),
*it makes me angry* (feelings), *and I lose respect from the other
students* (effect) *and I lose a lot of valuable teaching time.*

---

### I-MESSAGE

A technique of expressing to a student that a behavior is having a negative effect on you. This statement must contain three elements: the student's *behavior*, its *effect* on you, and your *feeling* as a result of the behavior.

---

The I-message is a way to inform the student of the problem that *you*, the teacher, are facing. The I-message is not saying "You did something wrong" (the word *you* is not permitted in an I-message) and it is not saying "Here is how I want you to change." It *is* saying, "Student, *I* want to let you in on how my world is being affected by your behavior." This nonjudgmental statement still gives the student the power to reflect on her actions and come up with her own solutions on how she will change, and so there is no coercion by the teacher.

---

### EXAMPLES OF POOR AND GOOD I-MESSAGES

*Poor Example:* "I want you to get your feet off that table now!"
This is a you-message implying guilt. It contains a poor definition of the improper behavior, no example of the effect, and a lack of expression of the teacher's feelings.

*Good Example:* "When feet are put on the table *(behavior),* dirt comes off our shoes and gets on the table. We must rewash the table before we eat *(effect),* and I get aggravated *(feeling)* having to do more work."

*Poor Example:* "When the school books are torn *(behavior),* I don't like it!"
This message starts well with a good statement of behavior, but no effect is given, and "I don't like it" is a value judgment rather than an expression of the teacher's feelings.

*Good Example:* "When the school books are torn *(behavior),* other students cannot use them *(effect),* and that makes me very concerned for their care *(feeling)."*

**Examples of Good I-Messages**

- "When backpacks are left on the floor *(behavior),* people might trip over them and fall *(effect),* and I worry *(feeling)* that someone will get hurt."

*(Continued)*

---

### EXAMPLES OF POOR AND GOOD I-MESSAGES *(Continued)*

- "When tables are not cleaned after lunch *(behavior)*, spilled milk and other 'gooey stuff' will make it uncomfortable for other groups to eat there later *(effect)*, and I am afraid *(feelings)* we will have a health problem."

- "When I am told to 'shut up' when I am speaking in our class meeting *(behavior)*, I am not able to explain the rules to everyone *(effect)*, and I worry *(feelings)* that someone will get hurt using this new equipment."

- "When students stand on the table *(behavior)*, I am afraid *(feeling)* that they will fall and get hurt *(effect)*."

- "When people scream in the hallways *(behavior)*, it hurts my ears *(effect)* and I get uncomfortable *(feeling)*."

- "When people write or scribble on the desk tops *(behavior)*, it destroys them *(effect)*, and I am afraid *(feeling)* we soon will have no good writing surfaces."

- "When objects are thrown *(behavior)*, there is a real possibility they could hurt someone's eyes *(effect)*, and that scares *(feeling)* me because I am the teacher and I must keep people safe."

- "When children climb over the fence and leave the playground *(behavior)*, I can't see them to keep them safe *(effect)*, and that frightens me *(feeling)*."

---

Generally, after you deliver an I-message, the student might respond in one of three ways. First, she might simply stop the misbehavior (Cindy returns to her math seatwork), thereby ending the encounter. Second, the student might continue to defy you, prompting an escalation of power along the Teacher Behavior Continuum to the *Questioning* stage of the Confronting-Contracting Face (see Chapter 5). Finally, the student might begin to respond to the teacher with some form of language. This back talk language is typically of two types: defensive language (verbal aggression, denial, or attempting to distract the teacher to a side issue) or real verbal communication (how the student may wish to solve a specific dilemma).

Here is an example of defensive language:

*Two sixth-grade students are "play-fighting" and pushing each other at one of the science lab tables.*

***Teacher:*** *"When friends push and fight with each other* (behavior), *other people may get hurt, equipment can get broken, or it could turn into a real fight* (effect). *I need to keep people and equipment safe, and it alarms me* (feeling) *when people fight."*

> **Student:**  *"We weren't doing anything, we were just playing!!*
> (denial) (the teacher simply looks on). *You're such a butt-head!*
> (verbal aggression). *Carl and Ted were slap-fighting at the
> beginning of class and you didn't say anything to them!"* (side-
> tracking).

In viewing this sixth-grader's defensive verbal response, you must
simply see these statements as an immature child's attempt to find some
defensive way of handling the situation. You must not view "we weren't
doing anything" *(denial)* as lying. Instead, you should simply ignore
these denials. This may be nothing more than the student's natural tendency to deny reality as he is faced with it. In addition, some students
emotionally "flood," causing a fight-or-flight response of the reptilian
brain, and they are quite frightened. These students actually may not
remember what they did, even though it occurred just moments before.
Here are some examples of I-messages responding to specific situations:

---

### I-MESSAGES

| **Student's Action** | **Teacher I-Message** |
|---|---|
| Joe starts to talk during seatwork while the teacher is reading to a small group. He talks loudly enough that it starts to disturb everyone listening to the story. | "When someone talks during seatwork *(behavior),* I have a hard time reading so everyone can hear *(effect),* and that makes me feel frustrated *(feeling).* |
| After getting up from the art table, Joanne leaves her supplies and trash behind. | "When students leave their supplies behind *(behavior),* I'm concerned *(feeling)* that these materials will be lost or broken *(effect).* |
| Kate finishes eating and departs, leaving behind her trash. | "I get frustrated *(feeling)* when I have to clean up the lunch table *(effect)* after trash is left behind *(behavior).* |
| When the door is opened to go to the next class, Jeffrey runs through the door and down the stairs. | "When students run down the stairs *(behavior),* I'm concerned *(feeling)* that people will fall and get injured *(effect),* and my job is to keep people safe." |
| Sara is taking a test when she stops, begins to cry, and comes to talk to the teacher through the crying. | "When children cry and talk to me at the same time *(behavior),* I can't understand what is being said *(effect),* and I am disappointed *(feeling)* that I can't help." |

*(Continued)*

## I-MESSAGES (Continued)

| | |
|---|---|
| The teacher is talking to a parent when Tim interrupts and starts talking. | "It makes me sad *(feeling)* when I cannot understand two people who are talking to me at the same time *(behavior)*, and I become confused *(effect)*." |
| Brett deliberately splashes a classmate while they are washing their hands. | "When water is splashed *(behavior)*, people's clothes get wet and the floor gets wet and dangerously slippery *(effect)*, and that frightens me *(feeling)* because I need to keep people safe." |
| Geri and Kendra fight over a book by pulling it back and forth. | "When books are pulled *(behavior)*, I am concerned *(feeling)* that they will get damaged or be destroyed and we won't have them any more *(effect)*." |

## FEELING WORDS FOR TEACHERS AND STUDENTS

When using I-messages with students, your encoding of feelings at times may seem repetitive, such as overusing the phrase "that scares me." At the same time, you are helping students learn to put words and labels to their own feelings. This list of feeling words (Dinkmeyer, McKay, & Dinkmeyer, 1989) might help broaden your feeling vocabulary.

| **Negative Feelings** | | **Positive Feelings** | |
|---|---|---|---|
| angry | sad | appreciate | great |
| confused | scared | better | happy |
| disappointed | sorry | enjoy | like |
| frightened | unfair | excited | love |
| hate | unhappy | glad | pleased |
| hurt | want to give up | good | proud |
| left out | worried | | |
| mad | | | |

Do not be frightened, angered, or offended by the "you're such a butt-head" comment (or sexual or swear words) or by verbal abuse such as that thrown at Ms. Sanders by Cindy. Through the fight-or-flight construct, note that verbal aggression is a more productive response than a physically aggressive response from the reptilian brain. You might respond, "Cindy, when those words are said to me *(behavior)*, I hear anger, but I don't know why you're so angry *(effect)*, and I feel disappointed *(feeling)* that I am not able to help you *(I-message)*. What words could you use to help me understand what you want?" *(door opener)*.

---

### DOOR OPENERS

When a student is having difficulty expressing something that is troubling him or her, you use a question (as a "door opener") to invite the student to talk about his or her concerns.

---

You must not be drawn into a power play by the student's attempt to make you feel guilty ("Carl and Ted were slap-fighting at the beginning of class and you didn't say anything to them!"), which could lead you to respond to this assertion by trying to deny the student's criticism or explain your behavior to him. It has been said that the best defense at times is a good offense, so you should just see this as an attempt—and a fairly sophisticated one—to sidetrack you down a blind alley and take the focus off the student and his actions. You may simply ignore this sidetracking statement or use some of the following techniques to respond to denial, verbal aggression, or guilt statements used by students to sidetrack you. The statement "I don't like it when so-and-so is done!" is not an I-message. It is an expression of the teacher's value judgment or preferences.

## Active Listening/Door Openers/Acknowledgments

Students can become emotionally flooded as a result of adults' sanctions on their behavior. When this happens, their response toward adults might be verbal aggression. Calling the teacher a "butt-head" or shouting out "I hate you!" should simply be viewed as the student's first attempt at using language; he or she is attempting to communicate with you by taking a step up from the reptilian response of physical aggression. Teachers should not be offended or frightened by this immature behavior, but instead accept the verbal aggression as an attempt at verbal communication. By avoiding reprimanding the student and encouraging him or her to verbalize or speak more, often the hostile feelings soon leave his or her language and greater reasoning and verbal problem solving begins.

Effective communication is a very difficult process among adults, but it is even more difficult for middle grade students with their budding powers of abstract thinking and ability to use language accordingly. The first surface communication is not always what the child really means. An example follows:

> **Student:** *"Mom, did you get the car back from the garage yet?"*
>
> **Mother:** *"Ann, you know that the car will not be ready until Friday."*

The young adolescent has failed to communicate her real need, and the mother has failed to hear what was *really* being said—thus, poor communication occurs. What the child really meant to say was, "Mom, I forgot about my science project and have to get it to school tomorrow."

---

### ACTIVE LISTENING

The process of mirroring back to a student his or her emotional feelings and the problem being expressed, to the extent that you can understand them.

---

When a student has an inner need, he or she must express it externally, and try *verbally encoding* that need to express his or her wants.

Now, let's replay the discussion, this time with the mother using *active listening:*

> **Student:** *"Mom, did you get the car back from the garage yet?"*
>
> **Mother:** *"No, it will be ready on Friday, but do we need it sooner?"* (active listening).
>
> **Student:** *"They'll probably not even have it ready by then."*
>
> **Mother:** *"You're worried that the car won't be ready by Friday"* (active listening).
>
> **Student:** *"Yeah. Uh-h-h . . . "*
>
> **Mother:** *(looks at student, nods and smiles)* (acknowledgments)
>
> **Student:** *"My science project is too big to take on the bus."*
>
> **Mother:** *"You're science project is done and you want me to take you to school so you can turn it in by Friday?"* (active listening).
>
> **Student:** *"Yeah. Uh-h-h . . . "*
>
> **Mother:** *"You would like to tell me more?"* (door opener).
>
> **Student:** *"Well, I have to finish it tonight, but I forgot it was due last week. Ms. Smith said she'd let me turn it in but it has to be in by tomorrow."*
>
> **Mother:** *"Oh, that* does *make a difference. The rule is that we try to keep up with our work, but if you'll finish it tonight, we'll see if Dad can go into work a little late tomorrow so he can take you and your project to school."*

*Active listening* is a technique for improving communication between student and teacher whereby the student is encouraged to "talk out" repeatedly. The teacher's role is to attempt to mirror back to the student the emotional feelings the teacher thinks he or she is hearing from the student. If you take first or surface communication statements from the student as fact, especially when the student is emotionally flooded, you may not hear what the student is really attempting to communicate. The nonverbal behavior of nodding your head *(acknowledgments)* and asking questions, such as "Would you like to tell me more?" *(door openers)*, simply serve to encourage the student to continue to talk and attempt to communicate.

---

### ACKNOWLEDGMENTS

A modality behavior, such as making eye contact or nodding your head, to indicate that you are listening to what the student is saying and you are encouraging him or her to continue.

---

Here is another teacher-student example, this time involving the "play-fighting" student we met earlier.

> **Teacher (using Naming):** *"Nathan, play-fighting can escalate into a real fight when one participant gets hurt or decides he's through playing before the other one is through. I need to keep all my students safe, and I feel frustrated when I have to keep stopping my teaching for this"* (I-message).
>
> **Nathan:** *"Charlie keeps messing with me"* (referring to the other student involved in the play-fighting).
>
> **Teacher:** *"Charlie began your play-fighting?"* (active listening).
>
> **Nathan:** *"Uh, no, I started it. But Charlie won't stop. I don't want to play anymore."*
>
> **Teacher:** *"You want the play-fighting to stop?"*
>
> **Nathan:** *"Yes, but he's my best friend and I don't want to make him mad at me."*
>
> **Teacher:** *"You don't tell Charlie that you want to stop play-fighting because you are afraid he'll be mad at you"* (active listening).
>
> **Nathan:** *"Yes, can you tell him to stop so I don't have to?"*

The teacher's efforts to determine the cause of Nathan's aggression have exposed a deeper problem Nathan is facing, and now the teacher can begin dealing with it from a new perspective.

## LIMIT SETTING AND RELATIONSHIP-LISTENING TECHNIQUES

Limit setting is a process for taking action toward a student whose actions are preventing the teacher from teaching and preventing other classmates from learning, or who is failing to follow required procedures and rules. The tools available to the teacher for limit setting, within the Relationship-Listening techniques, are I-messages, active listening, and, to a lesser extent, door openers and acknowledgments. Verbal statements, such as an I-message, would be delivered to the student while adhering to Cardinal Rule 1: Make a desist as private as possible. This normally requires the teacher to use these techniques in the proximity position of *intimate,* softly whispered in the student's ear.

> *Cindy, the neighbor, now joins Jamie's power team and attempts to gang up on Ms. Sanders, stating, "Get out of her face. Are you gay or something? F--- off!!"* (back talk: profanity).
>
> *The teacher now escalates to the slightly more powerful Relationship-Listening technique of* Step 2: Naming:
> *"Cindy, those words are telling me that you are angry* (active listening) *and there is something very wrong, and that we need to talk. I need you to return to your math work now, and we will meet after lunch to talk more about this."*

As part of the limit-setting system, the teacher does not take time to do extensive active listening, door openers, or acknowledgments. The teacher primarily delivers the I-message or, as in this case, an active listening statement. If necessary, he or she promises to meet later with the student, as part of the backup system, to discuss it further. Through *Naming,* the student has been given a desist request without guilt or anger.

## SUMMARY

The "face" or attitude of Relationship-Listening takes the position that when students act out in a negative manner, there must be some form of need being blocked, causing an inner emotional disequilibrium. The emotional tension, also called *flooding,* is ineffectively expressed by the youngster's negative behavior. In using the Relationship-Listening techniques, the student is seen as a capable person with the inner strength and ability to solve his or her own problems; through solving such problems, with our nonjudgmental help, the child becomes more empowered as an adaptive maturing person. The student can find the solution for his or her own problems; if a teacher provides the solution, the student becomes dependent and weakens his or her future problem-solving ability.

The Relationship-Listening techniques are part of a limit-setting system and deal with misbehavior by first using the techniques of *Step*

*1: Looking.* If this fails to work, escalate to *Step 2: Naming.* In carrying out the teacher techniques under *Naming,* as a form of verbal encoding or active listening, an *I-message* (behavior-effect-feeling) may be necessary to make the student aware of his or her actions. If these minimal verbal techniques are not effective in getting a desist from the student, escalating to other steps or systems as part of the TBC may be the most effective discipline. A summary of the major points in using the TBC's *Naming* is shown on the first page of this chapter.

If these techniques are effective, the end result will be a student who is free to express inner thoughts and feelings, knowing a teacher will respond in a nonjudgmental manner. In this way, a binding relationship is formed between teacher and student. It is through this relationship and the ability to express needs that the student now becomes free to solve his or her own problems and gain greater maturity.

At a time of life when adult role modeling is of paramount importance, the Relationship-Listening Face can facilitate helping young adolescents identify their feelings and deal with them appropriately. In addition, this attitude puts the teacher in a binding relationship with a student rather than in an adversarial or confrontational mode. Confronting feelings and solving problems rationally is an important developmental task (Milgram, 1992): The way in which teachers respond to verbal outbursts, which are sometimes offensive, is an excellent opportunity to model more mature behavior.

## REFERENCES

Dinkmeyer, D., McKay, G., & Dinkmeyer J. (1989). *Parenting Young Children.* Circle Pines, MN: American Guidance Services.

Milgram, J. (1992). A portrait of diversity: The middle level student. In J. L. Irvin (Ed.), *Transforming Middle Level Education: Perspectives and Possibilities* (pp. 16–27). Boston: Allyn and Bacon.

# 5

# Questioning
## The Confronting-Contracting Face

Minimum Power ◄————————————————————► Maximum Power

*Relationship-Listening Face*  *Confronting-Contracting Face*  *Rules and Consequences Face*

| LOOKING | NAMING | QUESTIONING | COMMANDING | ACTING |
|---|---|---|---|---|
| 1. Square off <br> • slow down <br> • shoulders to shoulders <br> • broad foot stance <br> • unbroken eye contact <br> 2. Relaxing breaths <br> 3. Close space <br> • far <br> • near <br> • intimate | 1. Limit setting <br> • I-message <br>   – student behavior <br>   – teacher feeling <br>   – effect of student behavior <br> • Door openers <br> • Active listening <br> • Acknowledgments | 1. Limit setting <br> • stop statements <br> • what/how questions <br> 2. Backup system <br> • contracting <br> • time out <br> • notifying parents | | |

The Relationship-Listening Face, through a process using the limit-setting techniques of *Looking* and *Naming,* calls for minimal intervention. Relationship-Listening techniques rely on a process of talking it out, facilitated by the teacher in an attempt to encourage the student in the direction of appropriate behavior. When those minimal supportive actions do not achieve the desired results, the teacher escalates across the Teacher Behavior Continuum to the Confronting-Contracting Face by moving to the use of *Step 3: Questioning.*

This Confronting-Contracting Face and its accompanying attitude are much more demanding of the student and call for a greater use of power by the teacher. The goal of Confronting-Contracting is to have the student mentally reflect on his or her past behavior and its negative effects, and project the negative future outcome if such misbehavior continues. The student is also confronted and asked to come up with an idea of how to deal with the realities he or she faces and to "live within the rules."

*Note:* Many of the techniques found in this chapter can be found in the works of Dreikurs and Glasser (see References).

Many misbehaving students fail to take time to evaluate their own behavior, to use their rational capacities to make decisions and control their actions. Instead, they are reactive, being easily triggered to act in an inappropriate manner. The Confronting-Contracting Face draws on and attempts to use the cognitive and rational capacities of the student. The teacher does not solve the problem for the student; rather, the teacher expects the student to come up with an acceptable solution, thus strengthening the student's problem-solving abilities. One of the major developmental tasks of early adolescence is to learn appropriate social skills with adults and peers. All young adolescents struggle with social interaction at one time or another. However, some students, particularly those who do not feel accepted at home, need more help from positive role models. Often, the only adults who can offer them guidance and patience are encountered in school. The Confronting-Contracting Face uses five major steps: "stop" statements, what-how questions, contracting, time out, and notifying parents.

## CONFRONTING-CONTRACTING LIMIT SETTING

The first two steps of the Confronting-Contracting process involve limit setting:

- Step 1: "Stop" statements

- Step 2: What-how questions directed at the student (see Figure 5.1)

The remaining steps, because they take much time and become public, involve the use of a backup system, which is discussed in detail in Chapter 8, as well as an incentive system (Chapter 9) and an encouragement system (Chapter 10). These steps are:

- Step 3: Contracting

- Step 4: Time out (circumstances may call for this step to be employed *before* Step 3)

- Step 5: Notify parents (see Figure 5.1)

## LIMIT SETTING

A variation on the squirt gun incident from Chapter 1 will be used to introduce the process of *Questioning*:

*Suddenly, Sean, a normally quiet student, springs from his seat with a loud, "Hey, what was that?" The students around his group begin to laugh as Mr. McDaniel makes his way to the area. Mr. McDaniel moves to Sean and asks quietly, "What's the matter, Sean?" Sean replies, "Someone just spit on the back of my chair or something! Look, it's wet." Carla, who sits next*

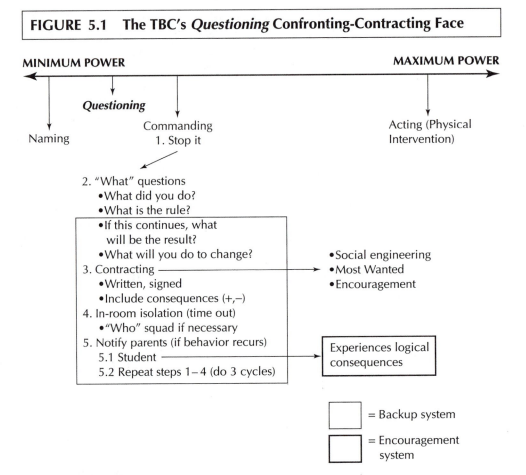

**FIGURE 5.1   The TBC's *Questioning* Confronting-Contracting Face**

to Sean, says, "It was Mark. He's got a squirt gun and has been squirting it all day!" Mark yells, "Man, I don't have a squirt gun!" Carla disagrees, "Yes, you do and you just squirted Sean's chair with it."

Mr. McDaniel moves closer to Mark (closing space) and makes eye contact, and then notices the green handle of a squirt gun slightly sticking out of Mark's back pack. (TBC Step 1: Looking). The teacher moves in, placing both hands on Mark's desk (proximity: intimate). Mr. McDaniel waits patiently, taking relaxing breaths, maintaining a Queen Victoria pose, and holding his visual focus. Mark rolls his eyes and gives a slight smile. Mr. McDaniel visually prompts him by pointing to the handle of the squirt gun and then to himself. The gesture is to signal Mark to give the squirt gun to Mr. McDaniel. Again, Mark rolls his eyes as if in disgust, and slumps deeper into his chair. Mr. McDaniel waits, permitting the "visual burn" to continue.

Other students who were working now begin to detect that something is happening, and they begin to stop their work to *watch the action. Mr. McDaniel leans over and gives Mark an ear warning that others do not hear. "Stop, Mark, This may not continue (Stop statement). When you display something that you should not have here at school, like a squirt gun, and disturb another student by squirting it, you also disrupt the rest of the class so that everyone stops their work. We then lose valuable time, and I find that quite annoying" (TBC Step 2: Naming—I-message). Mr. McDaniel backs out of Mark's "personal space" and gives him several seconds to respond. Mark takes a squirt gun from his backpack, squirts it up into the air, and then puts it back into his backpack with a grin on his face. Again, Mr. McDaniel places his hands on Mark's desk and quietly asks, "What is the rule regarding toys at school? What are you going to do to solve this problem, Mark, so that we may all get back to our work?" (TBC Step 3: Questioning). Mark responds, "F--- off!"*

In this squirt gun vignette, the entire class is busy doing seatwork until Mark, by his actions, causes a disruption. Cardinal Rule 3 is: Discipline comes before instruction. If Mr. McDaniel is busy working with a single student or a group of students, he may become aware that a disruption is beginning, but he chooses to ignore it in order to finish the teaching he is doing. However, if these small disruptions are not dealt with immediately, more and more of them will erupt (Kounin, 1970). The teacher must break off instruction and deal with this incident.

Mr. McDaniel must also keep in mind Cardinal Rule 1: "Make a desist as private as possible." If he shouts directly across the room or moves in a hostile manner toward Mark, it will alert the entire class; the students will stop their work, and as a result the teacher will have become a bigger classroom disruption than Mark's misbehavior had been. Handling the squirt gun incident takes skilled intervention as to how much power the teacher should use and how he should respond.

Cardinal Rule 2 is: "Use as little power as necessary to get positive change in the misbehaving student's behavior." We saw Mr. McDaniel starting with the first steps on the TBC and then escalating up the continuum. Initially, he attempted to use *Looking* through a process of *closing space* and moving to *intimate proximity,* all the while using teacher self-control activities (*squaring off* and *relaxed breathing*). Next, Mr. McDaniel escalated to *Naming* as an *I-message* ("When you display something that you should not have here at school, like a squirt gun, and disturb another student by squirting it, you also disrupt the rest of the class so that everyone stops their work. We then lose valuable time, and I find that quite annoying"). He then gave Mark some time to comply and respond. Mark escalated his defiance, flaunting his power by squirting the gun into the air and returning it to his backpack. In this way, Mark nonverbally challenged the teacher.

Finally, the teacher escalated to the Confronting-Contracting technique of *Questioning,* using Step 1: Stop statements and Step 2:

What-how questions. The teacher asked, "What is the rule regarding toys at school? What are you going to do to solve this problem, Mark, so that we may all get back to our work?" Notice that the teacher did not tell the student what *not* to do, but simply stated, "Stop." The what-how questions related only to what the student did, to the rule, to how this behavior might result in negative outcomes for Mark, and to a challenge for the student to come up with his own ideas of how to change.

---

### CONFRONTING

You respond to misbehavior with a verbal instruction to the student to stop the action.

---

Because of stress in the confronting process and the teacher's recognition of the student's misbehavior, after such a confrontation the student does not necessarily reflect on his entire sequence of behavior (especially when it is emotionally charged, as with Mark's swearing). The student simply knows he is being confronted by the teacher, and most likely his mind is racing through thoughts of "Will the teacher punish me?" or "How can I get out of this situation and away from the teacher?" or "Will other students feel that I am a coward because of my actions if I don't save face?"

The what-how questions ask the student to be reflective. If the student cannot remember what happened—and sometimes he will not, or cannot, articulate it—the teacher will tell the student what did occur. However, it would be preferable to have the student verbally state his own actions.

Mark is a "high-stakes player," and when he uses profanity directly at the teacher with classmates as witnesses, the teacher may also feel emotionally flooded and angry and could regress to a fight-or-flight position with an *adrenaline dump*. It is imperative that the teacher use all of the self-controlling activities explained in the previous chapter on *Looking*. He must use controlled breathing, posture, eye contact, and slow movements in an attempt to stop any regression to fight or flight. If, because of his anger, the teacher begins using the paleocortex brain, he will lose control of this confrontation.

---

### WHAT-HOW QUESTIONS

Questioning language that confronts the misbehaving student to reflect on his or her past misbehavior or to reflect on the rules, and to consider how he or she will change.

---

## CONFRONTING-CONTRACTING ORIENTATION

The Confronting-Contracting Face reflects the attitude that the teacher is the adult and knows what is acceptable and unacceptable behavior. When a student is misbehaving, the teacher clearly confronts that student to get him or her to desist and makes it clear that the behavior will not be permitted to continue. The Confronting-Contracting view is that there is *one* central motivation for all students: the attempt to find ways of belonging. If this social acceptance is blocked and the student feels unwanted and left out, the student will begin to disrupt the social situation in the classroom with a host of negative behaviors in an attempt to get excessive attention or to control the teacher and others through power techniques. By inappropriate actions, the student gets attention and shows power by misbehaving or challenging authority figures.

It is almost as if the student is saying, "If I can't get recognition for being the best *good* kid, I will get it by being the best *bad* kid!" Being the most difficult student brings social acknowledgment and recognition, even though it is negative. This misbehavior, motivated by a sense of not belonging, produces a self-defeating cycle in which the teacher and peers begin to have feelings of dislike for this student because of these offensive misbehaviors. The student now feels even more rejection and may become revengeful or so hurt that he or she retreats into a shell of passive helplessness (Albert, 1989).

In short, the misbehaving student is likely to be someone who feels unwanted and unaccepted by others and who cannot find social acceptance. Admittedly, this may be very hard to remember when feeling threatened by the student. The teacher's role is to take clear actions to (1) stop the misbehavior, (2) confront the misbehaving student with questions designed to get him to reflect on the wisdom of such negative behavior, and (3) challenge the student to think of new ways of behaving that are socially acceptable. (Further steps of Confronting-Contracting will be described in Section III of this book—in the backup system.)

With such misbehaving students a repetitive host of misbehaviors and aggressive actions may occur that, on the surface, do not appear to be related to immediate behavior by other students. Such a person may harass other students without any provocation. The first feelings of acceptance for all children come from the home setting. Children who feel they were rejected in early family interactions may assume they will be similarly rejected in a classroom situation and will set out with negative actions to prove that others do not like them.

The less skilled teacher might bring Mark aside and verbally reprimand and lecture him for his actions, applying large doses of guilt for the behavior or hand out punishment. Worse still, the teacher might issue a very public reprimand in front of the entire class. Such actions might unknowingly cause the teacher to fall into the student's power trap, as these behaviors are precisely what the student expects and wants from the teacher to make him the center of attention or permit him to show how powerful he can be. Alternatively, if the teacher disciplines the student with harsh punishment consequences, the student might regress and become revengeful toward those around him in more subtle ways that the teacher will not see or detect. Instead, this student must become the target for the teacher's positive efforts to help him acquire the social skills that will enable him to find acceptance.

A number of techniques can enable the teacher to be proactive in helping students acquire social skills. Before these are presented, however, it may be helpful to explain the outside aggressor phenomenon.

## THE OUTSIDE AGGRESSOR PHENOMENON

*The first period bell just rang in an eighth-grade classroom. The teacher is calling the role and mispronounces a student's name. The name, Luscious, is pronounced by the teacher as she has always pronounced this word, with the short u sound. However, to her dismay, and the amusement of the other students, the name is intended to be announced with the long u sound. All of the students, with the exception of Luscious, chuckle and make remarks such as "Oh, how Luscious that color is" or "Your long hair is so Luscious." In each of the classes for the rest of the day, the same scene ensued, with the teacher mispronouncing Luscious's name, and the other students teaming up in the taunting.*

You have just witnessed the phenomenon of the outside aggressor. Young students have two large islands of emotional extremes: When they love, they love totally, and when they hate, they hate totally. Their feelings of rivalry are still very strong, thus they have a difficult time coming together in groups. One of the more primitive and base levels of social interaction, which first develops during the early years, is coming together in a group and finding an outside person, object, or fantasy object against which to project the group members' strong competitive feelings and aggression. This creates an implicit agreement not to take aggressive action against each other and establishes a temporary feeling of belonging. In the previous classroom incident, Mr. McDaniel could become the outside aggressor if Mark is able to challenge him publicly in class and cause the class to identify with Mark and against the teacher.

Although the outside aggressor phenomenon begins in early childhood (Isaacs, 1972), examples can be seen among older students and adults. Young adolescents seem to perpetuate the role of the outside aggressor because of their fierce loyalty to friends and their own need for social approval (George & Alexander, 1993). Perhaps you can recall an interaction at a dinner party when one person must depart early, leaving everyone else behind to talk about him in a most negative manner. The "leaver" becomes the dinner group's outside aggressor. Members of the group have, by default, informally agreed to project their aggressive criticism at the departed person, and not to speak ill of one another. The game works if almost everyone says something derogatory. Thus, for a short period of time, the members of the "dinner gang" have a superior feeling of being above someone else, a feeling of primitive belonging to this "in" group. Politicians throughout history have used this outside aggressor phenomenon to gain control of groups; perhaps the most glaring and frightening example was the way in which Hitler controlled an entire nation by casting one ethnic group as the outside aggressor.

Reaction to the outside aggressor is an expectable, normal behavior among school-age students. Every substitute teacher's greatest fear is that the students will make the substitute their outside aggressor—after all, they know each other but do not know him or her. Some misbehaving students develop the skill to turn the entire classroom of peers against the teacher by challenging the teacher's power, thereby making the teacher the outside aggressor. A misbehaving student also may become the school's outside aggressor, disliked by peers, teachers, school crossing guards, bus drivers, cafeteria workers, and anyone else who has daily contact with him or her, becoming the "best bad" student in the school. The teacher who is forced to deal with this kind of misbehaving student, of course, is to engineer ways through which this student can learn to be social in a more healthy manner, and to help him or her find belonging and acquire social skills. Most of this help will come to the misbehaving student as a part of the backup system, (Section III of this book), which will require the use of much more time to counsel the student through private meetings or conferences.

## LIMIT-SETTING TECHNIQUES

Returning to the squirt gun vignette and picking it up where Mark hurls his verbal obscenities at the teacher, Mr. McDaniel can now respond. However, it is critical that he not fall into a power confrontation with Mark by *going public*. If Mark is motivated by the desire for power, he attempts to demonstrate his power to the teacher and his classmates by controlling the teacher's actions and getting the teacher angry (regressing to *fight or flight*). If this happens, the teacher's voice becomes harsh and shrill, and he begins to issue threats or warnings—he snaps and snarls by using his paleocortex brain. When the teacher loses his composure, it is *"show time"* for Mark and the classmates, and most likely the teacher will demonstrate fear and very unskilled, exasperated behavior. In this way, the teacher could become the outside aggressor.

When a teacher verbally "slam-dunks" a misbehaving student like Mark in front of peers by going public, the so-called ripple effect (Kounin, 1970) punishes not only Mark but all students. Because they have witnessed the teacher snapping and snarling and because they are in a less powerful position, the students feel vulnerable to the teacher's tirade. Even though they might dislike Mark and his behavior, they now identify with him and, through this ripple effect, feel just as verbally punished as Mark. In fact, because they are more socially sensitive, they may feel even more punished than Mark. The immediate goal for the teacher who has just been the object of Mark's verbal aggression is to get himself or Mark out of the immediate situation—which provides the public interaction of the classmates as spectators—and to get back to teaching or learning. The teacher may deescalate to *Naming,* such as, "Mark, that language is not acceptable to me and we must talk. I will need you to stay when class is dismissed." The teacher slowly moves back to helping students doing seatwork or other forms of instruction. If Mark sits passively, even if he still has the squirt gun, he is ignored. The teacher knows that at least Mark is no longer preventing others from learning. Mr. McDaniel will retrieve the squirt gun and deal with the swearing later, without the classmates as an audience, through the use of the backup system.

## DISENGAGING

Although most teachers will not openly admit it, student misbehavior can be frightening. Suppose Mark hits Jill, a classmate, producing a large bruise on Jill's arm. Now suppose Jill's mother is the most vocal member of the school board or the school's PTO. Under these circumstances, the teacher would feel "under the gun" and, of course, quite sympathetic to Jill's plight. When this happens frequently, the teacher must acknowledge his or her own feelings of becoming frightened of Mark, and gradually feeling hurt or angry. Teachers are not robots who are emotionless, who never get angry, who always have good feelings toward all students. This is an unrealistic picture and simply does not happen. Some students are appealing and some are very unappealing; the unappealing students generally are the ones who cannot find acceptance in their homes or from fellow classmates. The nonsocially adjusted misbehaving student, because of feelings of rejection, seeks excessive attention and power, becomes revengeful, and, finally, retreats into a passive state of helplessness (Dreikurs, 1964, 1968; Dreikurs & Cassel, 1972; Dreikurs & Grey, 1968). Teachers are human beings with a range of feelings. Excessive attention getting by students may produce feelings of annoyance and cause the teacher to feel beaten by the power-needy student. Feeling hurt by a revengeful student, and feeling inadequate in working with a passive-helpless student are normal reactions (see Table 5.1).

Teachers all have these feelings toward certain students. These feelings only become a problem when they begin to regress into becoming revengeful and feeling helpless toward these students. Therefore, it is often desirable to use isolation to become *disengaged.* If a teacher gets angry and overcome by feelings because of the repetitive demands of a problem student, the teacher becomes emotionally flooded in the middle of an incident. Skilled confronting is necessary, yet a teacher may not be able to handle the situation successfully and professionally because clear thinking has been flooded by emotions. The misbehaving student should be placed in isolation—a "relax chair" or a time out—for a period

**TABLE 5.1   Student's Motivations Resulting in Teacher's Feelings**

| Student's Motivation | Behavior Characteristics | Teacher's Feelings |
|---|---|---|
| Attention getting | Repeats actions to make him the center of attention. When asked to desist, he will comply but will start again later. | Annoyed |
| Power | Repeats actions to make him the center of attention. When asked to desist, he becomes defiant and escalates negative behavior and challenges the adult. | Beaten |
| Revenge | Hurts others for no apparent reason. | Hurt |
| Helplessness | Wishes not to be seen; passive and lethargic; rejects social contact. | Inadequate |

*Source:* Works of Dreikurs (see References).

of time. As an emotionally flooded individual, space is placed between the teacher and this student for several minutes, or even an hour, until the teacher has disengaged from his or her strong emotions. Once the teacher is calm and relaxed, he or she will have the energy to approach the difficult student to begin steps of confronting. *You cannot do Confronting-Contracting when angered.* Use the self-controlling techniques under the TBC's heading *Looking*, including relaxing breaths, slowed actions, squaring off, physical distance, and others.

The private meeting, as a part of the backup system, ends with a contract between the student and the teacher. The student at a future time will likely find himself or herself in a similar situation and will be faced with the possibility of again acting with such destructive behavior. The question What will you do to change? permits him or her to think out and anticipate these future situations. The student has determined and contracted with the teacher how he or she can act in a more productive manner in future incidents. The contingency contract for change between the teacher and student could be sealed with a simple handshake and smile in the first attempts, but it is advised that this agreement be stated in writing and have both the teacher's and student's signatures on the contract, with each getting a copy. The contingency contract may also contain a logical consequence to be employed if the student fails to live up to this contract.

If the use of time out is ineffective, or if the student fails to live up to the terms indicated in the contingency contract, the teacher may need to notify the parents. It is important for the teacher to contact the parents when he or she is calm and relaxed. The teacher should try to avoid generalizations such as "Mark is being disruptive" or "Cindy is misbehaving." Describe specifically what has happened and what has been done in attempts to solve the problem. To avoid a negative confrontation when speaking with the parent, focus on the misbehaving student's behavior and not on the student himself or herself. Let the parent know that it is the student's behavior that you disapprove of, not the student.

## SUMMARY

The techniques of the Confronting-Contracting Face require the teacher to face a misbehaving student with a demand to stop and, through what-how questions, get the student to reach an awareness of his or her actions, a clear recognition of the rules, and a plan for solving the problem through change. If the student is flooded, the teacher uses a "relax chair" or a time out as part of the backup system, until the student feels he or she is now ready to join the group, and has contracted to do so. Finally, the teacher may need to notify the parent of the specifics of student's misbehavior, noting his or her disapproval of the misbehavior and not of the student. Most misbehaving students are motivated by four needs (attention getting, power, revenge, or helplessness) because they lack the social skills to obtain recognition and belonging. If the *Questioning* techniques fail to be effective, following the TBC construct, the teacher will now move to *Commanding*.

## REFERENCES

Albert, L. (1989). *Cooperative Discipline.* Circle Pines, MN: American Guidance Service.

Dreikurs, R. (1964). *Children: The Challenge.* New York: Hawthorn/Dutton.

Dreikurs, R. (1968). *Psychology in the Classroom: A Manual for Teachers* (2nd ed.). New York: Harper and Row.

Dreikurs, R., & Cassel, P. (1972). *Discipline without Tears: What to Do with Children Who Misbehave.* New York: Hawthorn Books.

Dreikurs, R., & Grey, L. (1968). *Logical Consequences.* New York: Meredith Press.

George, P., & Alexander, W. (1993). *The Exemplary Middle School* (2nd ed.). Orlando, FL: Harcourt Brace Jovanavich College Publishers.

Glasser, W. (1975). *Reality Therapy: A New Approach to Psychiatry.* New York: Harper and Row.

Glasser, W. (1986). *Control Theory in the Classroom.* New York: Harper and Row.

Glasser, W. (n.d.). *Glasser's Approach to Discipline.* Los Angeles: Educator Training Center.

Isaacs, S. (1972). *Social Development in Young Children.* New York: Schocken Books.

Kounin, J. (1970). *Discipline and Group Management in Classrooms.* New York: Holt, Rinehart and Winston.

# 6

# Commanding
## The Rules and Consequences Face

Minimum Power ◄─────────────────────────────► Maximum Power

*Relationship-Listening Face*     *Confronting-Contracting Face*     *Rules and Consequences Face*

| LOOKING | NAMING | QUESTIONING | COMMANDING | ACTING |
|---------|--------|-------------|------------|--------|
| 1. Square off<br>  • slow down<br>  • shoulders to<br>    shoulders<br>  • broad foot<br>    stance<br>  • unbroken eye<br>    contact<br>2. Relaxing breaths<br>3. Close space<br>  • far<br>  • near<br>  • intimate | 1. Limit setting<br>  • I-message<br>   – student<br>     behavior<br>   – teacher<br>     feeling<br>   – effect of<br>     student<br>     behavior<br>  • Door openers<br>  • Active listening<br>  • Acknowledg-<br>    ments | 1. Limit setting<br>  • stop<br>    statements<br>  • what/how<br>    questions<br>2. Backup system<br>  • contracting<br>  • time out<br>  • notifying<br>    parents | 1. Assertive<br>  • name<br>  • gesture<br>  • touch<br>  • eyes<br>2. Broken record<br>3. State<br>   consequences | |

The Three Faces of Discipline model is designed to heighten the awareness of the actions the teacher takes toward a misbehaving student. The Relationship-Listening Face accepts that the misbehaving student is rational and may be made more purposeful and cooperative through a supportive nonjudgmental approach requiring the student to talk out the problem. The Confronting-Contracting Face, primarily through the use of questioning techniques, presents a clear use of power and demands that verbal techniques can be used to stop the misbehavior and get the student to become aware of his or her action and how it is socially unwelcome. The student is permitted almost total control to choose how he or she will change, but the teacher engineers ways to help the student gain social skills. These two faces should work to deal with most behavior problems. With some students, however, these techniques will not be enough, and escalating to the more powerful techniques of Rules and Consequences will be required.

*Note:* Many of the techniques in this chapter can be found in L. Canter and M. Canter, *Assertive Discipline: A Take-Charge Approach for Today's Educator* (Los Angeles: Lee Canter and Associates, 1976).

## RULES AND CONSEQUENCES

The Rules and Consequences Face, and its movement to *Commanding* on the TBC, comes into play when the student is flooded and in a defensive stance; escalating to a greater use of power now becomes necessary. Even with your *Questioning* and mediation, the student generally does not view his or her own behavior accurately nor does the student have the ability to change his or her actions on his or her own free will. To help such students requires strong intrusion and management techniques that demand that the teacher first be assertive in order to help the student gain self-control and a reawakening sense of trust.

Returning to the earlier vignette involving Mark, Mr. McDaniel, and the squirt gun will provide an example for the Rules and Consequences Face.

*Other students who were working now begin to detect that something is happening, and they begin to stop their work to watch the action. (Recall that the teacher has already used the nonverbal techniques of proximity and eye contact from the TBC's Looking.) Mr. McDaniel leans over and gives Mark an* ear warning *that others do not hear: "When you display something that you should not have here at school, like a squirt gun, and disturb another student by squirting it, you also disrupt the rest of the class so that everyone stops their work. We then lose valuable time, and I find that quite annoying" (TBC Step 2: Naming—I-message). Mr. McDaniel backs out of Mark's "personal space" and gives him several seconds to respond. Mark takes a squirt gun from his backpack, squirts it up into the air, and then puts it back into his backpack with a grin on his face. Again, Mr. McDaniel places his hands on Mark's desk and quietly asks, "What is the rule regarding toys at school? What are you going to do to solve this problem, Mark, so that we may all get back to our work?" (TBC Step 3: Questioning). Mark responds, "F--- off!"*

***Mr. McDaniel:*** *(makes eye contact, stands at the edge of Mark's comfort bubble, squares off, and gestures as a visual prompt): "Mark, take the squirt gun out of your back pack and hand it to me"* (Step 4: Command).

***Mark:*** *(takes a quick glance at the teacher and at his classmates, and smiles)*

***Mr. McDaniel:*** *"Mark, take the squirt gun out of your back pack and hand it to me!"* (broken record).

***Mark:*** *(makes no response)*

***Mr. McDaniel:*** *"You now have a choice. I want you to stand, walk to the back of the room, and seat yourself in that chair for the remainder of the class, or I will call in Mr. Carlson, the assistant principal, and we will remove you to the discipline*

*office (promises a follow-through by stating consequences).
Mark, move to the chair now!"* (time out).

In this incident, the teacher first uses the Relationship-Listening Face with *Naming,* then escalates to the Confronting-Contracting Face with *Questioning,* and then further escalates to the Rules and Consequences Face with *Commanding.* Through the techniques of the Rules and Consequences Face, the teacher plays a more specific role in demanding appropriate behavior by the student. While using the Rules and Consequences Face, the teacher *assertively demands* through a *Command,* that the misbehaviors desist and the student's behavior change to more desired behaviors.

## THE ASSERTIVE POSITION

The assertive position, as a part of the Rules and Consequences Face, supports the following message to the teacher: *You are the teacher and this is your classroom; you have a perfect right to get your needs as a teacher met.* As a part of the limit-setting process, the teacher arrives at this assertive position by (1) attempting to use the minimum amount of teacher power—*Looking, Naming,* and *Questioning*—but being forced to escalate to these stronger techniques or (2) seeing that the student's action was potentially dangerous to self or others or could lead to the destruction of property, requiring the use of the *severity clause.* The cardinal rules of "Make a desist as private as possible" and "Use as little power as necessary to get positive changes in the misbehaving student's behavior" must be *dropped when genuine danger or property destruction* are involved and time is of the utmost importance. Implementing the *severity clause* requires the teacher to move straight to directive statements as a *Command* and, if need be, to *Acting* with *Physical Intervention,* also through the use of the Rules and Consequences Face.

The Rules and Consequences Face takes the position that the misbehaving student is taking away your right to teach and other students' right to learn, and thus a teacher must assert control. Determining the rules and behavior in the classroom and making them clear to the students is the first step. When a student breaks these rules, an assertive action is taken by stating clearly the expected behavior and then demanding compliance from the student. If there is no compliance, the teacher is prepared to take actions to decrease misbehavior through the use of time out or by physically intervening. A *Commanding* teacher is one who communicates her wants and needs to students and is prepared to reinforce her words with appropriate actions. She responds in a manner that maximizes her potential to get her needs met, but in no way violates the best interest of the students.

## Characteristics of Assertive Teachers

The assertive teacher, using the TBC's *Command,* is one who can state his or her wants and needs clearly to the student without violating the child's rights, initially done through an assertive command. In the process of delivering an assertive command, the teacher:

1. Moves to the student and makes direct *eye contact.*

2. *States the child's name.*

3. *Gestures.*

4. *Touches* the student (on the shoulder when appropriate).

5. Verbally demands that the student stop *(demands a desist).*

6. *Demands change* for positive behavior by the student (tells the student what to do, rather than what not to do).

7. Promises a *follow-through consequence.*

Note that nearly all modalities are used to communicate with the student in an assertive command: visual (through eye contact and gesture), auditory (by stating the child's name and demanding he desist), and tactile (through touching). The following vignette serves as an example to see how the teacher uses the assertive command:

> *Mark responds, "F--- off!"*
>
> ***Mr. McDaniel:*** *(takes two* relaxing breaths *and moves to* proximity: intimate*):* "*Mark* (states the child's name, *makes direct* eye contact, *stands at the edge of Mark's comfort bubble, squares off, gestures as a visual prompt, places a hand gently on Mark's shoulder* [touches the student]*, take the squirt gun out of your back pack and hand it to me*" (demands a desist, *telling the student what to do rather than what not to do).*
>
> ***Mark:*** *(takes a quick glance at the teacher and at his classmates, and smiles)*
>
> ***Mr. McDaniel:*** *(takes two* relaxing breaths*):* "*Mark, take the squirt gun out of your back pack and hand it to me!*" (broken record).
>
> ***Mark:*** *(no response)*
>
> ***Mr. McDaniel:*** *(takes two* relaxing breaths*):* "*Mark, this is your last warning. Follow my instructions, now!*"
>
> ***Mark:*** *(no response)*
>
> ***Mr. McDaniel:*** *(takes two* relaxing breaths*):* "*You now have a choice. I want you to stand, walk to the back of the room, and seat yourself in that chair for the remainder of the class, or I will call in Mr. Carlson, the assistant principal, and we will remove you to the discipline office* (promises a follow-through by stating consequences). *Mark, move to the chair now!*"

Once the teacher has delivered this assertive *Command,* he does not allow himself to be sidetracked by excuses as back talk or other discussions by the student. He repeats the *Command* two or three times as a *broken record* and then promises a follow-up action—if the student does not comply, he is placed in time out in an out-of-classroom setting.

---

### ASSERTIVE COMMAND

A command used to communicate to the student the direct behavior that the teacher wants, incorporating the following elements:

- A statement of the child's name

- A gesture, in which the teacher signals through hand movement and/or nodding of her head

- Eye contact, whereby the teacher positions herself in front of the student, close enough to ensure that they are looking into each other's eyes

- Touching, whereby the teacher touches the student to make him aware of her presence and her need for his attention

- A demand that the student desist the improper behavior

- A statement of the consequence, whereby the teacher tells the student what punishing action will occur if the student does not perform the desired appropriate behavior (or continues to perform inappropriate behavior)

---

### BROKEN RECORD

The process by which, after a student fails to act on your request for a particular behavior, you repeat the command over and over in a controlled manner (as if a "broken record").

---

This strong assertive *Command,* as a limit-setting technique, is a very powerful intervention technique. It is public and very time consuming, and can quickly lead to very public backup system steps involving the principal, parents, and other professionals. For these reasons, it should be used only when the other, less powerful limit-setting techniques have not worked over a reasonable period of time or when the student is endangering himself or classmates or taking actions that may lead to property damage. For day-in, day-out classroom management, once having used the assertive *Command,* the teacher may now be forced to use the TBC's *Acting* in the form of physical intervention by isolating the student, physically transporting him out of the classroom, or—in the worst case—physically restraining a student who has become assaultive.

## THE NONASSERTIVE OR HOSTILE TEACHER

Many seemingly assertive commands by a teacher are actually nonassertive and generally ineffective. The passive, or flight, response brought on by the teacher's own fear ("Tommy, behave yourself!") merely pleads and begs for students to behave and change their ways. This teacher appears to be unclear as to what behavior she does want and has no plan to obtain that behavior from the students. The hostile, or fight, teacher responds by screaming at the students ("Shut up and sit down. I don't want to hear any more from you today!") or might grab, shake, or even strike the misbehaving student. This teacher has regressed either to the paleocortex or the "reptilian" brain. The hostile teacher knows what she wants, but her actions in attempting to get that behavior violate the best interest of the student.

### Characteristics of Nonassertive Teachers

Nonassertive teachers generally display two types of behavior: passive or hostile. The *passive teacher* takes these unproductive actions:

1. Asks the student to achieve an intermediate but nonspecific behavioral goal (*Example:* Asks the student to make an effort, as in "Try to be good!")

2. Makes statements to the student about his behavior that do not communicate what she wants the student to do (*Example:* "I can't imagine why you are doing that!" or "What is wrong with you?")

3. Says all the right words ("Stop fighting!") but does not back up the words with the necessary consequences to impress the student and influence him to choose to eliminate the improper behavior

4. Demands the student to stop and threatens to follow through, but fails to do so (*Example:* "The next time you do that, you're going to time out!" A few minutes later: "I am warning you—one more time and out you go!")

5. May plainly ignore the behavior as if it never occurred, hoping it will go away

The *hostile teacher* takes these unproductive actions:

1. Uses a you-statement that conveys a negative "put-down" message, but in no way clearly communicates to the student what the teacher wants, leaving the student simply feeling guilty (*Example:* "I am sick of your behavior. How many times am I going to need to tell you?")

2. Expresses a negative value judgment of the student and/or his behavior (*Example:* "You are acting like a little monster this morning")

3. Threatens the student in an angry manner, with no evidence of consistent follow-through (*Example:* "You just wait. I'll get you for this!")

4. Uses follow-through consequences that are overly severe (*Example:* "You are going to stay after school for two weeks")

5. Physically responds to a student out of anger (*Example:* Pulls the child's hair; squeezes the child's arm; shakes, throws, or hits the student)

## THE BACKUP SYSTEM

### Time Out

Limit setting is intended to remove a noncompliant student from the educational environment and quickly return to the learning process so that time is not wasted. When all the limit-setting techniques fail to work, the teacher drops the limit-setting approach and moves to time out, removing the student to some extent from the educational setting and beginning the use of a backup system. The backup system makes use of isolation and gradual removal of the student from the classroom, with the eventual involvement of the principal and others. It is used when the limit-setting system has failed to be effective.

Time-out procedures deny a student, for a fixed period of time, the opportunity to receive reinforcement. This removal of stimuli is actually time out from positive reinforcement—those activities that serve to reinforce the student's inappropriate behavior. Time out generally is used when the classroom activities reinforce the student and the teacher's application of the limit-setting techniques is ineffective. In the vignette of Mark and the squirt gun, the class may unknowingly be reinforcing Mark to continue to act in such a defiant manner by giving him the attention he so dearly seeks. Recall this portion of the vignette:

> ***Mark:*** *(takes a quick glance at the teacher and at his classmates, and smiles)*

The next option for the teacher would be to remove the student from some or all of the reinforcement he is receiving. The teacher may then choose from among four distinct categories of time out: nonseclusionary time out, contingency contracting observation, exclusionary time out, and seclusionary time out. In a middle school, this may entail a seat away from the other students at the back of the classroom, an arrangement with another teacher to move the disruptive student to his or her classroom, or even removal to a supervised time-out room such as an "in-school suspension" room. These will be described in detail in Chapter 8, which details the backup system.

## SUMMARY

The Rules and Consequences Face uses the central technique of assertive *Commands*. The teacher asserts himself or herself with the use of an assertive command that makes it quite clear to the misbehaving student what actions the teacher wants immediately. If the student fails to respond positively to the command, the teacher must move to the TBC's *Acting* as a last step before dropping the limit-setting system and moving to the time-consuming backup system, which uses various forms of isolation or time out.

# 7

# Acting
## The Rules and Consequences Face

Minimum Power ◄─────────────────────────► Maximum Power

*Relationship-Listening Face*    *Confronting-Contracting Face*    *Rules and Consequences Face*

| LOOKING | NAMING | QUESTIONING | COMMANDING | ACTING |
|---|---|---|---|---|
| 1. Square off<br> • slow down<br> • shoulders to shoulders<br> • broad foot stance<br> • unbroken eye contact<br>2. Relaxing breaths<br>3. Close space<br> • far<br> • near<br> • intimate | 1. Limit setting<br> • I-message<br>  – student behavior<br>  – teacher feeling<br>  – effect of student behavior<br> • Door openers<br> • Active listening<br> • Acknowledgments | 1. Limit setting<br> • stop statements<br> • what/how questions<br>2. Backup system<br> • contracting<br> • time out<br> • notifying parents | 1. Assertive<br> • name<br> • gesture<br> • touch<br> • eyes<br>2. Broken record<br>3. State consequences | 1. Physical intervention<br> • restraining<br> • transporting |

Another version of the squirt gun incident shows Mark's growing defiance and belligerence toward his teacher:

> **Mr. McDaniel:**   *(takes two relaxing breaths) "Mark, take the squirt gun out of your back pack and hand it to me!"* (broken record).

> **Mark:**   *"Why should I?"* (defensive response as verbal escalation).

> **Mr. McDaniel:**   *(takes two relaxing breaths) "Toys are not allowed at school, and squirting it in class causes conflict and disrupts my teaching, and that is really frustrating to me"* (I-message).

> **Mark:**   *"But why do I have to give you the gun? I quit squirting it and put it away"* (back talk and verbal escalation as questioning).

*Note:* Many of the techniques in this chapter can be found in F. Jones, *Positive Classroom Discipline* (New York: McGraw-Hill, 1987) and in Nonviolent Crisis Prevention Institute, *Nonviolent Crisis Intervention for the Educator: Volume III—The Assaultive Student* (Brookfield, WI: Author, 1994).

> *Mr. McDaniel:* *"Mark, this is your last warning. Follow my instructions now!"*
>
> *Mark:* *(no response)*
>
> *Mr. McDaniel:* *(takes two* relaxing breaths*) "Now you have a choice. I want you to stand, walk to the back of the room, and seat yourself in that chair for the remainder of the class, or else stand and go to the principal's office. If you do not move, I will call in Mr. Carlson, the assistant principal, and we will trans-port you to the discipline office (promises a* follow-through by stating consequences*). Mark, move to the chair now!"* (time out).
>
> *Mark:* *(snickers)* *"I'd like to see you make me! You touch me and you're a...(unintelligible threats)!"* (verbal escalation as refusal).

The hostile student may display a passive or active refusal, or even threats, during a teacher command for time out, as with the example of Mark and his attitude of, "I'd like to see you make me! You touch me and you're a...(unintelligible threats)!" This action of refusal and threat takes both the student and the teacher into high profile and very public techniques and actions. The teacher gives a final private warning, intended to be a promise preparatory to a consequence:

> *Mr. McDaniel:* *"Mark, stand and go to the chair and seat yourself* (broken record). *This is the last request, and if you fail to move, I will need to bring the assistant principal in here to remove you, and if that is done you'll be in much more serious trouble* (promise of a consequence). *Let's keep this between us. Now, move!"*

## ACTING (PHYSICAL INTERVENTION) AND THE BACKUP SYSTEM

Once the promise of a consequence, as part of the limit-setting com-manding process, is made, the teacher must follow through and the stu-dent may become defiant or potentially assaultive. At this point, the limit-setting system stops and the backup system must be employed. The classroom activities are clearly disrupted, and the educational pro-gram cannot continue with the student behaving in the classroom in such a manner. The help of others is needed, such as the principal and fellow teachers (get backup).

### The Response Team

We have observed Ms. Sanders in her dealings with Cindy *("Yeah, get out of her face. Are you gay or something? F--- off!!")* and Mr. McDaniel in his dealings with Mark *("I'd like to see you make me!")*. Each teacher has reached the point of having to move to the backup system. The teachers have previously prepared three envelopes that they keep in their lesson plan books. When necessary, they take the envelopes out, write the classroom number on each, and give one to each of three students they know to be very dependable and who are seated near the door. These students now deliver one letter across the hall, a second to the next-door neighboring teacher, and the final letter to the principal or assistant principal. The letter says simply, "Help. I need the Response Team immediately—Room B-17, Ms. Sanders (or Mr. McDaniel), Crisis code A." If a classroom telephone is available, of course, the teacher would simply telephone the administrative office. The principal and teachers (some schools have resource officers) arrive, asking "Who?" The teacher identifies the student who needs to be removed from the classroom and transported to the office.

The Response Team will again follow the cardinal rules concerning the use of power and privacy. These rules are followed as the situation escalates along the Teacher Behavior Continuum from *Looking* to *Naming, Questioning,* and *Commanding,* before escalating to the point of nonviolent crisis management through the use of *Acting (Physical Intervention).*

The removal of a defiant and potentially acting-out student places both the teacher and the student in a fight-or-flight stance involving an adrenaline dump. It has the highest probability of producing an assault by the student and an overuse of physical power by the adults, potentially leading to an injury or property damage.

Experts have identified four distinct levels of crisis in situations involving confrontation and noncompliance by a student such as Cindy or Mark: (1) anxiety, (2) defiant, (3) physically aggressive, and (4) tension reduction (or calming) (McMurrain, 1975). These levels have been modified for the *Three Faces of Discipline* approach (see Table 7.1). A new example clearly shows an assaultive behavior by a student and the ensuing levels of crisis and teacher behavior.

**TABLE 7.1    Levels of Crisis, Student Behavior, and Teacher Techniques**

| Crisis Level | Student Behavior Characteristics | Teacher Goals and Techniques |
|---|---|---|
| *1: Anxiety Phase*—Attention getting | As a result of some frustration, possibly as a result of the teacher's limit setting, the student appears as if he is a tightly wound spring, ready to snap. His hands may be clenched into a fist with white knuckles, and he may drop his eyes or glare intently, his gaze either focusing sharply on a peer or teacher or, instead, alternately focusing on his subject and then darting away. He may become physically restrictive, pulling inside himself and turning away, or he may become active, pacing like a caged cat and exhibiting nervous tics. His actions clearly attract the *attention* of peers and observant adults. | The student, if caught quickly, is still rational enough to respond to the teacher's language. Have the student ventilate representationally through language (talk it out). Redirect the student away from social interaction, giving him his "personal space." If possible, make few or no demands. With the use of language, employ Relationship-Listening techniques (active listening, I-messages, and door openers and promises to problem solve). |

*(Continued)*

| TABLE 7.1   Levels of Crisis, Student Behavior, and Teacher Techniques *(Continued)* | | |
|---|---|---|
| 2: *Defiant Phase*—Power | In order to maintain his *power* over a teacher or peer, the student now verbally escalates up a continuum by (1) *Questioning*—asks manipulative questions of "Why?"; (2) *Refusal*—refuses to cooperate; (3) *Release*—verbally releases pent-up feelings through screaming or shouting verbal aggression in the form of swearing, name calling, and similar verbal outbursts that may help to release or ventilate stored-up tension. The student may also use (4) *Intimidation*—a verbal attempt to intimidate threatening to do harm to the teacher or himself. Finally, if the conflict is able to be contained, there is a (5) *Tension Reduction*—whereby the student lacks energy, feels guilt, and is embarrassed about his behavior. | The teacher positions herself in an alert *supportive stance* and permits the child's ventilation through verbal aggression. If the verbal aggression turns to defiance, the teacher moves to provide a *Command* as the Rules and Consequence techniques (assuring the student of potential consequences) and promises of safety. Give the student time and space to ventilate, and if possible, do not physically intervene. |
| 3: *Physically Aggressive Phase*—Assault/ revengeful | The student now becomes totally *revengeful* and nonrational, and cannot control his own actions. He physically strikes out in a direct assault toward peers or the teacher by a *strike*, as a hit or throwing, or a *grab*, such as holding, hair pulling, choking, or biting. | In response to the assault, the teacher defends herself with defensive actions from a position of a supportive stance and accompanies her physical actions with a *command*, sending two messages: a command to desist action in a way the teacher desires, and verbal reassurance through a *promise of safety* and nonaggression toward the student. If the student appears to be attempting to injure himself or others or do major property damage, the teacher may be required to use team restraining techniques to stop and then transport the student. |
| 4: *Tension Reduction (Calming) Phase*—Helplessness | After the violent action, the student is deflated and becomes passive with little energy. He has feelings of guilt and feels *helpless* as to how others might respond to him. | Help cognitively recapitulate the happenings for the student, first by having him verbally talk about it using the Confronting-Contracting techniques, "What-how" questions, and contracting. Reestablish the relationship verbally and by touching (shaking hands, hugging, or other forms if possible). |

## Crisis Level 1: Anxiety Phase

When the student is in the anxiety phase, he or she is still rational. The teacher may still be able to appeal to the student's rational abilities to reflect on the situation and use the power of reason to prevent the situation from escalating to a more serious confrontation.

> *Mr. Griffin's third period physical education class is about to begin as he walks through the gym area. He sees a sixth-grade student, Anthony, attempting to "score" as he hurls his lock from his gym locker toward the basket and glass backboard. Not only is the lock smacking against the glass with the potential of breaking it but there are also other students around that could be injured if hit by the heavy lock.*
>
> ***Mr. Griffin:*** *"Anthony (name), stop! (He points to the lock in Anthony's hand* [gesture] *and moves face to face* [eye contact *and* proximity near]. *The lock could hurt someone or even break the glass backboard. Put the lock away in your backpack"* (Command).
>
> *(Because we have a potential danger to others or school property, the severity clause comes into play and the teacher moves straight to the Rules and Consequences Face with a command).*
>
> ***Anthony:*** *(stands still, holds the lock tightly with both hands, glares directly at Mr. Griffin, and then looks up at the basket, and—in direct defiance—repeats the throwing activity)*
>
> ***Mr. Griffin:*** *"Anthony (name), stop! (He again points to the lock* [gesture], *moves face to face* [eye contact] *and places himself between Anthony and the basket). Put the lock in your backpack or give it to me"* (broken record).

## Crisis Level 2: Defiant Phase

Any time a student regresses to the defensive phase by shouting, swearing, clenching a fist at the teacher, and so on, the teacher should shift her feet from a square position to a supportive stance, and begin making statements to the student to assure him of safety: "We will not hurt you *(promise of safety).* We need you to quiet down and move to the door, and go to the office." If the student is permitted to ventilate by shouting and swearing, the student will wear himself or herself out. Then, if necessary, a verbal desist through the Rules and Consequences Face can be effective.

> ***Anthony:*** *(screams)   "You asshole! Keep your damn hands off me! Keep your damn hands off me! No, let me go—don't touch me!"* (verbal escalation as release).
>
> ***Mr. Griffin:*** *(lets 45 seconds pass but maintains the unbroken eye contact with Anthony)* "Anthony (name), *stop, calm down. I am not going to touch you! Put the lock in your back-*

*pack or in my hand!"* (broken record). *(Mr. Griffin waits for a few minutes, giving Anthony an opportunity to think and comply.)* *"If you cannot, I will need to bring another teacher and the assistant principal here to transport you to the office, and if that is done, you'll be in much more serious trouble* (promise of a consequence). *Let's keep this between us. Now, put the lock in your backpack or in my hand!"* (preparatory statement).

**Anthony:**   *"You asshole! You're going down!"* (Anthony now pushes through the gymnasium door, leading into the school building, and Mr. Griffin follows.)

**Mr. Griffin:**   *(signals to a teacher in the building to call the administrative office to declare a Crisis Code A* [for potential assault]).

## Suggested Codes

Emergency codes can be communicated to the office or announced over the school public address system. They will communicate to the teachers, staff, and school personnel but will not be understood by the students (who otherwise might panic and become overly concerned).

- *Code W (for Weapon):* A student, or any person, has a weapon and the school resource officer or police need to come to the teacher's assistance. When announced on the school public address system, this could signal all personnel to take classroom and schoolwide actions to protect themselves and the students under their supervision (e.g., pull all window blinds or curtains [this might stop flying glass]; barricade the classroom door with a heavy object such as a filing cabinet so it cannot be opened; move the students as a group on the floor and away from windows or doors; keep students occupied by reading them a story until the all-clear is given).

- *Code A (for Assault):* The teacher is being or is about to be assaulted, and the Response Team must immediately come to assist.

- *Code H (for Help):* Response Team help is needed within the next hour, but the teacher is not in a dangerous crisis situation.

- *Code R (for Runner):* A student has run out of the classroom and is leaving the campus. The teacher would include the student's name and age and the possible direction of the student when last seen.

Many other codes may be used as needed by the school, but the use of more than five could create a list too long for good memory and communication.

## Crisis Level 3: Physically Aggressive Phase (Assault)

Techniques for the proper way to approach a potentially out-of-control student may include, when necessary, transporting the assaultive student. Once the student is so flooded emotionally that he or she is on the very edge (acting out), the student regresses through the paleocortex brain to the "reptilian" brain and becomes an irrational reflexive being not hearing commands or processing verbal communication. Instead, he or she tends to be on a sensory defensive alert, now receiving about 90 percent of incoming messages by what he or she sees and interprets from body posture and motion, voice tone, volume, and cadence. The manner in which this irrational student is approached will assist in calming him or her down, or, on the negative side, trigger him or her to act out.

> *Anthony turns and with both hands—including the one still holding the lock—suddenly and forcefully pushes Mr. Griffin at shoulder level and strikes him, causing him to fall back three full steps. Mr. Griffin quickly catches his balance.*
>
> ***Mr. Griffin:***  *"Anthony (name), stop. Calm down!"*
> ***Anthony:***  *"No—f--- off, asshole, you're going down!"*
>
> *Anthony screams at full volume, and again attempts to push Mr. Griffin with both hands. Mr. Griffin grasps both of Anthony's arms at the wrist to restrain him. Anthony drops the lock and attempts to butt Mr. Griffin with his head. Anthony now lashes out with his right leg in three quick kicking motions, one of which strikes Mr. Griffin squarely in the shin, causing him definite pain. (Note: After reading the full explanation that follows, you will see that the teacher in this example made a number of mistakes in handling this incident and dealing with a revengeful child. He should have used supportive demand and stance rather than assertive demand and stance (explained later). But if the teacher has had little past experience and does not know the history of this child, he might judge the student's actions as an attempt to grab attention or power, and then might find himself handling the revengeful incident as best he can once it begins.)*
>
> *Mr. Griffin now releases Anthony to see if he will quiet down. Instead, Anthony runs into a nearby classroom, knocking over furniture that is in his path. Mr. Griffin prevents Anthony from leaving by physically blocking the door. Anthony kicks the door, to his discomfort, and runs his arm across a storage shelf holding a globe, vase, and books, knocking all of these items onto the floor with a great crashing noise. Anthony now moves to the window and violently strikes it with his fist; it cracks, but the window pane stays intact. This action carries the real potential for Anthony to injure himself, and before a*

*second blow can land, Mr. Griffin again grasps Anthony's wrists and pulls him away from the window. He now runs out the unblocked door and into the arms of Mrs. Mitchell, who has arrived to assist. Anthony steps back and attempts to punch Mrs. Mitchell, who blocks Anthony's blow with a raised arm and then steps aside.*

*After the full blow has been thrown by Anthony, Mrs. Mitchell quickly steps behind Anthony and grasps his right wrist with her right hand. The second member of the Response Team, the assistant principal, Mr. Haigs, grasps Anthony's left wrist in a parallel fashion. At the same time, Mrs. Mitchell takes her open left hand and places it on Anthony's right shoulder from behind. Again, Mr. Haigs parallels Mrs. Mitchell's hand movements.* (See Drawing 7.11, Team Restraint, later in this chapter.) *With their arms on Anthony's shoulders, the adults push Anthony's head and shoulders down until his head is below his waistline. From this position, it is impossible for him to pick up his feet to kick. Each teacher places the foot closest to Anthony in front of his body and between his feet, thus preventing him from walking out of the restraining hold. The third member of the team moves in front of Anthony and holds up his shoulders to keep him from falling forward on his face. Anthony is now standing flat-footed, bent over with his head below his waist, and each of his arms is held upward and wrapped around a teacher. He is wedged between the teachers, immobilized, and unable to kick or strike.*

**Mrs. Mitchell:** *(whispers)* "*Anthony, we are not going to hurt you, and we are not going to let you hurt us. You are safe. We are trying to keep you safe. We will not hurt you* (broken record). *We are teachers; we will not hurt you. Anthony, we are restraining you like this to keep you safe*" (broken record). *(Anthony attempts to struggle free, but the team holds him firmly.)* "*We are holding you but we are not hurting you* (broken record). *We need to hold you like this until you can relax. Quiet down, Anthony. Relax. Breathe and relax.*" *(Anthony continues to struggle violently but without success. His head is below his waist, but he still screams a list of profanities at the teachers. Mrs. Mitchell, however, continues to speak to him in a whisper.)* "*We are not going to let you hurt us, and we are not going to hurt you. You are safe. We are the teachers. We are going to hold you like this until you quiet down.*" *(Anthony now begins to cry and slowly stops struggling.)*

*The restraining teachers slowly permit Anthony to straighten himself and stand upright, but as he does, both Mrs. Mitchell and Mr. Haigs—who still are grasping his wrist— take their nongrasping hands, swing them under Anthony's arms, and grasp their own wrists. They now are holding Anthony in a transporting position. Holding him firmly by each of his wrists and pushing with their shoulders, they quickly turn Anthony around, go out the door, and transport him to the office. The third team member remains in close pursuit and ready to help by restraining Anthony if he physically struggles again.*

---

### RESTRAINING TECHNIQUES

Nonviolent methods of holding students so they will not hurt themselves or others.

---

One of the most demanding teacher-student interactions is one that involves a clear assault on the teacher, a danger to the student, and the potential for destruction of school property. When forced to deal with such a student, the heart pounds and the adrenaline rushes through the body, pushing to a state of hyper-alertness and creating a defensive stance for one's protection and the student's safety. Out of one's own understandable fright, a teacher may emotionally flood, thus causing real difficulty in thinking correctly and acting constructively as these sudden and quick actions unfold.

Experts (Nonviolent Crisis Prevention Institute, 1994) who have studied such violent actions by students recognize a general level-by-level progression in the behavior and actions of a potentially assaultive student. If these levels of crisis progression are understood, then when the sudden quick developments do occur, they can be better recognized and thus less frightening. Previous mental and physical rehearsal will permit responding constructively.

Under emotional stress, the student will regress from the rational neo-cortex brain (Crisis Level 1: Anxiety phase) to the paleocortex brain where he snaps and snarls (Crisis Level 2: Defiant phase). Finally, he or she will regress to the reptilian brain (Crisis Level 3: Physically aggressive phase) with physical assault. Eventually, this thinking will begin the process of returning to rational activity (Crisis Level 4: Calming phase).

---

### SUPPORTIVE STANCE

When a student is about to be violent, you approach to calm him or her down. You face the student at a 45-degree angle and, without gesturing, attempt to communicate that you are not going to physically confront or assault the student.

---

This defiant verbal behavior by the student, as it gets more and more out of control, may also progress through escalation stages that can be recognized and displayed on a Verbal Escalation Continuum, as follows (see Figure 7.1):

1. *"Why?" questions:* The first stage, *Questioning,* is where the student asks "Why?" questions when he or she already knows the answer. This is a subtle defiance ploy by the student.

   *Intervention:* First give a real answer to the question, and then repeat the command; if necessary, repeat the command again as a broken record response.

2. *No response:* A further verbal escalation is when the student moves to verbal defiance: "No, I won't do it, and you can't make me!" The student at the No Response stage is losing rational ability.

   *Intervention:* The response is to assure the student that no one will attempt to "make him" (or her) and that the student can be powerful. Then the command is repeated. If the refusal continues, move to a promise of a consequence, but always said in such a manner as to give the student a clear choice. "Mark, you can either do so-and-so, or I will need to call Mr. Carlson, the principal, and we will do so-and-so! Take your choice."

3. *Flooding:* Still escalating further, the student performs a verbal release or "flooding" by screaming, shouting profanities, and appearing to become generally hysterical. Giving the student information and talking to him is useless because he has regressed to the paleo-cortex brain, is "snapping and snarling," and is clearly not rational.

   *Intervention:* The appropriate response is to do nothing; simply hold tight in a supportive stance. The student, by the verbal release, is just eating up his or her energy, and in two or three minutes will tire and may become quiet.

4. *Threatening:* In this form of verbal escalation, the student makes threatening statements in an attempt to intimidate. These threats

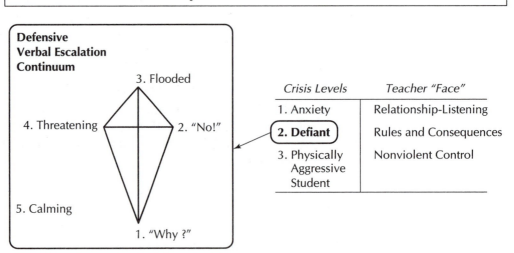

**FIGURE 7.1   Crisis Development**

may be to do injury to person or property, or even a threat to hurt himself or herself. These threats must be treated as real and clear action must be taken.

*Intervention:* Take all necessary actions to get assistance through school policies and regular training practices. The school should have in place a severity crisis code system understood by all teachers, administrators, and staff. When it receives a call or note from a teacher with the crisis code A, for example, the administration knows that a teacher is in danger of being assaulted, and a Response Team will come to the teacher's assistance immediately.

5. *Calming phase:* After any of these verbal outbursts or an acting-out behavior, the student normally will retreat to a stage called the *calming phase.* He or she may feel a large amount of remorse or guilt for his previous verbal outburst or physical aggression. The previously violent or verbally threatening student is deflated. He or she appears introverted, quiet, and flat in facial expression, and will have difficulty speaking. The child becomes withdrawn, with little energy. He or she may have feelings of guilt and helplessness as to how others might respond to him or her—especially the teacher that the student may have assaulted or verbally abused or threatened.

*Intervention:* In dealing with the student in the middle of the calming phase, the Relationship-Listening Face is appropriate before moving to the *Confronting-Contracting Face.*

## Crisis Level 4: Tension Reduction (Calming) Phase

Some students will begin self-abusive activities such as pulling out their hair, biting themselves, or some similar act of inwardly directed physical abuse. Since the student is more relaxed and is now rational, he or she may need help to recall what has happened, for he or she may not actually remember what started the crisis incident or what transpired once it began.

Two goals characterize the calming phase: (1) enabling the student to reflect on what occurred and challenging the student to consider or contract how he or she might act differently in the future and (2) reestablishing equilibrium in the relationship between the student and the teacher. The student must realize that the negative behavior is unacceptable but that he or she will still be accepted as a worthy person. These two goals are achieved through a private meeting, which clearly moves into the backup system (see Chapter 8).

---

### CALMING PHASE

After a violent act, the student feels guilty and remorseful, and you approach the child to reestablish friendly relations and dispel negative feelings.

---

## Private Meeting (Semi-Private)

During the calming phase, the teacher and the student should be eye to eye in a very close proximity-near setting. This can be done by sitting on chairs without a table or any other object in between. During this stage, it is important that the student be able to state cognitively—or for the teacher to describe—the events that have occurred in a way that imparts no guilt, and for the relationship between the teacher and the student to reach a new emotional equilibrium free of hostility. This reunion is important for both the student and teacher.

Teachers should be very cautious about forcing a verbal apology that requires the student to say "I'm sorry." This verbal statement may be something the teacher needs, but if it is forced, the student will begin to have feelings of guilt and start a new crisis. If the calming phase goes well, the student will have feelings of remorse and will wish to apologize, but he or she may express it in a nonverbal form. A feeling of warmth generally accompanies the remorsefulness. He or she may meet eyes, saying nothing but smiling affectionately. Teachers should feel free to return the smile. Forgiveness can be expressed back to the student through similar smiling, but the teacher must also convey these feelings in the form of verbal expression as a statement of a promise of safety. As a general rule, after a significant isolation or assaultive event, a private meeting should occur between the teacher and the student (the principal and others may also be included if appropriate).

> *Minutes later, the bell rings and the students depart, passing Ms. Sanders as she stands at the door. When Cindy arrives, the teacher signals her to move to a nearby desk, then closes the door to the now empty classroom* (private meeting). *It is time for Ms. Sanders to deal with Cindy regarding her use of profanity* (Don't go public!). *Ms. Sanders has not forgotten Cindy's words, "Yeah, get out of her face. Are you gay or something? F--- off!"* (This swearing and behavior would be classified as Crisis Level 2: Defiant phase, and seen as Intimidation on the Verbal Escalation Continuum.)

Again, the teacher has the decision as to what "face" to wear and what parallel techniques to use in carrying out this meeting. Cardinal Rule 2 is to use the least powerful technique necessary, so at first the teacher might try a private meeting using Relationship-Listening techniques. If later incidents occur involving isolation and future private meetings, the teacher may escalate to Confronting-Contracting meeting techniques, and then finally to a Rules and Consequences approach.

## The Relationship-Listening Meeting

Because the techniques are taken from a counseling model, this face is ideally suited for one-to-one interaction between student and teacher. Go slowly, continuing to use such *Looking* techniques as eye contact and relaxing breaths. You and the student are seated so that you are knee to knee, which places you at the edge of the student's comfort bubble. (A meeting between Mr. McDaniel and Mark, or Mr. Griffin and Anthony, would follow similar teacher techniques.)

The Relationship-Listening teacher (see Figure 7.2) might open with an I-message: "Cindy, when a student swears at me like you did *(behavior),* such harsh words stop me from talking and working with a student *(effect).* It also causes me to lose the respect of your classmates *(effect),* and I feel first frustrated and then angry *(feelings).* We need to talk about this" *(door opener).* In dealing with Anthony, a door opener is necessary: "Anthony, we have had a terrible experience in the band room, and I feel a need to talk about it with you."

You are now free to use:

- Acknowledgments

- Verbal encoding of the student's feelings through critical listening

- Door openers

- The Six Steps to Problem Solving (see Chapter 8)

For a short private meeting, a no-lose plus/delta technique may be used by simply having both the teacher and the student write out a list of all the items that are going well and all that are not. Through no-lose problem solving, the student is asked how both the teacher and the student can move the minuses into the plus column: What actions can we take to work this out so that we are both comfortable and so we will not have to face such a situation in the future?

---

**FIGURE 7.2    Relationship-Listening Face**

The objective in using the Relationship-Listening Face is to maintain the relationship with the misbehaving student and work things out in a nonpunitive, no-lose manner. The attitude, or face, is one that allows your actions to say, "I will nonjudgmentally express to you *(I-message)* how your actions may be taking away my rights and impacting on me as a teacher. I am here to listen to you empathetically and uncritically. I will help by listening and attempting to get clarity, through active listening, and when you wish, I can help through my guidance to permit you to solve your own problems. I will not do this for you."

Sometimes issues may arise out of the private meeting that do not have a concrete effect on you or the school. The student wishes to share these issues or seek guidance in matters related to values that will translate to later student behavior, so you may use the preceding techniques to have the student think out clearly about these important issues.

### The Confronting-Contracting Meeting

The Confronting-Contracting private meeting begins with a series of "What?" questions: "Cindy (or Mark or Anthony), this must stop. This shall not continue to go on! What are you doing? What is the rule? I want you to think about this behavior; is it helping you?" Again, it is best to continue slowly to use nonverbal limit-setting behaviors such as eye contact and relaxing breaths, and seat the student knee to knee with the teacher at the edge of the student's comfort bubble. The Confronting-Contracting attitude is to give the student time, with counseling, to reflect on what he or she is doing—requiring the brain's neocortex to be engaged. If the student is in a state of fight or flight, it may be necessary to have him or her relax, so that real thinking can take place. This is not a meeting to scold the student, but to think.

Finally, ask, "What will you do to change?" and then push for a contract. The student likely will be faced with another opportunity in the future to act in a similar misbehaving manner. Now is the time to use rational thinking to have the student come up with his or her own appropriate strategy so he or she will know how to behave the next time this incident occurs. The contract may be informal and sealed with a handshake if it is done in a mini-meeting within the classroom. When contracting is done in an after-class meeting, the contract is written and signed by both the student and teacher, and may include a logical consequence if the contract is broken. The original contract is given to the student and a copy is stored in the teacher's grade book or student filing system for later retrieval if necessary. The teacher can also require a student to obtain a parent's signature on his or her copy of the contract.

### The Supportive Stance

While the teacher controls his or her own body actions, wishing to communicate a nonhostile position, it is advisable to use the supportive stance, to calm the student. The body is turned at an angle to the student, with the preferred foot pointed toward the student and the other foot at a 45-degree angle. Do not place yourself square shoulder to shoulder for two reasons: (1) the squared-off stance communicates a power challenge and will likely be viewed as hostile by the irrational student and may trigger him or her to act out and (2) if you were to be grabbed or receive a blow, such as being kicked, from the irrational student while in this squared-off power stance, all of the vulnerable parts of the body—face, neck, stomach, and groin—would be exposed to the blow. The angled supportive stance (see Drawing 7.1) is interpreted by the irrational student as nonhostile. Also, if assaulted, any blow would be against the side of the body (shoulder, hip, or leg). Taking an unexpected blow against the side of the body may hurt, but these body parts are less sensitive and less prone to injury. The supportive stance also gives the best footing to block and move to deflect any action by the acting-out student and to remove yourself from the situation—to escape. The squared-off stance, on the other hand, leaves you flat-footed and exposes you to any quick blows.

During a potentially threatening situation, use the supportive stance and, placing both hands in front and facing the student with a palms-up position, be ready to use your hands to block and assault. Be careful not to gesture or make any threatening moves with your hands, such as wagging your finger or similar hostile gestures. It is also important not to conceal your hands by placing them behind your back, which the irrational student may interpret as a sign that you may be holding something dangerous behind you. Also, do not put your hands on your hips, clench your fist, or point. Move in a slow manner, moving to the

**DRAWING 7.1    The Angled Supportive Stance**

edge of the student's comfort bubble, about one leg length away from the student, but be careful not to invade this bubble of space.

---

## A COMPARISON OF BODY STANCES

**"Squared Off" Power Stance**
*Purpose: Communicates and maintains power*

- Shoulders squared off
- Eye contact (visual burn)
- Hands behind the back
- Face is flat and expression-less (slack jaw)
- Say nothing
- Close space

**Supportive Stance**
*Purpose: Communicates support and nonhostile attitude*

- Feet positioned as in an "L"
- Open hand, palms up in front
- Nonglaring eye contact
- Control of voice (tone, volume, cadence)
- Promise of safety
- Give command and promise of consequence
- Repeat as "broken record"
- Stand at the edge of privacy bubble (proximity-near)

---

While employing the supportive stance, make eye contact, promise the student safety, and state a command, repeating it two or three times *(broken record)*, attempting to get the emotionally flooded student to hear you. If a change in the student's behavior does not occur, clearly state a preparatory statement for possible consequences: "Anthony, I am not going to hurt you or touch you! I want you to calm down, take a couple of breaths, and relax *(promise of safety)*. Anthony, lower your voice, put the lock in your pocket, and go to the cafeteria *(command)*. Lower your voice, put the lock in your pocket, and go to the cafeteria *(broken record)*. (A few seconds pass.) If you do not, I will need to call the assistant principal and two other teachers and we will escort you to the office. Take your choice."

---

## PROMISE OF SAFETY

When the student has been violent, you repeatedly tell him or her that you are not going to return that violence (hit) and that the child is safe with you.

In response to the student's assault, the teacher will defend himself or herself by using blocking and release techniques. If the student is endangering self or others or doing severe damage to property, use the restraining techniques described next (with the help of a second or third adult if one is nearby to form a Response Team). Physical actions should accompany a command, sending two messages: a directive to desist the unwanted action and a promise of safety and nonaggression toward the student.

## ASSAULT

Experts have studied the nature of assault in order to design ways that teachers may act to keep themselves safe and in turn not injure the student—called *nonviolent crisis intervention*. They have discovered that a student typically assaults in two ways: a strike or a grab. Each is described here, along with some suggested teacher actions.

## A Strike

A strike occurs when a weapon (foot, fist, object, etc.) comes in contact with a target (the teacher's body). The general techniques for defending against a strike are to block and move.

### Assault by Kicking

From a supportive stance with your feet at a 45-degree angle, lift your foot that is pointing toward the student, balancing on the other foot. While holding your foot up as a barrier, attempt to block the kick with the back of your foot or shoe and deflect to the side and behind you. If this kicking continues, you may need to get help, and a restraining hold may be required (see Drawing 7.2).

### Assault by Hitting and Throwing

The three-foot space at the edge of the student's privacy bubble in the supportive stance may provide the teacher with some room to anticipate a punch that is delivered by the student. This punch can be blocked and deflected with the backside of your arm by holding it across your body. When a student throws a blow with a fist, he or she has a forward momentum. Once the blow is deflected, you may grab the back of the student's arm and pull him or her past you with the aid of his forward momentum. You may then exit to get help, or may choose to position yourself with your back to an exit door permitting an escape, return to the supportive stance, and command the student to desist.

When the student is throwing something at you, there are two ways of handling an incoming object that has the potential to do you bodily harm. You can either move out of its path and dodge, or block and deflect. If time permits, an object can be picked up, such as a book, or perhaps a small chair you can hold like a lion tamer and be used to block and deflect the blow or thrown object.

| DRAWING 7.2    Kick Block |
| --- |

## A Grab

Besides being assaulted by a strike, you may also experience a grab, which is defined as a strike that clings to a target. Under this definition, every grab begins as a strike, and continues in the form of choking, biting, or grabbing.

### Assault by Choking

If a student assaults you by a front choking—placing his or her hands around your throat and squeezing—respond by standing erect, thrusting both arms upright above your head, taking one step back to put the student off balance, and turning suddenly to the right or left so the student's hands will be pulled. It is not wise to grab the student's hands and pull them off your throat; this will simply be inefficient or ineffective, and the student might dig his or her fingernails farther (see Drawings 7.3 and 7.4). Accompany the quick movement with a psychological response by shouting or screaming, startling the assaultive student and throwing him or her slightly off balance, permitting a short second to get free.

### Assault by Biting

If the student has caught you off guard and has sunk his or her teeth into some body part (most likely an arm), put the edge of a flat hand

---

**DRAWING 7.3  Front Choke Release**

---

**DRAWING 7.4  Rear Choke Release**

under the student's nose and against his or her upper lip, quickly vibrating the hand up and down with sufficient force to break free without injuring the student. Do not pull away from the bite but rather lean into it. Pulling may cause more damage by tearing than the bite itself. If the student has turned in such a manner that the upper lip area is not available, the fingertips of a flat hand can be pushed firmly into the student's cheek, finding the teeth between the upper and lower jaw and again vibrating a hand in an up-and-down motion to break free (see Drawing 7.5). The release attempt can be accompanied by a psychological response such as a shout.

## Assault by Grabbing

An assault by grabbing will usually come in the form of the student doing a one- or two-handed grab of arms or hair.

**One- and Two-Hand Grabbing Release.**   When the student uses either one or two hands to grab an arm, there is a weak link in the grab between the student's thumb and forefinger. Simply take a free hand, bring it over the top of the student's grab, lock the fingers of your two hands, and pull directly up (see Drawings 7.6 and 7.7). Again, accompany this release with a shout.

**One- and Two-Hand Hair-Pulling Release.**   If the student grabs hair, either with one hand or two, clasp his or her hand and push it into or against your head as a platform, while at the same time turning toward the student and bending your upper body down in a 45-degree angle. The student's wrist is bent backwards, causing a loss of strength in his or her hands and enabling you to break free and physically move away (see Drawings 7.8 and 7.9).

If, after an incident of choking, biting, kicking, grabbing, or hitting/throwing, the student retreats and moves to a protective corner or space out of the way of classroom activities, presenting no danger to self or

---

**DRAWING 7.5   Bite Release**

**DRAWING 7.6    One-Hand Grab Release**

**DRAWING 7.7    Two-Hand Grab Release**

| DRAWING 7.8    One-Hand Hair Grab Release |
| --- |

| DRAWING 7.9    Two-Hand Hair Grab Release |
| --- |

others, you should simply leave him or her alone, moving to the calming phase. However, if the student is still endangering others, property, or self, nonviolent restraining techniques can be used to stop his or her dangerous actions.

## NONVIOLENT RESTRAINING

### Basket-Weave Hold Restraint

If the student is small enough and you have a strength advantage, you may choose to use the basket-weave hold, which is a preferable restraining technique for a small student. This hold is accomplished by getting behind the assaulting student and putting your arms around him or her, grasping the student's right wrist with your left hand and his or her left wrist with your right hand, and pulling in a way that causes the student's arms to cross over the front of his or her body (see Drawing 7.10). Standing, your body can be moved sideways to the student with your feet at a 45-degree angle. This places the student's back at your right hip, and then pull his or her arms back toward you and lift up. This causes the student's heels to come slightly off the floor, forcing the student to stand on his or her tip-toes with his or her weight supported by your thigh. The student may also be held or restrained in a seated posi-

---

**DRAWING 7.10    Basket-Weave Restraint**

tion. Only a minimum amount of force is needed, so that the student is not injured.

The basket-weave restraint is the most powerful hold suggested for a small student, where you have a substantial physical strength advantage. If the student is too big and strong, a team restraint may be needed.

## Team Restraint

Once a full blow has been thrown by the assaulting student, and two other members of the Response Team have arrived, quickly step behind the student and grasp his or her right wrist with your right hand, with the thumb side of your hand facing down and in. At the same time, take an open left hand and place it on the student's right shoulder from behind. The thumb of the left hand should be positioned in the "V" formed by the student's arm and rib cage (see Drawing 7.11). Also, the left foot should be placed in front of the student's body and between his or her two feet, thus preventing the student from walking out of the restraining hold. Now push down with your left hand on the student's shoulder, while gently turning the student's wrist clockwise with your right hand. Only the needed pressure should be applied so that the student is not hurt. The second member of the Response Team parallels your actions with the student—her left hand on the student's left wrist, her right hand on the student's left shoulder, and her right foot parallel to your foot in front of the student. Again, this is all coordinated, and the two of you grab, move your feet, push down, and hold in one smooth action. The student is pushed head-down until his or her head is below

---

**DRAWING 7.11   Team Restraint**

his or her waistline. From this position, it is impossible for the student to pick up his or her feet to kick. The third Response Team member moves in front of the student, places his hands palms-up under the student's shoulder and holds the student to prevent him or her from falling forward. The acting-out student is told to calm down and advised that he or she may get up when he or she assures the Response Team that there will be no more resistance or acting out. Once the team members are assured that the student is calmed, he or she is now permitted slowly to stand erect, but the first two teachers maintain their hold on wrists and move into a transporting hold.

## Transporting Techniques

If the student does stop struggling and is in an upright position, quickly take the hand that had been holding his or her shoulder and move it under his or her arm. Being careful not to release the student's wrist, use a free hand to grasp the inside of the elbow of the student's other arm (see Drawing 7.12). Now walk quickly, bringing the student at the fastest manageable pace, applying a forward pressure with your inside shoulder that touches the student. A second Response Team member can get behind the student, place both hands on the student's shoulder blades and push (see Drawing 7.13). If at any time during the transport-

| DRAWING 7.12    Single Transport |
|---|

**DRAWING 7.13   Two Person Transport**

ing process the student excessively struggles to get free, simply reapply the team restraint. Never transport a student who is struggling and acting out.

It is important to accompany a physical restraint with parallel language of supportive command, preparatory directive statement, and promise of safety. During this crisis management, as with the removal of a student, the classroom teacher will be the Response Team leader and will use verbal mediation to attempt to calm the acting-out student. The classroom teacher plays the lead role for the following reasons:

1. The assistant principal and the Response Team members do not have a relationship with the student and know very little background as to what had happened to precipitate the event.

2. Giving up the power to an administrator or another teacher weakens the classroom teacher's power with the student and his or her authority in the eyes of the classmates.

3. With the classroom teacher maintaining the leadership, there is continuity of action during escalation and deescalation of power through the Three Faces of Discipline techniques.

4. Power does not involve physical strength, and the yielding of leadership to a physically larger male faculty member or administrator (which historically has been the practice) suggests that this is a physical power confrontation.

A potentially assaultive student's behavior with a weapon (knife, gun, explosives) may also be viewed through the crisis construct. However, disarming such a student is clearly outside the role and skill of a teacher. The police should be called. It is mandatory that the school have predetermined steps and procedures to deal with a student carrying a weapon, with all teachers and staff drilled in the procedures and emergency codes.

If the armed student is restricting departure through threats, and an evacuation cannot be carried out, the teacher is forced to deal with that student through this defiant phase level. These guidelines will help if you are caught in such a situation:

- Do not challenge with eye contact.

- Do not close space or invade the student's comfort bubble.

- Use repeated relaxing breaths to keep under control so that an adrenaline dump is not experienced.

- Do not square off with the student, but use a supportive stance (feet placed in an "L" position).

- Do not cross arms over your chest or make any gestures; simply put hands behind your back.

- Send for help if at all possible.

If the student wishes to talk, this usually is an encouraging sign. Use Relationship-Listening door openers and active listening to encourage ventilation. If the student appears to be attempting to think through his actions, use the "What?" question from the Confronting-Contracting techniques. When in doubt in dealing with an armed student when evacuation is impossible, the best action is to do nothing.

What has been described here is how one may deal with the *Level 3: Physically Aggressive* student by gradually escalating your power with the use of the TBC, from *Looking* (eye contact and proximity) to *Naming* (Relationship-Listening), to *Questioning* (Confronting-Contracting), to *Commanding* (Rules and Consequences with assertive commands), and, ultimately, to *Acting* (Physical Intervention) (nonviolent crisis management). The use of outside help from a Response Team involves very public techniques. Return repeatedly to a controlled use of verbal limit setting, with its minimal use of power, escalating only gradually from Relationship-Listening to Confronting-Contracting, and, when warranted, Rules and Consequences.

After the violent act, the student feels deflated and becomes withdrawn *(Crisis Level 4: Calming Phase),* with little energy. The student has feelings of guilt and feels helpless as to how others might respond to him or her, especially the teacher that he or she may have assaulted. The teacher techniques for handling the student during tension reduction were described in the previous discussion of verbal escalation; you might wish to reread that section.

## CLASSMATES AS ONLOOKERS TO THE ASSAULT

Whenever possible, the teacher should take steps to remove onlooking classmates by having the other students move to another room, by sectioning an area off from the view of other students, or (if possible) moving the misbehaving student to another room. Witnessing the irrational, flooded student can be very frightening for classmates, and seeing the teacher's restraining actions on the assaulting student may appear to students as if the student is being hurt by the teacher.

It is important to deal with the classmates who were onlookers to an assault on the revengeful student. Witnessing such aggression can cause an individual student or an entire group of students to move to *Level 1: Anxiety*, whereby they become highly anxious with accompanying behavior that might escalate through the crisis levels. Ventilating techniques previously suggested work with *Level 1: Anxiety* students. "Talking it out" often helps and involves holding one or more class problem-solving meetings, using the Relationship-Listening techniques.

### Class Meetings (Verbal Ventilation)

The entire class is seated in a circle. The formerly assaulting student is included in the meeting, and should be seated if possible. Just as the Confronting-Contracting techniques were used for the *Level 4: Calming Phase* to enable the teacher to establish an emotional equilibrium with the previously assaulting child, this tension reduction will also need to be reestablished with the student's classmates. They have seen or heard the frightening event, and have identified themselves as a part of the action. Through verbal ventilating in the class meeting, an attempt is made to reach the point where the teacher and students have gotten rid of any feelings of hostility. If the teacher does not conduct this meeting, the classmates, out of their fear of the acting-out student, will begin to make the misbehaving student the outside aggressor. Here is an example of a class meeting. Notice that the meeting begins with the teacher wearing a Relationship-Listening Face with its accompanying techniques, before moving to Confronting-Contracting.

> ***Teacher:*** *(opens the meeting)* *"Class, I would like to talk about the frightening things that happened this morning"* (door opener).
>
> ***Students:*** *(no one speaks for several moments, but then a discussion begins)*
>
> ***Tammy:*** *"Anthony went ballistic!!"*

**Alfred:** *"He hit the teacher."*

**Teacher:** *"Anthony was very angry. And when he gets angry, he hits"* (active listening).

**Dara:** *"Keep him away from me!"*

**Teacher:** *"When people hit, it is hard to like them."*

**Alfred:** *"You hurt Anthony's arm."*

**Teacher:** *"When I held Anthony, you thought I was hurting him"* (active listening).

**Jim:** *"You didn't hit Anthony."*

**Teacher:** *"What else did you see and feel?"* (door opener).

**Marsha:** *"I saw Anthony hit you and kick you. He cried and screamed swear words."* (This verbal ventilation may continue for 5 to 10 minutes with the teacher maintaining a Relationship-Listening Face and its techniques. Now the teacher moves to Confronting-Contracting and does not hesitate to deal with the realities of the situation and explain misinformation.)

**Teacher:** *"What happened first . . . Tammy?"* ("What?" questions).

**Tammy:** *"Anthony was throwing his lock at the basketball goal."*

**Teacher:** *"What happened next?"* ("What?" questions).

**Jim:** *"You told Anthony to stop, and he pushed you and hit you."*

**Teacher:** *"What happened next?"* (Confronting: "What?" questions).

**Dara:** *"Anthony screamed and hit, and you held him. And there was a big crash."*

**Teacher:** *"What happened next?"* ("What?" questions).

**Alfred:** *"You hurt Anthony's arm."*

**Teacher:** *"No. Because Anthony got so mad that he could hurt me, and he could hurt others, and he could hurt himself, I needed to hold him tightly to keep him safe. I am the teacher, but I do not hurt students. I am a friend, but when students get very angry, I need to hold them tight to keep them safe"* (a reality explanation and promise of safety).

**Alfred:** *"You hurt Anthony's arm."*

**Teacher:** *"No, Alfred. I was holding his arm and hands tightly so that his hands would not hurt me. I did not hurt Anthony; I was keeping him safe. Come up here, Alfred. (Alfred stands before the teacher.) Let me show you how safely I was holding Anthony."* (The teacher now demonstrates the basket-weave restraint on Alfred and two other children. Alfred giggles as if it is a game, and now a number of other students want a chance. The teacher demonstrates the basket-weave restraint *on all students who have requested it—including Anthony, who wants to be a part of this new game.)*

***Teacher:*** *"When students get very angry, they sometimes try to hurt other people. I am the teacher, and I keep people safe. And no matter how mean people are, I will not hit them, I will not hurt them, I will not kick them, and I will not bite them. I am the teacher and I hold students to keep them safe* (reality explanation and promise of safety). *Now we need to make some promises—we need to have an agreement. What should we do when others make us angry?"*

***Several of the students, in unison:*** *"Use words."*

***Teacher:*** *"Yes, when others make us angry, the rule is, 'We do not hit, but we tell that person with words,' and we can come to the teacher to get help. Hitting, biting, kicking, and spitting are against the rules. Also, how can we help Anthony when he gets mad?"*

***Dara:*** *"We can share with him."*

***Jim:*** *"We can include him in our activities."*

***Teacher:*** *"Does everyone agree with this? Good! We all now have an agreement. We are going to use words when we are angry, and we are going to include Anthony in our activities as a friend"* (contracting).

This vignette, of course, is for purposes of modeling teacher techniques, and is certainly rather artificial. This ventilation process and the Confronting-Contracting might take many minutes, or even many meetings, and may need to occur throughout the year if aggression is high in the classroom. But the techniques to be used, and the general attitude and processes to be employed, should develop in a direction much as the one demonstrated here.

This class meeting will serve a number of purposes: (1) it ventilates any pent-up anxiety and feelings that a student might have after witnessing the aggression; (2) it helps the assaultive student and his or her classmates reestablish an emotional equilibrium through tension reduction, potentially preventing the assaultive student from becoming the outside aggressor; (3) it helps students understand that if they, too, should become angry (and they may), the teacher will not take aggressive action against them but instead will help; and (4) it dispels any misinformation and misperceptions the students may have ("You hurt Anthony's arm").

## SUMMARY

There will be times that some students emotionally flood, creating a crisis that may lead to an assault by the student against the teacher or others. This behavior represents four levels: anxiety phase, defiant phase, physically aggressive phase, and calming phase. If you understand the behavior and these levels, you are more empowered to know how to act and how to intervene with such out-of-control students. Generally, a teacher can employ TBC techniques, first with the techniques of controlling his or her behavior and using proximity, eye contact, and the supportive stance. If the teacher needs to escalate, she or he would again use as little power as necessary, moving from the *Naming* techniques of the Relationship-Listening Face to *Questioning* and its accompanying Confronting-Contracting techniques. If necessary, the teacher can move to *Commanding* and the Rules and Consequences Face. Also, if it is unavoidable, the teacher may be required to *Physically Intervene (Acting)* by first protecting herself or himself from the student's assaults and then restraining and transporting the student to areas where he or she may be isolated. Finally, once the student is calmed down, the teacher may reestablish the teacher-student relationship through a progression of discussion techniques.

## REFERENCES

Jones, F. (1987). *Positive Classroom Discipline.* New York: McGraw-Hill.

McMurrain, T. (1975). *Intervention Is Human Crisis.* Atlanta: Humanics Press.

Nonviolent Crisis Prevention Institute. (1994). *Nonviolent Crisis Intervention for the Educator: Volume III: The Assaultive Student.* Brookfield, WI: Author.

# The Professional-Administrative Backup System

When all the limit-setting methods and techniques have failed to stop a student's misbehavior and his or her actions continue to disrupt the classroom learning environment, it may be time to call for help from others. The first step in moving to the professional administrative backup system is recognizing that some student action and behavior is beyond your skills and abilities. This situation forces more public action with a misbehaving student who has resisted attempts to resolve the problem in private. The student may then need to be isolated, or you may need to seek help from other professionals outside your classroom (other teachers, the school counselor or psychologist, perhaps even mental health organizations and law enforcement.)

The professional-administrative backup system involves two parts: a *professional sphere,* with specific procedures designed to resolve the problem within an academic setting, and an *administrative-legal sphere,* for problems that go beyond the realm of the educational setting (see Figure III.1).

Among the procedures used as part of a backup system are isolation/time out, private conferencing, contracting, professional staffing, and a technique called the Six Steps to Problem Solving. These concepts will be explained in detail in subsequent chapters.

The backup system, as part of the *Three Faces of Discipline* philosophy, draws on the series of techniques previously learned in the three categories of Relationship-Listening, Confronting-Contracting, and Rules and Consequences. Techniques for managing violent and assaultive student behavior are also included.

FIGURE III.1   Professional and Administrative Spheres of Responsibility

**Professional Sphere**
(e.g., a psychological need)

**Administrative-Legal Sphere**
(e.g., committed a criminal act)

Teacher

Counselor

School Psychologist

Mental Health Clinic

Institutionalized Care

Principal

Superintendent

School Board

Police

Court System

# 8

# The Backup System

The professional-administrative backup system involves two parts. The first entails a *professional sphere,* with clearly delineated steps and procedures designed to permit the primary deliverer of educational services to gain professional consultation, through staffing, from colleagues. The objective is to enable you to increase your skill and become more effective with a particular very difficult student.

The second part uses an *administrative-legal sphere* involving a yielding of primary responsibility for the management and restraint of the student's behavior. The administrative-legal sphere is necessary when the student action becomes severe, which may be criminal or at least threaten the safety and well-being of teachers and students alike—or even the disruptive student. Understandable and clearly defined steps and procedures must be established to dictate when such crisis students should be referred to the administrative authorities or legal system.

## DOCUMENTATION OF THE BACKUP STEPS: THE BACKUP SYSTEM CHECKLIST

To guide the teacher through suggested steps, a backup system checklist is provided (see Figure 8.1). By writing in dates and checking appropriate boxes, the teacher can easily document his or her own actions. The checklist, when followed, helps in these ways:

1. It provides a pathway for the teacher to follow.

2. Because it records the dates of actions and techniques, a time line of events can later be created to document the attempts that the teacher has made to help this misbehaving student.

3. It provides legal and professional documentation for the parents, the administrator, the professional (school psychologist, counselor), and legal authorities who may question any of the procedures.

## FIGURE 8.1 Backup System Checklist

Date (beginning) _____

Grade _____

Student's Name _____

Teacher's Name _____

| | Relationship-Listening | Confronting-Contracting | Rules and Consequences |
|---|---|---|---|
| **Limit Setting** | • I-Message<br>• Active Listening<br>(Proxemics—far, near, intimate) | • Stop ("this may not continue!")<br>• "What" questions ("…will be the consequences?")<br>(Proxemics—far, near, intimate) | • Assertive Command (tell what to do!)<br>• Promise a Consequence<br>(Proxemics—far, near, intimate) |

Severity Clause → → → → → → → → → → → → → → → → → → → → → → → → → → → → → → → → → → → →

| | Relationship-Listening | Confronting-Contracting | Rules and Consequences |
|---|---|---|---|
| **Backup System** | **1. 1st Knee-to-Knee Conference**<br>a. I-Message<br>b. Active Listening<br>c. Door Openers (acknowledgments, critical listening)<br>d. No-Lose Problem Solving<br>☐ _____ Date<br><br>**2. 2nd Knee-to-Knee Conference**<br>(Repeat a, b, c, d)<br>☐ _____ Date<br><br>**3. 3rd Knee-to-Knee Conference**<br>(Repeat a, b, c, d)<br>☐ _____ Date | **1. 1st Conference**<br>1.1 "What" question<br>☐ "What did you do?"<br>☐ "What is the rule?"<br>☐ "What is the consequence?"<br>☐ "How will you change?"<br>1.2 Contract<br>☐ handshake<br>☐ written _____ Date<br>☐ 1.3 (if broken) Logical Consequences _____ Date<br>• *Level 1 Time Out*<br>(Mediate afterwards with R-L or C-C)<br>• *Level 2 Time Out (In Room)*<br><br>**2. 1st In-Room Time Out/Conference**<br>2.1 "What" questions<br>☐ 2.2 Contract (written-enclose) _____ Date<br>☐ 2.3 (if broken) Logical Consequences _____ Date<br><br>**3. 2nd In-Room Time Out/Conference**<br>☐ 3.1 Repeat 1 and 2 (above) _____ Date<br>☐ 3.2 (if broken) Logical Consequences _____ Date<br>• *Level 3 Time Out (Out-of-Room)*<br><br>**4. 3rd In-Room Time Out/ Conference**<br>☐ 4.1 Repeat 1 and 2 (above) _____ Date<br>☐ 4.2 (if broken) Logical Consequences _____ Date | **5.** ☐ **Telephone Parents** _____ Date<br>5.1 (Begin Encouragement System) _____ Date<br>*Level 3 Time Out (Out-of-Room)*<br>**6.** ☐ **1st Out-of-Room Time Out**<br>(Repeat 1, 2, and 3, enclose Time Out Form) _____ Date<br>**7.** ☐ **2nd Out-of-Room Time Out**<br>(Repeat 1, 2, and 3, enclose Time Out Form) _____ Date<br>**8.** ☐ **Telephone/ In Writing**<br>(Enclose/copy to principal/parents) _____ Date<br>*Level 4 Time Out (Principal)*<br>**9.** ☐ **Office**<br>(Repeat 1, 2, and 3) _____ Date<br>(Repeat 1, 2, and 3) _____ Date<br>**10.** ☐ **Conference with Parents**<br>(Repeat 1, 2, and 3) _____ Date<br>**11.** ☐ **Staffing (members)** _____ Date | ☐ 11.1 "Who" squad _____ Date<br>☐ Members: _____<br><br>Severity Code Called<br>☐ Weapon _____ Date<br>☐ Assault, _____ Date<br>☐ Crisis _____ Date<br>☐ Runner _____ Date<br>☐ Transporting (performed) _____ Date<br>(enclose form)<br>☐ _____ Date<br>(enclose form)<br>☐ _____ Date<br>(enclose form)<br>☐ Restraint (performed) _____ Date<br>(enclose form)<br>☐ 11.2 Out-of-School Time Out _____ Date<br>or<br>☐ 11.2 Mental Health Referral _____ Date<br>or<br>☐ 11.2 Legal Referral (HRS/Police) _____ Date |

126

4. The checklist, with its boxes to be checked and its spaces for dates, means less paperwork for the teacher, who otherwise would have to write this documentation in anecdotal records.

## Procedures

The teacher begins using the backup system checklist by taking the checklist form (Figure 8.1), dating it, giving the student's grade level or home room, and including the student's and the teacher's names. The checklist is kept in the teacher's lesson plan book within easy reach of the teacher. It contains boxes to be marked whenever the teacher has performed one of the actions, and a line for dating its completion.

Generally, the teacher begins with Step 1 under the left column (Relationship-Listening techniques) and progresses down the column and across the checklist, following a plan of action. The Relationship-Listening column guides the teacher to progress through a sequence of three private (knee-to-knee) conferences. The student has been so disruptive (that is, preventing the teacher from teaching) that the teacher needs to call the student aside for a private conference. At each of the conferences the teacher would use the following procedures:

1. I-messages

2. Active listening

3. Door openers

4. No-lose problem solving

A box is provided so the teacher may place a check to document his or her actions. The teacher also writes the date of each private conference.

---

### RELATIONSHIP LISTENING

**1. 1st Private Conference**
- ☐ a. I-Message
- ☐ b. Active Listening
- ☐ c. Door Openers (acknowledgments, critical listening)
- ☐ d. No-Lose Problem Solving   Date_____

**2. 2nd Private Conference**   (Repeat a, b, c, d)

Date_____

**3. 3rd Private Conference**   (Repeat a, b, c, d)
Date_____

---

## PRIVATE CONFERENCES

In handling a backup system private meeting with a student such as Mark (in the squirt gun incident), the teacher meets with Mark after class and again begins to escalate up the TBC, first using the Relationship-Listening techniques. These techniques can also be used if a team conference is preferred because the student is having problems in other classes as well, or in the case that a second or third conference is needed. (*Reminder:* The Relationship-Listening Face during these techniques is one that views the student as (1) logical and rational, (2) able to control herself or himself, (3) able to be trusted, (4) able to solve his or her own problems, and (5) having a right to express strong feelings/anger.)

---

### PRIVATE CONFERENCING

A meeting, either planned as part of the backup system or spontaneous, held between the student and teacher to work out either person's problem and how behavior might be changed accordingly.

---

### Looking (Relationship-Listening Face)

*Both Mark and the teacher are seated in chairs, squared off, with the teacher's knees at the edge of Mark's comfort bubble (proximity: near). Mr. McDaniel maintains unswerving eye contact with Mark but is not hostile, aggressive, or unpleasant to him in any manner (such as finger pointing and gesturing). The teacher's face takes on the Queen Victoria look that says "I am bored" as he takes two controlled breaths. Mr. McDaniel may wish to permit a little time to go by as he maintains his eye contact and says nothing—he does not rush this, as a minute used now may save hours later.*

### Naming (Relationship-Listening Face)

*Mr. McDaniel says calmly, "Mark, we had a very unpleasant morning" (active listening). The teacher now says nothing, and lets the heat of the relationship simmer to see if Mark will begin to speak first. In this first step on the TBC, Mr. McDaniel is returning to his Relationship-Listening Face and wishes Mark to talk it out and externalize what is bothering him so that real problem solving may occur. The teacher may choose to stay in the Relationship-Listening Face and use door openers ("Let's talk about what happened in class this morning"), acknowledgments, I-messages ("When I am told to f--- off (behavior), it hurts our relationship (effect), and I feel frustrated (feelings) because it cuts off our communication"), and active listening ("I could tell that something was bothering you this morning"). Mr. McDaniel may also use the Six Steps to Problem Solving process to settle any difficulties in his relationship with Mark.*

If the student remains disruptive after the first private conference and the use of the Relationship-Listening techniques, the teacher would continue to use Relationship-Listening techniques for two more private meetings carried out in a similar manner (Steps 2 and 3). If the teacher believes this is not effective and feels the need for more power, he or she may turn to *Questioning* in private meetings.

## Six Steps to Problem Solving

To help a student learn to think through a problem logically, the teacher might lead the student through a six-step process while using the Relationship-Listening techniques to carry out these private meetings. The example that follows is a meeting using the Six Steps to Problem Solving using the example of Cindy, who has been offensive to the teacher.

> ***Ms. Sanders:*** *"You had some good friends where you used to live"* (active listening).
>
> ***Cindy:*** *"Yeah. Really good friends...and my best friend, Rose."*
>
> ***Ms. Sanders:*** *"You miss the friends that you used to be with, especially Rose"* (active listening).
>
> ***Cindy:*** *"Yeah, I've been friends with Rose since we were five years old. She was never a snob and we did lots of things together."*
>
> ***Ms. Sanders:*** *"You wish you could go back to your old school to be with your friends."*
>
> ***Cindy:*** *"Well, that would be nice but it's not going to happen. But if I could even just go to visit Rose, I think I'd feel better...that I wasn't losing my best friend. But my parents said that if I didn't bring up my math grade, I couldn't go to visit Rose, and I'll probably fail this stupid math."*
>
> ***Ms. Sanders:*** *"Failing math would keep you from being allowed to visit Rose."*
>
> ***Cindy:*** *"Yeah, I don't understand this stuff!"*
>
> ***Ms. Sanders:*** *"Ah, I see. You have a problem here—and that is passing math so you can visit Rose (Step 1: Defining the Problem). Let's work together to think of ways you might solve this problem. What are your ideas?"* (Step 2: Generating Solutions).
>
> ***Cindy:*** *"I was trying to get Carolyn to help me with my homework."*
>
> ***Ms. Sanders:*** *"That may work—getting a person to tutor you. But let's think of a lot of other ways, too"* (door opener).

**Cindy:** *"Well, my dad's pretty good at this stuff."*

**Ms. Sanders:** *"OK, we have two solutions: getting another student to tutor you and getting your father to help. What else can you think of?"*

**Cindy:** *"Well, I could take math in summer school."*

**Ms. Sanders:** *(nods her head in acknowledgment)*

**Cindy:** *"Carolyn lives next door to me and we ride the same bus. Maybe I could get her to help me before or after school or on the bus."*

**Ms. Sanders:** *"It sounds like you have generated a number of solutions: getting a tutor, getting help from your father, taking math in summer school, and getting Carolyn to help you at home or on the bus. Which of your ideas would be best?"* (Step 3: Evaluating the Solutions).

**Cindy:** *"Getting Carolyn to help me. Sometimes, I could get my dad to help too, when he has time."*

**Ms. Sanders:** *"Do you want to evaluate your other possibilities?"* (door openers).

**Cindy:** *"Well, if I took summer school, I still wouldn't be able to visit Rose until that was over and I had passed it. I don't want to wait that long. And I don't know any tutors or have any other time to meet with a tutor."*

**Ms. Sanders:** *"So getting Carolyn to help you and getting help from Dad—is that what you will do?"* (Step 4: Deciding on a Solution).

**Cindy:** *"Yes."*

**Ms. Sanders:** *"Remember, that I am available for help some afternoons as well."*

For the next two weeks, the teacher notices that Cindy's homework is completed, she has scored well on two quizzes, and her off-task behavior in class has stopped *(Step 5: Implementing the Solution)*. After class, the teacher talks to Cindy.

**Ms. Sanders:** *"Was your solution to your problem a good one?"* (Step 6: Evaluating the Solution).

**Cindy:** *"Yes, it was great, and I figured it out all by myself! You know, my Dad is a whiz at this math stuff."*

### The Six Steps to Problem Solving

1. *Defining the problem:* Before any discussion may occur in a conference, a clear statement of the problem must be given by the teacher or the student.

2. *Generating solutions:* All parties—teachers and students—are encouraged to come up with a creative list of solutions, no matter

how unrealistic the solutions may be, without evaluating the merits of the suggestions.

3. *Evaluating the solution:* All solutions are openly evaluated for the "goodness" or "badness" of the solutions.

4. *Deciding on a solution:* All parties—teacher and student or the students as a group—must decide on a solution that is acceptable to everyone.

5. *Implementing the solution:* All parties must decide what their roles are in carrying out the solution and commit themselves to the actions required. They must agree on when a later evaluation of the effectiveness of the solution will occur.

6. *Evaluating the solution:* A later follow-up meeting will occur to see if the solution was effective and what other actions might now be needed.

The teacher has used the Six Steps to Problem Solving to help Cindy through a process of on-the-spot conferencing or private meeting as part of the backup system. First, Cindy was an off-task and verbally hostile student. Active listening revealed that Cindy had an inner disequilibrium, or "blocked," need—she missed her best friend and wanted to be allowed to visit her, which required her to pass math for her parents to allow this. The teacher did not solve this problem for her, but was willing to take the time to listen, as part of the backup system, and encourage Cindy to communicate (speak out) about this problem until a solution was developed.

## Problem Ownership

Notice that with Cindy, who wanted to be allowed to visit her friend Rose and pass math, the teacher did not take ownership of these problems, nor did the teacher use roadblocks to communication by lecturing, giving solutions, or issuing warnings. Cindy owned the problem, and the teacher facilitated her thinking through the problem solving and then encouraged her to act. Teachers are solidly motivated to nurture and help children. They may be super-teachers who see their role as being the person who solves all problems. To classify the problems that are seen involving the students in the classroom, the teacher must determine whether the student owns the problem or the teacher owns the problem. These questions may help:

1. Do student's actions or problems take away the teacher's or classmates' rights? *(The student moves to the head of the line, past the other students waiting to use the pencil sharpener. This requires teacher intervention.)*

2. Is the safety of the materials, the classmates, the teacher, or the student involved? *(The student is stabbing the end of a dissecting*

*knife into the science lab table near other students who are also working at the same table. This requires teacher intervention.)*

3. Is the student too young and incapable of "owning" or solving this problem? *(The student is attempting to slide a heavy wooden cabinet away from the wall to retrieve a pencil that rolled behind it, which takes more strength than an average 11-year-old has. This requires teacher intervention.)*

If the answer to any of these questions is yes, the teacher owns the problem and must respond. Response techniques will be I-messages, active listening, door openers, acknowledgments, and possibly the Six Steps to Problem Solving. The concept of problem ownership transmits the clear message that teachers should inhibit their "rescuer" tendencies.

> **Student:**  *"Michael took my baseball cap!"*
> **Teacher:**  *"What are you going to do to get your cap back?"* (door opener).

From 80 to 90 percent of all problems faced by students in the classroom belong to them. The guidelines for problem ownership suggest that teachers must not allow their need to help or their fear of chaos to prompt them to move too quickly and without thinking, thus robbing the students of the experience of solving their own problems.

## Questioning (Confronting-Contracting Face)

If three private or team conferences using the Relationship-Listening techniques have been conducted and the student's behavior has not improved or is getting more destructive, the pathway of teacher action suggested by the checklist now requires the teacher to move to the Confronting-Contracting Face. Again, another series of conferences between the teacher and student will be held, but this time it will be carried out in a very different manner. If this first conference fails to be successful, the teacher holds a second and then a third conference, repeating the suggested techniques of I-messages, active listening, door openers, and no-lose problem solving.

In the Confronting-Contracting Face, the teacher attempts to maintain an adult relationship with a misbehaving student, by requesting the student to stop and change. The solution for how the student will change remains in his or her own hands. During the first conference, the student and the teacher are seated facing each other, literally "knee to knee" *(proximity-near)*:

- The teacher maintains eye contact.

- The teacher's face or attitude changes to Confronting-Contracting.

---

## CONFRONTING-CONTRACTING FACE

1. **1st Conference**
   1.1  "What" question
   ☐ "What did you do?"
   ☐ "What is the rule?"
   ☐ "What is the consequence?"
   ☐ "How will you change?"

   1.2  Contract
   ☐ handshake
   ☐ written
   Date_____
   1.3  (if broken) Logical Consequences
   Date_____
   • *Level 1 Time Out (Mediate afterwards with R-L or C-C)*
   • *Level 2 Time Out (In Room)*

2. **1st In-Room Time Out/Conference**
   ☐ 2.1 "What" questions
   ☐ 2.2 Contract (written-enclose)
   Date_____
   ☐ 2.3 (if broken) Logical Consequences
   Date_____

3. **2nd In-Room Time Out/Conference**
   ☐ 3.1 Repeat 1 and 2 (above)
   Date_____
   ☐ 3.2 (if broken) Logical Consequences
   Date_____
   • *Level 3 Time Out (Out of Room)*

4. **3rd In-Room Time Out/Conference**
   ☐ 4.1 Repeat 1 and 2 (above)
   Date_____
   ☐ 4.2 (if broken) Logical Consequences
   Date_____

---

• The teacher wants the student to think about past behavior:
   a. What is the rule?
   b. What will be the negative results if the student continues such negative behavior?
   c. The student will commit himself or herself to a rational response if similar incidents occur in the future.

d. The student will commit to a contract or agreement (a contract form is provided here).

---

**CONTRACT**

Date _____ Class _____ Semester _____

Location _____

Behavior _____

_____

I will _____

Signature _____    Time Out

Signature _____    Total time:_minutes

Signature _____    Type (level):

Signature _____    _1.   _2.   _3.   _4.   _5.   _6.

---

In the conference discussion, the teacher uses "what-how" questions and contracting, and suggests possible logical consequences. In addition, isolation and forms of time out may be used, with the degree of separation increasing with each incident of isolation.

Steps 1 through 4 suggest three "in-room" isolations followed by questioning and contracting. If the student does not live up to the contract, he or she would experience this logical consequence of his or her actions. The Confronting-Contracting Face, during these techniques, is one that says to the student:

- You are "over the line" and must be stopped.

- Your behavior must change.

- Control is still in your hands.

- You must be aware of what you are doing.

- You must think about the future (cause-effect).

- You may need time away to think (isolation: time out).

- You and I must agree on future behaviors.

*Mr. McDaniel:*  *"Mark, what are you doing?"* ("What-how" questioning).
*Mark:*  *"Huh?"*
*Mr. McDaniel:*  *"Mark, what are you doing?"* ("What-how" questioning).
*Mark:*  *"I dunno!"*

> **Mr. McDaniel:**  *"Well, you had a toy in school which you were using to disturb others with, and you swore at me. I want you to think about your behavior, and decide whether you really want to act this way and what will be the future consequences if this behavior continues. How is this behavior helping you?"* ("What-how" questioning).

At this point, the teacher attempts to engage in an open discussion with the student about the behavior. Mark will use many examples of back talk (denial, statements of helplessness, blaming, accusing the teacher, insults, profanity, crying, and tangential statements [see Chapter 3]). The teacher does not get caught up in a debate over back talk or allow himself or herself to be sidetracked, but uses "fogging" techniques by agreeing in general.

> **Mark:**  *"You're always picking on me. Get off my d--- back."* (back talk).
>
> **Mr. McDaniel:**  *"My actions may be seen by you as 'picking on you'* (fogging—agreeing in general), *but what were you doing?"*

The teacher keeps repeating, as a broken record, the questioning of: "What did you do? What is the rule? How is this helping you? What will be the result of your action if you continue acting this way? What will you do to change?"

The teacher does not stop the confronting process when the student responds by crying (sometimes humorously called "water power") or throwing a temper tantrum. Some students have discovered that such strong expressions of emotion can serve as a power technique to get the adult "off their back" and for them to avoid facing up to their behavior. The teacher responds to this emotional flooding by returning the student to a time out or a relax chair or an isolated space for the sole purpose of permitting him or her to calm down and get relaxed. The teacher reassures the student that this is a safe space and no one will bother him or her. This is not a punishment, for when the student is ready to make a contract and to discuss the incident rationally, he or she is free to return. The teacher's voice inflection and nonverbal expressions (paraverbals) are not ones of guilt, but take a rather matter-of-fact problem-solving attitude toward the student. The teacher is not sidetracked by the student's claims of unfairness or denial, or by another emotional outburst or crying. Instead, the teacher remains focused on the student's behavior in this particular incident, attempting to limit any implication of guilt. The teacher's approach in using the Confronting-Contracting Face toward the student is: "Look, this is not appropriate behavior here. We are faced with a problem, and I want to work with you to understand the problem and your behavior. I want to give you the power to change. I want you to commit yourself to this change through a contract or agreement. And finally, I want you to understand the consequences of failing to live up to this contract or continuing to behave in such a negative manner."

If the student is defiant, still angry, still using the paleocortex brain, and will not talk and contingency contract, it would be advisable to permit the student to remain in isolation until talk of a contract seems reasonable. This course of action may involve keeping the student in the back of the room for an entire class period—missing out-of-classroom activities. The student may have books and may study, and is also in a position to hear discussions and other educational classroom activities. The isolation, as nonseclusionary time out, is not for the purpose of punishment when used in the Confronting-Contracting Face. The teacher withdraws all social activities and places the student in a nonthreatening and nonstimulating situation to facilitate time for reflection. When the student is ready to work it out, the teacher returns to the "What-how" questioning: "What did you do? What is the rule?" and so on, and then to contracting.

## UNDERSTANDING TIME OUT

The teacher has escalated across the TBC using up all the limit-setting techniques, and the student's actions have not changed—the student is stopping the teacher from teaching and fellow students from learning. As a result, the teacher has dropped the limit-setting system. He has begun the backup system, where he must move to isolating the student in some form—thus the teacher's actions become public. The degrees of isolation will escalate, as seen in the checklist, following these time-out definitions.

### Types of Time Outs

Time outs consist of four types: nonseclusionary, contingency contracting observation, exclusionary, and seclusionary (see Figure 8.2).

### Nonseclusionary Time Out

To deal with a minor disturbance, the teacher performs some action (physical intervention) to deny the student reinforcement by removing

**FIGURE 8.2   Time Out and Degrees of Aversion**

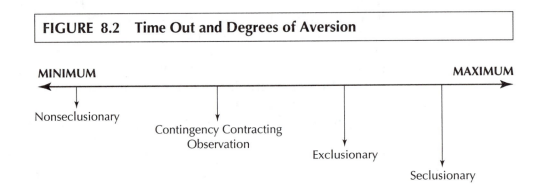

the materials that are being used inappropriately (e.g., paintbrushes in art class that are being used destructively, balls or similar physical education equipment used inappropriately, a personal item during seatwork that is disturbing the classroom environment) or an item that the student treasures. This time out is called nonseclusionary because the misbehaving student is not removed from the classroom or immediate environment. The object, rather than the student, is removed.

> *For a math lesson where students are allowed to use calculators, Joey has brought his calculator from home. In addition to doing the usual calculations, this particular calculator offers a simple video game, complete with bells and whistles. Joey has been warned once by the teacher about not doing his math and, instead playing the game with his calculator. "Joey, by playing games on your calculator, you are not only not doing your work but you are also disturbing those around you that are doing their work. If you continue to play, then you will lose your calculator for the rest of the class period and will not be able to use it for your math assignment" (if-then statement: "If you do X behavior, then Y consequence will happen").*
>
> *For the next five minutes or so, Joey works on his math problems as directed. However, Joey soon resorts back to his video game. The teacher takes away his calculator and places it on her desk (nonseclusionary time out).*

## Contingency Contracting Observation Time Out

Another form of time out is contingency contracting observation. The student is removed to the edge of an activity or at the back of the classroom. He or she can still observe the other students being reinforced and is only allowed to return contingent on his obeying the rules.

> *Students are learning how to play basketball in physical education class. They have been working on this unit for a week and are now beginning to play short games. Although he has been taught otherwise, Clyde insists on trying to "tackle" the person with the ball. He continually pushes, elbows, or bodily "slams" the player with the ball in order to get the ball away from them. The rules of the game have been repeatedly explained to Clyde, but he continues to hurt other students.*
>
> *The teacher sends Clyde to sit on the bleachers and requires him to sit passively and watch others obeying the rules. The teacher reinforces the other students (models) as they correctly obey the direction rules. After four minutes, she asks Clyde, "Do you now see how our rules work? Can you play basketball without physically abusing other students?"*
>
> *If he says yes, he is permitted to return; if he defiantly says no, he stays on the bleachers (the time out) for another two minutes and is again asked whether he is ready to comply. If*

*Clyde's response of no means that he simply does not truly understand the rule, the teacher would again teach it to him in the three-step directive lesson of say, show, and check, as explained later in Chapter 12.*

---

### MODELING

The demonstration by you or a student of a behavior or group of behaviors that you wish a targeted student to imitate.

---

The contingency contracting observation is nonseclusionary because the student is not removed totally from the environment, such as being required to go inside the school. Instead, the student is placed at the edge of the activity so he or she may observe others being reinforced. Here are some other examples of employing contingency contracting observation:

- Brad is pushing others while waiting in line at the water fountain. He is removed to the side to watch others standing in line and getting a drink. When the line of students is complete, he is now allowed to get a drink after agreeing (contingency contract) to do so without pushing.

- Elise is disrupting her peers at the cafeteria table by throwing small pieces of food for the purpose of getting her tablemates to respond. She and her chair are pulled away to approximately four feet from the table and out of reach of her food. After four minutes and following contingency contracting with the teacher, she is able to return to lunch and move her chair up to the table.

- Matthew is being reckless on the trampoline. He is removed from the apparatus and asked to sit nearby and watch. After four minutes, he is allowed to return, after a verbal contract.

- While seated in her work group, Juanita repeatedly disturbs others seated nearby. She is removed from the group and is instructed to sit on a chair out of her group. After three minutes and agreeing to obey the rule, she is allowed to return.

The criterion for returning or being released from the contingency contracting observation nonseclusionary time out, as in the preceding situations, is contingent on the student maintaining nondisruptive behavior for a minimum time requirement. Normally, the student is asked, "Do you know and understand the rule and will you obey it when you return?"

When the techniques of nonseclusionary time out have been tried but have failed, the teacher may recognize that the student's behavior is so serious that it demands a stronger form of response. Two other forms of time out are available in such a situation: exclusionary and seclusionary.

## Exclusionary Time Out

Exclusionary time out involves the removal of the student from an activity as a means of denying access to reinforcement but generally not access to the classroom. While the contingency contracting observation and modeling were used in the nonseclusionary time out, none of these procedures is used in exclusionary time out. The student may be placed near a corner facing the wall, or in an area of the classroom that is screened off from the room activities so the student's view is restricted—he or she is excluded.

## Seclusionary Time Out

Seclusionary time out involves the complete removal of the student from the classroom or environment to a time-out room or the principal's office because of the student's misbehavior (usually aggression or noncompliance). The student is denied access to any reinforcement from the classroom, including peers, adults, objects, or activities.

The justification for the use of any of the forms of time out is not for purposes of retribution as a morality form of punishment (based on the idea that the student has failed morally or has not lived up to the adult's values and expectations). The justification is that the environment and social context are too strongly reinforcing the student to continue his or her misbehaviors. The objective is to remove that reinforcement, and the only way to accomplish this is to use one or more forms of time out.

Time out and time-out rooms have historically been misused or mismanaged by teachers, causing real distrust of this technique among parents and the general public. A time-out record form documenting the procedure (giving witness names, circumstance, times, and dates), such as the one in Figure 8.3, should be required for each staff member who uses time out. This time-out record should be attached to the backup system checklist.

| **FIGURE 8.3    Time-Out Record** | | | |
|---|---|---|---|
| Student's Name: | Date: | Time of Day: | Total Time in Time Out:<br><br>_____ Minutes |
| Teacher's Name:<br><br><br><br>Other Adult Witness: | | | Type of Time Out (check one):<br><br>___ Contingency Observation<br><br>___ Exclusionary<br><br>___ Seclusionary |
| Description of the Situation: | | State Behavioral Change Wanted: | |

## Levels of Exclusion and Time Out

The teacher will follow a pathway of increased levels or degrees of isolation or time out, as explained in Table 8.1, which is a guide to follow

| TABLE 8.1 | Level of Time-Out Methods and Procedures | | | |
|---|---|---|---|---|
| **Level or Degrees of Isolation** | **Type of Isolation** | **Method** | **Parties Involved** | **Follow-Up Meetings** |
| Level #1 | **Nonseclusionary time out** | Remove toy or object or move seat 3 feet from table. | Teacher and student | May involve no discussion or private meeting by the teacher. |
| Level #2 | **Contingency contracting observation** | Isolate student at edge of classroom to observe. | Teacher and student | *Private Meeting* using R-L, then escalate to C-C, and/or R and C (normally a verbal contract is established). Experience the *logical consequence*. |
| Level #3 (recommend doing three cycles of this form of isolation) | **Exclusionary time out** | Isolate in the classroom, behind a barrier or turned toward a wall. | Teacher and student | *Private Meeting* using R-L, then escalate to C-C, and/or R and C (normally a verbal contract is established). Experience the *logical consequence*. |
| **Notify Parents** After three cycles of Level 3 time out, private meetings and contracting, call parents before doing an out-of-classroom isolation. The methods for handling this parent telephone call are presented in Chapter 5. | | | | |
| Level #4 (recommend doing three cycles of this form of isolation) | **Seclusionary time out** | Isolate in a time-out room or in another classroom across the hall. | Teacher, student, and supervisor of time-out room or teacher across the hall | *Private Meeting* using R-L, then escalate to C-C, and/or R and C (normally a verbal contract is established). Experience the *logical consequence*. |
| **Parent Conference** After three cycles of Level 4 time out, private meetings and contract, hold a parent conference. The methods for handling this parent conference call will follow. | | | | |
| Level #5 (recommend doing three cycles of this form of isolation) | **Seclusionary time out** | Isolate in principal's office. | Teacher, student, and principal | *Private Meeting* using R-L, then escalate to C-C, and/or R and C (normally a verbal contract is established). Experience the *logical consequence*. |
| **Professional Staffing** A staffing session involving the teacher, school psychologist and/or counselor, teachers, administrators, and possibly the student and parent is held. See methods and techniques to follow. | | | | |

in escalating the use of time out. The teacher starts in the classroom with minor nonseclusionary time out (levels 1 and 2). If the student does not change his or her behavior, the teacher gradually escalates to in-classroom isolation (level 3), calls the student's parents, and then moves to out-of-classroom isolation (levels 4 and 5), finally leading to a professional staffing. After most of these time outs, the teacher holds a private meeting with the student and uses techniques that involve a movement from Relationship-Listening to Confronting-Contracting, including experiencing logical consequences, and then moves to the use of the assertive techniques of Rules and Consequences. At levels 3, 4, and 5, the teacher moves through three cycles of time out.

A cycle is defined as a form of isolation that entails using the TBC for a private meeting and contracting, and then permitting the student to return with a clean slate. If the contract is broken, the student experiences the logical consequence of his or her actions. It is recommended that this be done three times, but the teacher and principal would have the flexibility to determine the number of reasonable cycles. Copies of the student-teacher or student-teacher-principal contract would be kept on file for documentation purposes.

## DISENGAGING

A misbehaving student can be frightening. Teachers are not emotionless robots who never get angry and who always have good feelings toward all students. This is an unrealistic picture and simply does not happen. Some students are appealing and some are unappealing; the unappealing students generally are the ones who cannot find acceptance in their homes and from fellow classmates. The nonsocially adjusted misbehaving student, because of feelings of rejection, begins to seek excessive attention and power, becomes revengeful and, finally, retreats into a passive state of helplessness. If a teacher gives vent to a full range of his or her feelings, this may allow the excessive attention-getting student to produce feelings of annoyance—a sense of being beaten by the power-needy student, hurt by the revengeful student, and inadequate in working with the passive-helpless student.

It is important to acknowledge that negative feelings toward these students exist. When a teacher regresses to revengeful (fight response) or feeling helpless (flight response) toward these students, then problems generally result. Therefore, isolation, as described under Confronting-Contracting, is often effective to get disengaged and emotionally neutral. If a teacher is angry and overcome by negative feelings because of the repeated demands that the problem student is presenting, then the teacher will need to confront the student skillfully. The misbehaving student may be placed in isolation (a relax chair or time out) for a period of time. As an emotionally flooded individual, a teacher must spatially move away from this student for many minutes or even an hour until the teacher has disengaged from these strong

| NONSOCIALLY ADAPTIVE STUDENTS | | |
|---|---|---|
| **Student's Motivation** | **Behavior Characteristics** | **Teacher's Feelings** |
| Attention Getting | Repetitively acts to become the center of attention. When asked to desist, will comply but will start again later. | Annoyed |
| Power | Repetitively acts to become the center of attention. When asked to desist, becomes defiant and escalates negative behavior and challenges the adult. | Beaten |
| Revenge | Hurts others for no apparent reason. | Hurt |
| Helplessness | Wishes not to be seen; passive and lethargic; rejects social contact. | Inadequate |

*Source:* Adapted from *Cooperative Discipline: A Teacher's Guide to Cooperative Discipline* by Linda Albert, pages 31–44, © 1989 American Guidance Service, Inc., 4201 Woodland Road, Circle Pines, MN 55014-1796. Adapted and published here with the permission of the publisher. All rights reserved.

emotions. Jones (1987) states that it takes at least 20 minutes for a teacher's body to clear the adrenaline from its system after he or she became angry or frightened as a result of a clash with a student. Once the teacher is calm and relaxed, he or she will have the energy to approach the difficult student to begin the steps of confronting. It is ineffective to assume the Confront-Contract Face when angered. The self-control techniques under the TBC's *Looking,* relaxing breaths, slowing down actions, squaring off, using the proper physical stance, and the host of related techniques described in previous chapters can be helpful at this time.

## Contingency Contracting

Contingency contracting is a form of time out in which the student is removed to the edge of an activity or at the back of the classroom so he or she can still observe the other students being reinforced and acting in an appropriate manner. The teacher demands from the misbehaving student that he or she reflect on past behavior and come up with a way to change to ensure that it does not occur again. The student must now commit to this as an agreement or contract, contingent on his or her reentering the classroom, and verbally sealed by shaking hands or in writing.

## Sealing the Contract

The private meeting ends with a contract between the student and the teacher. The student will at a future time likely find himself or herself in a similar situation and will be faced with a possible repeat of the undesirable behavior. The question "What will you do to change?" permits the student to think out and anticipate these future situations, knowing he or she has determined and contracted with the teacher regarding how to act in a more productive manner in future incidents. The contingency contract for change between the teacher and student can be sealed simply with a handshake and a smile, at first attempts, but it is advised to put this agreement in writing and to have both the teacher and student sign the contract, with each getting a copy. The contingency contract may also contain a logical consequence if the student fails to live up to this contract.

## COMMON QUESTIONS REGARDING CONFRONTING-CONTRACTING

Perhaps some of these questions and answers will help you with Confronting-Contracting:

- *What do I do if the student does not come up with a solution?* If the student is not simply being defiant, but really cannot think of a change in behavior, you may make two to three suggestions and ask him or her to pick one and commit to it. If a student agrees to your suggestion, be sure he or she knows the "motor rule" or response to which he or she has committed, by teaching the choice in a directive lesson of Say-Show-Check (explained in Chapter 12).

- *What if the student refuses to make a contract?* Permit the student to continue staying in the relax chair (time out) until he or she is ready to negotiate. The student's refusal indicates he or she is still angry or flooded.

- *What if the student's action endangers self, others, or valuable property?* Endangerment of any type calls into effect the *severity clause,* and you immediately move to *Acting (Physical Intervention).* The accompanying verbal response could be *Step 1: "Stop"* followed by Steps 2, 3, and 4, or an assertive command (explained in Chapter 6).

## Repeating Previous Steps

While using the Confronting-Contracting Face, interaction between teacher and student after an incident of misbehavior is confined to these four steps: "Stop" statement; "What-how" questioning; contracting with a statement of logical consequences; and, if needed, isolation. After a contingency contract is established with the student, the student is to return to the classroom with a clean slate, meaning that the teacher maintains an attitude of optimism. It is important that the teacher show, *by actions,* that the student can and will change his or her behavior. If you are angry with the student because of his or her actions and this anger is communicated nonverbally, the student and classmates will sense this, and he or she most likely will live up to your nonbelief in his or her ability to change—the power of expectations (Dinkmeyer, McKay, & Dinkmeyer, 1989).

It is inevitable that some contracts will be broken. When this occurs, the student will have to experience the logical consequence of his or her actions. After the student experiences this logical consequence, the previous steps should be repeated in a similar manner: "Stop it! What did you do? What is the rule? What will you do to change?" Again, ask for a contract with consequences, and use isolation if needed. The student will again return with a "clean slate," and the teacher will be optimistic.

## Clean Slate

After the teacher and student complete the step of contingency contracting, the student returns to the classroom activity as if nothing has occurred. The student has a "clean slate" whereby the teacher does not continually remind him or her of past misbehavior and is optimistic that the misbehavior will not be repeated.

If the student's behavior still does not become more positive, or even regresses to more destructive behaviors, the teacher should use the sequence of "Stop" statement, "What-how" questioning, contracting, and time out for at least three cycles. After three cycles of these Confronting-Contracting steps, escalating along the Teacher Behavior Continuum to Rules and Consequences techniques (or deescalating to Relationship-Listening techniques if the student's behavior becomes more positive) may be necessary. But before moving to the Rules and Consequences techniques, which may involve removing the student from the classroom, notify the student's parents of your difficulties and the actions you are taking.

---

## CONFRONTING-CONTRACTING FACE
### (see page 133)

**5. Telephone Parents**
Date_____
☐ 5.1 (Begin Encouragement System)
Date_____
*Level 3 Time Out (Out-of-Room)*

**6. 1st Out-of-Room Time Out**   (Repeat 1, 2, and 3, enclose Time Out Form)
Date _____

**7. 2nd Out-of-Room Time Out**   (Repeat 1, 2, and 3, enclose Time Out Form)
Date_____

**8. Telephone/In Writing**   (Enclose copy to Principal/Parents)
Date_____
*Level 4 Time Out (Principal)*

**9. Office**   (Repeat 1, 2, and 3)
Date _____
            (Repeat 1, 2, and 3)
Date_____

**10. Conference with Parents**   (Repeat 1, 2, and 3)
Date_____

**11. Staffing (members)**

_____

_____

_____

_____

Date_____

---

## Notifying Parents

After completing three rounds of in-room time out/conference, the teacher turns to telephoning parents (Step 5), informing them of the behavior of their child providing them with the details and facts regarding the student's behavior and the teacher's attempts to work with the student. The teacher is not prescriptive, telling the parents what actions they should take at home. If the parents respond to the teacher with, "Well what do you want me to do about it?" the teacher would state, "I am calling you to keep you informed." A hypothetical telephone call by Mark's teacher illustrates the facts and specificity that the teacher provides.

> ***Teacher:*** *"Hello, Mrs. Capps. I am Mark's teacher, Mr. McDaniel. I felt a need to call you and keep you informed about my attempts to work with Mark. On four occasions he has disrupted class by playing with games that disrupt others including using a squirt gun in class, pushing and striking other classmates, making disruptive remarks in class, and swearing at a classmate. When I confronted him, he has on three occasions told me to go f--- myself and referred to me as an asshole. I have counseled him, attempted to make a contract with him to change his behavior, and isolated him at the back of the classroom on three occasions. I am still optimistic that I can find a way to work with Mark, but I felt that at this point it was important to inform you and your husband as to his recent behavior and my actions."*

In using the Confronting-Contracting Face and attitude, it is important that the teacher be factual and reality oriented, both with students and parents, by not masking or soft-selling descriptions of the student's behavior. Describing it in clear terms with specific examples and not expressing value judgments or implying any guilt or anger helps keep the conversation informational. The teacher's position in notifying parents at this point is factual, so that they are informed. Asking the parents for a conference is not necessary until things have escalated to the Rules and Consequences Face. If they request a conference, the teacher will of course agree—preferably a meeting with both the parents and the student.

When parents receive such a call, they are likely to respond in one of three ways. They may accept the descriptions and offer to help; they may respond with a fight-or-flight response, failing to hear what you are saying (flight) or becoming verbally hostile (fight); or they may begin to use back talk (verbal aggression, denial, or attempting to distract the teacher to a side issue, accusing the teacher of professional incompetence). Back talk in the form of verbal aggression is to be expected because these parents have just done an "adrenaline dump" and are "snapping and snarling." The teacher's response in dealing with such angry parents is the same as with students.

Begin by retreating to Relationship-Listening techniques using the TBC's *Looking* and *Naming*. Take two controlled breaths and simply say nothing, permitting the parents to ventilate. All the information you wish to give to the parents has already been given, and being drawn into a heated debate regarding any issue is not productive. Move to nondirective techniques of active listening, I-messages, door openers, and acknowledgments. If the parents slowly become more rational and begin to ask, "How can I help?" moving through the Six Steps to Problem Solving is appropriate. When using the Relationship-Listening Face and even the Confronting-Contracting Face with students and parents, a prescriptive is not necessary. Telling the parents what you want them to do means that you would now own the problem. By using a process of problem solving, lead them through a discussion that enables them to come up with ways through which they think they can help such as by asking "What have you found that has worked with your child in the past?"

When a prescriptive is given to the parents, such as "Here is what actions I want you to do...," it is possible to hear from the parents, weeks later, "Well, we did what you said and it still didn't work." Such a statement suggests a lack of real ownership by the parents. The teacher was trapped into giving prescriptive solutions and then "slam-dunked" for those suggestions later by having them thrown in his or her face. If the parents truly insist that they are incapable of dealing with their child, a suggestion that they seek advice from school or private counseling services or a psychologist may be appropriate.

To summarize, parents should be notified after three cycles of in-classroom isolation (time out) and private meetings, with written contingency contracts and the use of logical consequences. If there is no improvement in the student's behavior or it has gotten worse, parents should be notified through a factual telephone call with a clear list of the student's and your past actions. If parents wish to help, the Relationship-Listening technique of Six Steps to Problem Solving is useful. On the other hand, if parents become hostile to the information, first getting control of your own behavioral response is necessary and, if need be, use the Relationship-Listening techniques to allow the parent to ventilate.

After phoning parents, an encouragement system, which will be discussed in Chapter 10, should begin. Note again that boxes for checkmarks and lines for dates are provided to document actions. In Steps 6 and 7, Out-of-Room Time Out, the student is removed to a separate room in the school for disruptive students or, by prior arrangement, is seated at the back of the classroom across the hall. Before the student is returned to full participation in the classroom, the teacher repeats "What-how" questions, contracting, and logical consequences if appropriate. A time-out documentation is completed for each of these out-of-room isolations, using the box on the bottom right corner of the contract form (see page 134). This box requires the teacher to indicate the date and time, the number of minutes the student was isolated, and the form of isolation used.

In Step 8, Telephone/In Writing, the teacher acts after the second out-of-room isolation to notify the parents for the second time by telephone. A follow-up letter would also be sent and a copy attached to the backup system checklist.

Next, the backup system would escalate to Step 9, Office (Isolation in the Principal's Office), and Step 10, Conference with Parents. These use many of the techniques previously described.

## MEETINGS AND CONFERENCING IN PUBLIC

When it is necessary to escalate to Steps 9 and 10, the backup system becomes public and time consuming because the principal, other professionals, and parents are now involved. For this meeting, it is essential to have total privacy and adequate time for a real discussion to occur. This process should not be rushed. Time spent in conferencing now can save much more time later and prevent the necessity of going to the much more time-consuming high-profile corrections processes. In carrying out this meeting, the teacher still maintains his or her power. The teacher is in charge and should not hand over the power for chairing the meeting to an administrator or other professional. The teacher chooses which "face" to wear and which parallel techniques to utilize in carrying out this meeting. Remember the cardinal rule to use the least powerful techniques necessary. This would suggest that, at first, the teacher attempts to conduct the meeting with Relationship-Listening techniques, before escalating to Confronting-Contracting and, if necessary, Rules and Consequences.

## The Relationship-Listening Meeting

Because the techniques are taken from a counseling mode, the Relationship-Listening Face is ideally suited for one-to-one teacher-student interaction, even with the setting of a meeting attended by parents and others. Go slowly, continue to use the nonverbal behaviors of limit setting (such as eye contact and relaxing breaths), and have all participants—the teacher, student, parent, and principal—seated so that they are knee to knee, or at the edge of each person's comfort bubble.

The Relationship-Listening teacher might start off with an I-message ("Mark, when I am told to f--- off *(behavior),* such harsh words stop me from working with a student *(effect),* and cause me to lose respect from your classmates *(effect),* and I feel first frustrated and then angry *(feelings).* We need to talk about this" *(door opener).)* The teacher is now free to use (1) acknowledgment, (2) verbal encoding of the student's feeling through critical listening, (3) door openers, and (4) active listening (see Figure 7.2).

For this meeting, the teacher may use the plus/minus method or may simply, with the student, list on a sheet of paper all items that are going well and those that are not. This, of course, is being witnessed by the principal and/or parent. Through no-lose problem solving, the teacher asks the student how he or she can move the minuses to the plus column. In essence, the teacher asks, "What actions can be taken to work this out so we are both comfortable and both get our needs met?"

If the student's behavior or the problems he or she is expressing are quite serious, it would be wise to take time to guide the student through the Six Steps to Problem Solving:

1. Define the problem.

2. Generate solutions.

3. Evaluate the solutions.

4. Decide on a solution.

5. Implement the solution.

6. Reevaluate.

By following this six-step structure, a teacher can help a student think out future problems, and thus be able to be an independent thinker leading to self-discipline. The objective in using the Relationship-Listening Face is to maintain a positive relationship with students, and work things out in a nonpunitive no-lose manner. The attitude, or face, is one that through action says, "I will nonjudgmentally express to you *(I-message)* how your actions may be taking away my rights and having an impact on me as a teacher. I am here to listen to you empathetically and uncritically. I will help by listening and attempting to get clarity, through active listening. And when you wish, I can help through my guidance *(Six Steps to Problem Solving)* to permit you to solve your own problems. I will not do this for you."

## The Confronting-Contracting Meeting

The teacher is free to choose which face or techniques to use during this public meeting. It is advisable to follow the rule of using the least power necessary, so the Relationship-Listening Techniques should be used first before escalating to more powerful faces and techniques. Some teachers may feel uncomfortable and insincere with Relationship-Listening techniques or cannot (or will not) use the amount of time necessary to carry out a Relationship-Listening meeting. These teachers, therefore, may choose not to begin with a Relationship-Listening meeting but decide instead to employ Confronting-Contracting or Rules and Consequences. Although the teacher has the freedom of choice to determine which of the methodologies from these three faces to start out with, the teacher who chooses one of the more powerful "faces" has already narrowed the range of techniques available. If the stronger techniques of Rules and Consequences fail, the teacher will be left with no choice but to move to the time-consuming and less constructive punishment techniques. Again, it is advisable to start the meeting using minimum power and then, only if necessary, gradually escalate to a Confronting-Contracting meeting or a Rules and Consequences meeting. Once the teacher is forced to spend time doing high-profile actions, the likelihood of success is diminished and the process is dramatically more costly in terms of the teacher's time.

The Confronting-Contracting private meeting begins with a series of "What?" questions: "Mark, this must stop. This shall not continue to go on! What are you doing? What is the rule? I want you to think about this behavior. How is it helping you?" Again, a teacher should proceed slowly and continue to use the nonverbal behaviors of limit setting (such as eye contact and relaxing breaths), and have both the student and the teacher seated knee to knee and at the edge of the student's comfort bubble. The Confronting-Contracting approach is to give the student time, with counseling, to reflect on what he or she is doing, requiring the neocortex of the brain to be in gear. If the student is in a state of fight or flight, taking some time to relax so the real thinking can take place is helpful. This is not a meeting to scold the student, but to have him or her think.

Finally, the teacher can ask, "What will you do to change?" and then push for a contract. The student is likely to be faced with an opportunity to act in a similar misbehaving manner in the future. Now is the time to have the student, who is using rational thinking, come up with a personal appropriate strategy so he or she will know how to behave the next time a similar incident occurs. The contract reached may be informal if it is done in a mini-meeting in the classroom, sealed simply with a handshake. If the contracting is done in a meeting after class, a written contract should be signed by both the student and the teacher—and even the principal and parent—and may include a logical consequence if the contract is broken. Copies of the contract are given to the student, teacher, principal, and parent, and a copy is stored in the teacher's grade book or student filing system for later retrieval if necessary.

To repeat, if the behavior of the student still does not improve, the teacher moves to conferencing with parents (Step 10). This conference is carried out with the student, the parents, and possibly the principal in attendance. The teacher goes through items 1, 2, and 3 while confronting the student and writing the contract. All members in attendance, including the parents, sign the contract.

Finally, the last step in Confronting-Contracting is staffing (Step 11). This is a meeting in which the teacher asks the school counselor, school psychologist, principal, fellow teachers, and any other teachers and professionals who may be able to contribute to provide information or help in designing a program to change this student's behavior.

## Professional Staffing

Simply put, many minds working together are better than one. Historically, teaching has been a rather solitary profession—one teacher closed in by four walls and a closed door. When the teacher's limit setting fails to be effective with a misbehaving student, she or he often feels like a failure.

Such misbehaving students can be like small grenades, and beyond the ability of a teacher to know when something or someone may pull the grenade pin and explode as small aggressive power forces that destroy the climate for learning and destroy the group's ability to live and work together as a healthy classroom of sharing people. Some teachers depend on being the conductor who can orchestrate this shared space through a limit-setting system. If a classroom is not conducive to learning, teachers generally feel helpless. A teacher in such a situation often feels out of control with no outlet for getting help. In fact, many teachers, are frightened to admit that they are having this disciplinary difficulty, for fear that they may be judged as ineffective and later evaluated negatively at the end of the school year.

The way to get help is to create a collegial team working. Rarely do other professions expect a professional to live and work in a four-walled island cut off from colleagues. Doing it alone should not be a virtue that defines your worthiness as a teacher. Students have changed in the modern world, and the knowledge base of psychology and education has exploded far beyond the ability of a day-in, day-out practicing teacher to keep pace. It is extremely difficult, if not impossible, for the classroom teacher to maintain constantly updated knowledge on the many problems faced by students, especially young adolescents, and new methods of educational discipline practice.

The collegial meeting of professional minds takes the form of a professional-administrative backup system leading to a staffing, or brainstorming, session that focuses on one student as well as how this professional (the classroom teacher) might become more effective at facilitating a positive change in behavior. Such staffing sessions must become a standard practice. This concept of a staffing team as a collection of problem-solving professionals is a structure to guide the collective minds, so that thinking is orderly and creative and includes everyone on the team. In all meetings that will follow—private and public meetings, and staffing sessions—the teacher will maintain his or her authority and power as the leader.

To overcome roadblocks to good collective problem solving, a clear orderly process will be proposed based on the Six Steps to Problem Solving (Gordon, 1974): (1) defining the problem, (2) generating a possible solution, (3) evaluating, (4) deciding on a solution, (5) implementing, and (6) evaluating the solution. To maximize the use of time, a clear staffing agenda procedure is proposed for the purpose of working as a team to use the host of techniques drawn from Chapters 1 and 2, the concept of *levels of crisis,* and the development of an *individualized discipline plan* for intervening with and helping the difficult student. The team approach uses a creative application of techniques and procedures to fit the needs of a particular school and a particular teacher working with one of his or her difficult students.

## Staffing Agenda: Steps and Procedures

Once the full range of time out has been used and a conference with the parents held without any real change in the student's misbehavior, a professional staffing process becomes necessary. Team members might include any or all of the following people: teacher, other teachers on the team, assistant teacher, teacher aides, special education teacher, school principal, school counselor and/or psychologist, social worker or home and family visitor, and any other person having direct contact with the student on a daily basis (including cafeteria supervisor, bus driver, and office staff). On some occasions, it is helpful to have the student's parents as members of this team. The teacher should decide, in consultation with the school administrator, just who is invited to this meeting. One thing to avoid in team staffing is the notion of rank (defined as administrative rank [principal] or expertise rank [psychologist]). If formally or informally asserted in the team staffing, rank is inhibiting to creative problem solving because those members feel less "in authority" and will hesitate to speak up or challenge a position of some member in a position of "higher rank."

The attitude or "face" of the staffing meeting is that roles are clearly defined but not necessarily according to rank. The meeting is for the benefit of the person who has daily responsibility for the difficult student and, of course, the student. All members are there to serve as consultants and advisors with a direct focus on what the teacher and others can do to help this particular student. It is preferable for meetings to be held at a round table, where all members can see each other face to face, suggesting an equal power relationship among team members, rather than at a rectangular table with a power figure seated at one end. A wall chart or chalkboard should be nearby and in clear view of all team members.

It is helpful at the beginning of a staffing meeting to appoint a timekeeper and a secretary. The timekeeper serves as a type of moderator, announcing before each step begins the purpose of that step, who may speak, the amount of time to be spent on that step, and the actions and results needed to be accomplished. A copy of Table 8.2 should be mounted on the meeting room wall or included in a handout in front of each member for easy reference. The secretary handles writing activities such as keeping notes, writing suggestions on wall charts, and writing the final plan. These duties should be rotated among the team members for each new meeting. The timekeeper will channel the discussion to conform to the stated goals and will signal when time periods are up. If the team is well disciplined, the entire team staffing activity can be accomplished in 60 minutes.

---

### TIMEKEEPER

A team member appointed by the difficult student's teacher, assigned responsibility for monitoring the time and keeping the staffing steps on task.

---

### SECRETARY

One team member appointed by the difficult student's teacher, assigned responsibility for carrying out the writing duties during the staffing process.

| TABLE 8.2     Six Steps to Team Staffing Agenda | | | |
|---|---|---|---|
| **Purpose** | **Speaker** | **Time** | **Actions** |
| **Stating the Problem** | | | |
| a. Background Information (Teacher) | Teacher | 5 mins. | State general description of the student's behavior problems and desired changes. Present background information using collected data. |
| b. Background Information (Team) | Team Members | 10 mins. | Present information from other team members who may have observed the student under various situations and time periods. |
| c. Clarifying Information | Team Members | 6 mins. | Team members question other team members on data presented and the final changes in desired student behavior. |
| **Generating Solutions** (in writing) | Team Members | 3 mins. | Each team member writes a list of solutions independently of all other members. |
| (oral) | Team Members | 10 mins. | Each member quickly reads her solution list without comment; the secretary writes each solution on a wall chart or chalkboard. |
| **Evaluating Solutions** | Team Members | 10 mins. | Members state their objections (in the form of an I-message) to a suggestion; if there is general agreement to these objections, the suggestion is removed. The secretary strikes out rejected suggestions. |
| **Deciding on Solutions** | Team Members | 5 mins. | Decide on a group plan with roles and each member's responsibility defined. Using the Individualized Discipline Plan, the secretary writes solution agreements and completes the IDP form. |
| **Implementing** (a commitment) | Team Members | 1 min. | All members sign the plan as a commitment to the strategies. |
| **Reevaluating Scheduled** | Teacher | 10 mins. | A time is established for a follow-up meeting, normally two to three weeks later, to reevaluate the success of the plan. |

*Source:* From *Solving Discipline Problems: Strategies for Classroom Teachers* by C. Wolfgang and C. D. Glickman, 1980, Boston: Allyn and Bacon. Reprinted by permission.

## Step 1: Stating the Problem (Overview of the Student's Behavior)

### a. Background Information—Teacher

**Purpose:**   The teacher clearly states to the team members a general description of the student's behavior and states clearly those behavioral changes she would like to see in the student.

**Time:**   5 minutes

**Actions:**   The teacher, having direct responsibility for the difficult student, begins the reporting by providing the team with a general description of the student's past behavioral problems. The teacher also summarizes the data on her Student Background Information Form (Figure 8.4) and gives a few vignettes to place this behavior in context. Each team member should have copies of these forms, previously completed by each member, during the reporting. Finally, the teacher states clearly the behavior changes she or he would like to see in the student's daily behavior—for example, "In the cafeteria, Brian will stop throwing food and hitting other students, and he will follow my directions and requests."

After completing three rounds of in-room time out/conference, the teacher turns to Step 5, Telephone Parents, calling the parents to inform them of the behavior of their child. This telephone conversation is conducted in a manner to inform the parents of the details and facts regarding the student's behavior and the teacher's attempts to work with the student. The teacher is not prescriptive, telling the parents what actions they should take at home. If the parents respond to the teacher with, "Well what do you want me to do about it?" the teacher would state, "I am calling you to keep you informed."

### b. Background Information—Team Members

**Purpose:**   Each team member adds any information not previously mentioned by the student's teacher.

**Time:**   10 minutes

**Actions:**   The team members report their data by summarizing their copy of the Student Background Information Form (Figure 8.4), moving clockwise around the table in a businesslike manner. It is important to get all data out and "on the table" and it is recommended that members refrain from asking questions of clarification until this is accomplished. This would also be the time for any other teachers on the team that have the student in class to offer any information that they have regarding the student's behavior in their classes.

| FIGURE 8.4  **Student Background Information Form** | | | | | |
|---|---|---|---|---|---|
| Student's Name: | | | Date: | | |
| Team Members: | | | | | |
| | | | | | |
| Student's Misbehavior(s): | | | | | |
| | | | | | |
| | | | | | |
| | | | | | |
| 1. Describe misbehavior(s) | 2. What activities was the student engaged in at the time? | 3. In what physical surroundings? | 4. How frequent is each type of misbehavior? | 5. What time of day? | 6. What peers/ adults were involved? |
| a. | | | | | |
| b. | | | | | |
| c. | | | | | |

## c. Clarifying Background Information

**Purpose:**  All members may now ask clarifying questions concerning background information previously presented.

**Time:**  6 minutes

**Actions:**  All members of the team have the right to question the teacher or any team member who presented information to discuss the child in greater detail. This is also time to identify and explore what techniques have previously been tried. Team members should also question the behavior change goals that the teacher stated in Step1, and discussion should occur to get a team agreement on the stated behavior changes desired. Once the goals are agreed on, the secretary will write these goals on the individualized discipline plan (IDP) form.

## Step 2: Generating Solutions

### a. Solutions (Written)

**Purpose:** All members write down their proposed solutions, listing the actions they and anyone else could take to help the child. During this process, each member should mentally review the teacher-child interaction models of the *Three Faces of Discipline*. This mental review will help the members decide what teacher methods and techniques would be most helpful and how these actions can be organized systematically. Writing these possible solutions creates active involvement by all members and establishes their active commitment to the problem solving process.

### b. Solutions (Oral)

**Purpose:** Each team member verbally presents his or her written ideas to the other members without evaluation or feedback.

**Time:** 10 minutes

**Actions:** Each member presents his or her ideas orally to the group. The discussion of these ideas is reserved for a later step, so as not to inhibit the free flow of each member's ideas. The attitude in this discussion is that there is no "crazy" idea—no matter how "off the wall" it might initially sound, it is nonetheless put on the table for consideration. Even the seemingly "crazy" idea might later trigger an idea from a team member as to how this idea can be turned into a practical and very real creative solution. Criticism in any manner during this step will stifle creative ideas and keep them from surfacing. While the members are reading their ideas out loud, the secretary writes them on a wall chart (or chalkboard) as a visual display of these ideas.

## Step 3: Evaluating Solutions

**Purpose:** To have all members verbally explore, in a "brainstorming" format, how each of the ideas presented in Step 2 can be interrelated and developed into a comprehensive, collectively agreed upon plan of action, to achieve both the short-term and long-term behavioral changes or other results desired.

**Time:** 10 minutes

**Actions:** This step begins with the team taking a quick vote to score the suggestions on the wall chart. One simple but effective method employs a "thumbs up–thumbs down" approach. The secretary writes a plus sign (+) before the number of a proposed solution if all team members vote "thumbs up." A question mark (?) is placed before the solution if the members' responses are mixed negative and positive. Finally, a minus sign (-) is added and a line drawn through the suggested solution if all members vote "thumbs down." This quick vote provides an immediate, overt display of the group's feelings about each suggestion, and members are now ready for meaningful discussion. However, even when a solution has been scratched out, any member may bring it back for further discussion.

---

### QUICK VOTE

A nonbinding process to gauge support for the list of proposed solutions in evaluating solutions. The solutions are ranked according to those the group likes (+), dislikes (–), or is not sure of (?).

---

Interaction among the members, which has been controlled and limited in previous steps, now becomes of primary importance as the members fully discuss how their ideas are interrelated or have some commonalties. The team might ask itself: Do our solutions cluster into one "face" or discipline? Do these suggestions indicate the amount of power at which we wish to begin our intervention? Do we need to make educational changes beyond the disciplinary actions?

It is important that the teacher and team members recognize in this step that they have progressed beyond the "personal wisdom" kind of speculative thinking in which the teacher attempts to solve problems by "stabbing in the dark." The constructs, methods, and procedures provided for the teachers and school staffs here have brought the professional out of the darkness in which she or he functions as a limited technician, and provide a framework for the scientific problem solving that is characteristic of a true professional.

## Step 4: Deciding on Solutions (A Final Written Plan)

**Purpose:**   To decide on an orderly plan of action and to put that plan into writing.

**Time:**   5 minutes

**Actions:**   The members agree on a plan of action, including their own responsibility for carrying out the various segments of this plan. The secretary writes out this individualized discipline plan, or IDP (see Figure 8.5), with a designation of each person's responsibilities. (All members should receive a copy.)

**FIGURE 8.5 Individualized Discipline Plan**

| Student's Name: | Summary of Present Behavior: |
| --- | --- |
| School: | |
| Date of Staffing: | |
| Long-Term Behavioral Changes Desired | (1) |
| (2) | (3) |
| (4) | (5) |

| Short-Term Behavioral Change | Specific Teacher Techniques | Person Responsible | % of Time | Approx. Date of Completion | Reevaluation Date |
| --- | --- | --- | --- | --- | --- |
| | | | | | |

## Step 5: Implementing the Solution (A Commitment)

**Purpose:** To have the members commit themselves to implementing the plan's procedures.

**Time:** 1 minute

**Actions:** Each staff member is asked to sign or initial the IDP, and by doing so agrees to actively carry out the procedures and return for a follow-up reevaluation. A time for a follow-up reevaluation future meeting should be established at a time convenient for all members.

---

**INDIVIDUALIZED DISCIPLINE PLAN (IDP)**

A written plan, created at the end of a staffing process, that details the specific techniques to be utilized in dealing with a difficult student and that identifies those who will be responsible for carrying out the techniques.

---

## Step 6: Reevaluation Meeting

**Purpose:** To have the members return for a meeting to evaluate the plan's effectiveness and call for any changes that might be necessary.

**Time:** 10 minutes (may vary)

**Actions:** This last step is to meet again to assess the progress of the IDP and to determine the effectiveness of the techniques proposed and the changes needed. The reevaluation meeting might simply require a short discussion, but if the teacher is still unsuccessful, the group might need to repeat the six-steps process described previously.

---

### STAFFING AGENDA

The established six-step process (stating the problem, generating solutions, evaluating solutions, deciding on a solution, implementing the solution, and reevaluating) that defines team members' roles, the purpose of each step, the amount of time to be used, and the actions needed to be accomplished.

---

The structured agenda with established procedures is a systematic process loosely based on a six-step problem-solving process, but it can be modified to accommodate team members' own unique working styles. However, it is important to have an agreed-upon structure for such staffing meetings. The solutions generated by the staffing process can be built out of an understanding of the techniques found in Chapters 1 and 2 and augmented by the individual and collective ideas of the team members.

## SUMMARY

The teacher drops the limit-setting system and moves to the use of a backup system when limit-setting techniques prove ineffective with a misbehaving student who continues to disrupt the educational setting. The teacher gradually escalates the use of isolation or time out, private meetings (teacher and student only) and public meetings (teacher, student, principal, and possibly others), and contracting (informal or written), and notifies the parents in a timely manner before removing the student to out-of-classroom isolation. In all conferences or meetings, the teacher maintains the leadership role and escalates up the TBC from the use of Relationship-Listening techniques, to Confronting-Contracting, and then, finally, to Rules and Consequences. If, at the end of all of the backup system steps, the teacher is still ineffective at finding ways to help the misbehaving student move to more positive behavior, the teacher seeks the help of school staff by holding a staffing meeting, to benefit from the professional experience and insights of his or her colleagues.

## REFERENCES

Dinkmeyer, D., McKay, G. D., & Dinkmeyer, J. S. (1989). *Parenting Young Children.* Circle Pines, MN: American Guidance Service.

Gordon, T. (1974). *T.E.T.: Teacher Effectiveness Training.* New York: David McKay.

Jones, F. (1987). *Positive Classroom Discipline.* New York: McGraw-Hill.

## RELATED READINGS

Alberto, P. A., & Troutman, A. C. (1990). *Applied Behavior Analysis for Teachers* (3rd ed.). New York: Merrill-Macmillan.

Engelmann, S., & Carnine, D. (1982). *Theory of Instruction: Principles and Application.* New York: Irvington.

Madsen, C. H., & Madsen, C. K. (1981). *Teaching/Discipline: A Positive Approach for Educational Development.* Raleigh, NC: Contemporary Publishing.

# The Incentive System

Young adolescents learn social skills both in and out of school. Although they have many years of school experience, learning how to interact positively with adults and peers is an important task for any student. The incentive system is a positive, deliberate way of teaching students appropriate ways to behave.

Dealing with student misbehavior is an important element in implementing any discipline plan, but stopping negative behavior is only half the equation for a well-run classroom. The other half lies in helping students demonstrate positive behavior and performance routinely. That is where the incentive system comes into play. The limit-setting system provides techniques for quietly getting students to stop their misbehavior so ongoing teaching is not disrupted, and the backup system addresses significant disruptions that require more public responses. The incentive system, on the other hand, is a classroom process for motivating students to increase the speed of their work and positive behaviors, or to acquire new behaviors not already in their repertoire. The incentive system, for example, can be used to get students to do their homework or to care for school property, and is a key element in establishing a healthy classroom environment.

# 9

# The Rights and Responsibilities Game

What motivates students? What is it that students want to do, and will do excessively, and with great passion? The answer, which will differ with age, lies hidden within an understanding of psychological development. If teachers understand these developmental "passions," they may harness this motivational steam to stimulate students to do the work and learn. An incentive system is a process that motivates students to work with great gusto, even with passion.

A young adolescent will not clean his or her room at home or take out the trash, but will spend hours running up and down a basketball court with a group of like-minded peers to put a ball through a hoop or playing endlessly with a video game; he or she is motivated to do these activities passionately. If aliens came from another planet and saw this competitive activity with its massive output of energy, they could easily conclude that the activity is utter nonsense. It is not work; it does not produce a product or provide a service to anyone, and, on the surface, it simply appears to be a use of excessive energy. Yet the student is passionate about these activities. Between the ages of 10 and 14, students undergo a transitional time in which they experience the most rapid changes of their lives, except for the time from birth to three months old (Brooks-Gunn & Reiter, 1990). Because of these changes, early adolescence is an opportune time to help students learn self-control and to interact positively with peers and adults (Bennett, 1997). The incentive system, through the Rights and Responsibilities Game, provides the structure for students to make a transition from an external to an internal motivation for positive behavior.

## DEVELOPMENTAL TASKS OF EARLY ADOLESCENCE

Young adolescents display individual differences in their cognitive, emotional, social, physical, and moral development. This variability, especially the emotional, increases the likelihood that these young adolescents will make decisions that may have a negative impact on their future health and/or success. Early adolescence is, indeed, a time when values are formed and behaviors, positive or negative, are reinforced (Milgram, 1992).

Young adolescents are egocentric. They believe that they are constantly being watched and scrutinized by an "imaginary audience" involving others who are deeply concerned about them. This imaginary audience explains why young adolescents are self-conscious, especially about their hair, clothing, and other aspects of their physical appearance (Elkind, 1984). Many young adolescents feel that they are continuously being judged by others. Their behavior may be directly related to what the young adolescent expects the reaction of the imaginary audience to be. Some of the members of that audience include teachers, parents, counselors, and friends.

Because early adolescence involves such change, this is a very vulnerable time for the young adolescent's self-esteem (Lipka, 1997; Lipka & Irvin, 1996). According to Kohlberg (1964) children who have a favorable self-concept are less likely to engage in at-risk behavior. In addition, self-consciousness peaks during early adolescence, and a young adolescent with poor self-esteem may not see this as a stage. At this time, young adolescents are particularly vincible to resorting to unfavorable behavior or even alcohol or other drugs while seeking ways to become part of the group or to please their imaginary audience. However, the audience influence is important, for it provides reinforcement in teaching young adolescents how to relate to others. This influence is an important part of what helps young adolescents generate their norms, values, and even their sense of morality.

It is the task of teachers, parents, and counselors to ensure that the imaginary audience's influence is as positive as possible. One way teachers can assist in providing a positive influence on young adolescents' values and sense of morality is in game playing. Piaget (1965) found that there is a positive relationship between playing games that have rules and the development of morality. Piaget defined *morality* as the internalization of rules, and began his investigation of morality in children with an examination of their progressive understanding of rules of games. According to Piaget, by the age of 11 or 12, children understand that rules exist to make games possible and that rules can be changed by way of mutual agreement. Many games used in schools are heavily controlled by rules not created by adults but generally handed down from an older generation of children to the next generation. These time-tested rules are adapted by the newly formed children's groups on the spot, before any competitive activity can begin. Without adult interference, elementary school children can even argue the rules for 15 minutes and play the game for 5 minutes. By the age of 11 or 12, children begin to accept gradually that rules are made by people and that they can be changed by players of the game if they decide to do so.

When a child learns a new task that is basic to his or her psychological and physical development, the child can appear "drunk" with enthusiasm to practice that new skill. The 12-month-old who learns to walk for the first time is "drunk" with passion and gusto to master this walking; when parents put the child to bed at night, those legs are still pumping with a need to practice—the child is "passionate" about walking. Even into adolescence, a student can be developmentally preoccupied with learning to understand and to obey rules and social relationships and to master his or her competitive nature. This shows itself in the passionate desire for playing games that have rules.

---

### THE VALUE OF GAMES WITH RULES

1. Morality (rules) is practiced at a motor/practice level without undue harm.
2. One must know and enact a role.
3. One must obey rules that define a role and the larger game.
4. A massive expenditure of energy can occur within the confines of rules and boundaries of the game (channeled aggression).
5. One must follow a leader.
6. Teams are made up of members with varying skills (the less-skilled are still accepted).

---

In considering the moral concepts of right and wrong, the elementary school child has a harsh conscience with a "black and white" sense of right and wrong. However, the middle school student, now capable of formal, or more abstract, thought processes, is now more likely to consider the motives and issues involved in those moral concepts. Due to the young adolescent's strong reliance on the judgments of the imaginary audience, it is still important to have rules that serve as safety devices. These safety devices help to create a collective reality—the game—that, for short periods of time, provides an equal arena for each student to demonstrate his or her skills and to challenge himself or herself safely against others. If the games and activities are not controlled or organized by adults, winning is only a minor goal of participating in these activities. More important is the young adolescent's quest to be accepted by his imaginary audience and to be accepted in groups of his peers. Teams will accept unskilled players, but they must "fairly" divide the skilled and unskilled players among the teams so they are balanced in ability. Then the game can begin.

The classroom incentive system helps students acquire new behaviors, maintain already learned behaviors, and increase the rate of their work activities. The motivation for such actions must be built on the developmental interest in group membership and identity, rules, "gaming," and competition for rewards that are real or symbolic. Middle grade students are highly self-conscious and concerned about being accepted by the members of their imaginary audience, especially their peers. In creating this motivation, care must be taken to assure that nothing will occur that might lower their prestige among their peer group and thus endanger their group membership. Nonetheless, practicing rules through games is important to the middle level student. Just as the toddler needs to practice walking and becomes "drunk" with this activity, the young adolescent needs to be provided with practice in group membership and rules, providing the developmental and psychological impetus for his or her passion for games with rules.

## Team Competition

*Mr. Martin, a seventh-grade teacher, is teaching a language arts lesson about Romeo and Juliet, when it becomes apparent that Casey and Steve are not paying attention. The boys are off task and are talking so loudly that they are disturbing their neighbors and disrupting Mr. Martin's lesson. Mr. Martin does not use a high-profile correction (Kounin, 1970) by stopping his lessons and reprimanding the two boys; instead, while maintaining the rhythm and continuity of his lesson, he walks to one side of the chalkboard, where a mounted score chart represents the five study groups by number. (If the cooperative group approach to learning is not being used, then the class could be divided into teams by rows.) The teacher places a check mark under groups 1, 3, 4, and 5, but does not put a mark under group 2—of which Casey and Steve are members. The boys look up to see what is happening, and realize that they have caused the other four classroom groups to score a point. They quickly return to the lesson, and Mr. Martin has lost no time or momentum.*

---

### HIGH-PROFILE CORRECTION

An intrusive process whereby the teacher stops his or her teaching to spotlight an off-task student, and in turn disrupts the ongoing activities and thought process. This interrupts ongoing activities and imposes guilt on the student, making all students feel reprimanded. High-profile correction is highly correlated with poor academic gains and ineffective classroom management (Kounin, 1970).

---

*Later, the students have lined up to leave the classroom for lunch. Just before they depart, Mr. Martin, along with most of the students, looks out over the empty room to find it neat and orderly—except for Larry's desk. On and under his desk are scraps of paper, library books, and similar items that were not put away. Mr. Martin goes to the team score chart and places a check mark under the columns for groups 1, 2, 4, and 5, but does not place one under the column of Larry's group, number 3. This elicits a small groan of disappointment from the other group 3 members. Groups 1, 2, 4, and 5 are dismissed to the cafeteria, while the teacher and group 3 members wait and watch as Larry cleans up his desk area.*

*Later in the day, after the students have returned to their classroom and taken their seats after arriving back from lunch, Mr. Martin takes out two 3-by-5 pink cards that were given to him by the teacher supervising the cafeteria that day. The teacher holds up the pink cards and announces that they are cafeteria score cards. He reads two names: "Steve Markelson and Larry Parker—throwing food and fighting in the cafeteria." He goes to the team score chart and places a mark for groups 1, 4, and 5, but none for Steve's group 2 or Larry's group 3.*

*At some subsequent preestablished time, we will see Mr. Martin adding up the check marks for each team; the four highest-scoring teams receive some form of reward as the "winners." Following this, a new game is started.*

To understand the rationale and dynamics of such a team competition process as a classroom incentive system, one can anticipate that the students in all groups, but especially in group 3, will quickly prompt those misbehaving or off-task students such as Larry to "get with the program—you're causing your team to not win." The socialization is coming from peer to peer instead of coming unilaterally from an authoritarian teacher to the student. The traditional classroom has generally worked with the premise of the teacher as the authority handing out rewards and, more likely, many more forms of punishment.

Today, many students are growing up with minimal or no family supervision, living much of their lives among their peers sometimes on the streets. More than at any other time, the modern child's emotional investment is in peer relationships and membership. Adult authority—in the form of punishment, reprimands, or even rewards—increasingly has little or no effect on such youth. Many misbehaving students will challenge the authority of the teacher, while those same students cannot stand against peers, both because of early socialization and because of the developmental interest and needs of the middle grades student—the peer group holds the power. If this dynamic is understood, peer pressure can form the incentive system. Ultimately, this will prove more effective than an adult authoritarian system, which the difficult student will challenge in an attempt to make the teacher the outside aggressor.

---

### OUTSIDE AGGRESSOR

Groups of students—out of fear, rivalry, or dislike—project their hate (their outside aggression) toward a fellow student or teacher who is not a member of the group.

---

### The Immature and Mature Moral Positions

The team competition incentive system called the Rights and Responsibility Game is based on the levels of a student's moral development. The child's first developmental moral reasoning is the immature moral stage, where she or he obeys rules out of love and fear of powerful adults, often beginning with the mother and then advancing to the mother and father. The mature moral position begins to develop during the elementary school-age period, when right and wrong are defined by the motive of the person and there is an understanding of empathy and reciprocity for others. As a person moves into adolescence, this position is enhanced by their increasing feeling of importance of peer and social relations. Therefore, students of this age group feel that moral behavior is behavior that receives approval from significant people such as parents, teachers, peers, and society at large.

The Rights and Responsibility Game has the potential of demonstrating to students how their actions can take away the rights of others and, in turn, feel what it is like to have others take away their rights. If the classroom discipline system is autocratic and based on punishment and fear, then the student's moral reasoning may be retarded. The Rights and Responsibility Game is a transitional process that gives the misbehaving student real day-in and day-out practical experiences of how rule-breaking actions cause fellow classmates, as a mini-society, to lose. At the same time, it helps to satisfy the young adolescent's need to understand how others, or the imaginary audience, are viewing the actions. When these peers are given the opportunity to express their dissatisfaction with a classmate's misbehavior, they begin to socialize the misbehaving student and provide an effective feeling for social interactions.

Of course, because there is a reward in the Rights and Responsibility Game, there is still an external locus of control. However, when carrying out this incentive system, the teacher fades the reward process until the feelings of belonging and being a part of the democratic group become the reward—the locus of control will gradually move internally. Maehr and Midgley (1996) found that when a student maintains an internal locus of control, they have higher levels of motivation and achievement. In addition, internal locus of control tends to correlate positively with self-esteem (Kohn, 1986).

For young children, the nearly total dependence on parents produces the first moral position in which they view adults as god-like or all-powerful. This produces an authoritarian view of what is right or wrong. What is right or wrong is determined by what parents allow or forbid, rather than by an evaluation of the motives of the person and whether the person intended to do a negative act—or even whether the person understands how his or her actions affect others. Children's beliefs about right and wrong have less to do with their behavior than the likelihood of their being caught or the gains to be made from their offense (Piaget, 1965). The young student obeys rules because of an external locus of control related to the love, as well as the fear of loss of love, from parents and adults such as teachers. As the student moves into adolescence, the fear of the loss of favor with peers is also a factor in adherence to rules.

## Locus of Control

When students make decisions, it is because they decide (internal locus of control) or because someone else (external locus of control) is insisting or coercing them to perform such action. A person's mature moral position does not fully develop until near the end of the elementary school and into the middle school years. This more mature moral position enables the older student to understand his or her behavior and actions and how those actions affect others. He or she has developed empathy for the feelings and rights of others. The student in this mature position understands that rules are collectively created and may be changed with mutual consent, and that the unilateral imposition of rules by someone holding more power (authoritarian) does not make these rules fair or right. The higher cognitive understanding of a mature moral position now enables the locus of control to be internal, based on the student's evaluation of concepts of right and wrong and not just because external authorities state it must be so.

The playing of games with rules that dominates children age 7 and older is a facet of human development, or nature's "built-in" process. Such play provides experience involving competition and rule-governed behavior and facilitates the movement to this more mature moral position. Just as the toddler was "drunk" with practicing the physical skill of walking, the older child developmentally learns to "obey" social rules by practicing through playing games with rules. In the incentive system, as the Rights and Responsibility Game, teachers build on this developmental interest and—through the incentive game—assist the student toward more socially mature understandings of socially acceptable behavior.

Simply defined, the Rights and Responsibility Game is a process through which the teacher places students into four to six teams or groups, balancing each team with well-behaving and misbehaving students as well as students of different sex and ethnic backgrounds. The groups accept a mascot symbol, color, or number with which they can be identified. This game is played daily for a period of six weeks, with acts of misbehavior causing the other team to win points. This approach permits the teacher to make a positive act, by rewarding teams and students who are behaving. Much like a sports referee, the teacher makes tally marks on a score sheet mounted on the classroom wall. Misbehaviors outside the classroom, such as in the cafeteria, are also counted as a part of the game.

After a period of time, the teams that "win" receive some form of reward, such as food treats, stickers, movie tickets, or special time for activities that they like to do (called preferred activity time, or PATs). Over a period of six weeks, these reinforcers are faded out and the rewards gradually disappear, thus enabling the students to move from an external locus (the reward) to an internal locus of control in the form of self-discipline.

Socialization occurs when well-behaving peers express their displeasure, during teacher-supervised problem-solving team meetings, toward a team member who is causing them to lose. These meetings, full of intense discussion, can help counsel the misbehaving student and can get commitments from all students to work more effectively together. The misbehaving student learns that he or she lives interdependently among others, that his or her misbehavior takes away the rights of others, and that the all-powerful teacher is not the only one who can punish. In contrast, the team members who are losing out because of their misbehaving team member must learn, as in a democratic society, to speak out and stand against misbehaviors that disrupt the social order. All students learn through the Rights and Responsibilities Game. It provides a bridge that leads students out of the immature moral position, the childish fear of authority and feelings of "I behave only because I might get punished," to the more mature moral position of reciprocity, empathy for others, and an understanding of how one's behavior affects the rights of others.

## Establishing Teams

On the first day of school, when students are generally unfamiliar to the teacher, they may arbitrarily be assigned to a team, by directly balancing team membership for sex, race, or other similar outwardly apparent variables, and then seating team members together, such as in the "double E" classroom seating arrangement (see Chapter 12). The desks or tables at which the students are seated are color coded so that a simple glance at the classroom makes it obvious where members of the red team, blue team, and so on, are seated.

Team members should not be all girls or all boys, nor all of the same race or ethnic group. Similarly, all the misbehaving students should not be on the same team. This balancing of team membership deliberately builds on the student's sense of fairness and engineers experiences that require each student to interact with peers who are very different from himself or herself. This results in learning experiences with others of diverse backgrounds.

Quickly, during the first few days of school (or with the aid of cumulative folders), the teacher will discover which students are going to have difficulty behaving within the demands of a classroom. The teacher can then reassign students to new teams with the "misbehaving" or target students being evenly divided among the teams. If you watch students choosing teams for a softball game, their sense of fairness becomes obvious, whereby players who are highly skilled and those who are unskilled are evenly distributed between the teams so the teams are balanced before the game begins. If too many star players or unskilled players play on one team, the children view this as unfair and they will not participate. The classroom teacher must be sensitive to this same fairness phenomenon, balancing all teams so they have a relatively equal chance of "winning."

When one team has a difficult misbehaving member and keeps losing points because of that one member, the teacher must first use this tension to do plus/delta meetings (counseling sessions) with the team. However, this one team eventually may feel so burdened that the team members feel they may never win; if this happens, they respond with "It isn't fair," and the whole team will become a discipline problem. Before this occurs, the team's membership will need to be reassigned, with the misbehaving student being moved to a new team. Ideally, the best balance is to have the misbehaving student on a team with one or two peers who are very verbal and are not afraid to speak up to the misbehaving student. These well-behaving team members must have a clear sense of right and wrong, including a sense of fairness, and must be liked and highly respected by all class members. These well-behaved students can help set a positive moral tone for the classroom.

Some teachers may see the Rights and Responsibilities Game as manipulative and as placing undue pressures on both the misbehaving student and the well-behaved team members. However, the Rights and Responsibilities Game may be defended, as an incentive system, with the following justification.

In modern society, the "kid" culture, supported by TV programs and TV marketing, has already obtained great control over the moral and value development of this country's children. By watching closely the way teachers, parents, and adults are portrayed on popular children's programs, it is easy to conclude that adults are portrayed as "geeks," ineffective, and "uncool." Certain "star" child actors are portrayed as sophisticated, and "really cool," and the children watching would like to emulate them. Increasingly, very little admiration of adults and wanting to be like adults is evident. In fact, the opposite seems to be true, with many adults wanting to wear the status clothing of youth.

This control by the peer group can become excessive, as can be seen in the violent street gangs that wear mascot symbols and colors of membership. The Rights and Responsibilities Game effectively uses the motivation of group-peer membership and accepts it as one central motivation, if not the most powerful motivation, of today's youth. Educators understand this phenomenon and must use it to promote positive, healthy, and mature ways of acting and belonging with others. The incentive system picks up today's student where he or she is socially and developmentally, and bridges to a more mature position of social responsibility. This classroom practice, through the Rights and Responsibilities Game under the guidance and supervision of the teacher, can prepare large numbers of students, when they are outside adult supervision, to speak up and stand up against destructive control of the peer group. Not only is the misbehaving student learning from the Rules and Responsibilities Game but the well-behaved peers and team members are also learning to stand against destructive behavior rather than to emulate or ignore it. The teenager who telephones her parents to be taken home from the teen party two hours early because drugs and alcohol have appeared is the one who has learned to make her own decisions and can stand against the peer group when it is wrong or potentially harmful. Where do children get practice in making such critical decisions? Ideally, the parent can teach this to the child, but the teacher has a classroom laboratory full of peers for practicing these skills in a real-life manner. The Rights and Responsibilities Game and other similar games-with-rules play have the potential for teaching students a host of greatly needed skills, such as:

Listening
Conversing
Planning
Joining in
Giving instructions
Following instructions
Apologizing
Convincing others
Controlling and expressing feelings
Understanding others
Dealing with someone else's anger
Expressing affection
Dealing with fear
Rewarding yourself
Asking permission
Sharing
Helping others
Negotiating
Using self-control
Standing up for your rights
Responding to teasing
Avoiding trouble with others
Keeping out of fights
Making a complaint
Answering a complaint
Sportsmanship after the game
Dealing with embarrassment
Dealing with being left out
Standing up for a friend
Responding to persuasion
Responding to failure
Dealing with contradictory messages
Dealing with an accusation
Getting ready for a difficult conversation
Dealing with group pressure
Deciding on what to do
Deciding what caused a problem
Setting a goal
Deciding on your abilities

Gathering information
Arranging problems by importance
Making a decision
Concentrating on a task

## Incentive Reinforcers

The teams may "win" reinforcers of three types: edibles, tangibles, and preferred activity times (PATs). The type 1 reinforcer (edible) is highly desired by students but is a less desired reinforcer for the classroom setting. It will be used first, but is then faded to a type 2 (tangibles), and finally faded to type 3 (PATs).

The classroom teacher should be aware that after a number of edibles, the student can become saturated and no longer interested. Additionally, edibles can be cumbersome, time consuming, and difficult to administer. Edibles, as a type 1 reinforcer, also appear more like bribes. They are initially very powerful and motivational to large numbers of students, but their use should be phased out over a six-week period.

| | INCENTIVE REINFORCERS | | |
|---|---|---|---|
| **Type** | **Category** | **Examples** | |
| 1 | Edibles | Foods and liquids (e.g., blowpops, pudding, juice, Popsicles, sugarless candies) | |
| 2 | Tangibles | Certificates, badges, stickers, balloons, movie tickets, discounts for videogame rentals, novelties, and other status or desired items | |
| 3 | Preferred Activity | Play and game activities, computer time | |

## Preferred Activity Time (PAT)

Preferred activity times should provide not only socialization benefits but also academic practice. A detailed example of one form of PAT, called Academic Baseball, is shown in Figure 9.1. Other forms of PAT may include variations of such popular games as Jeopardy, Family Feud, College Bowl, Tic Tac Toe, or Bingo, as well as any other activities that the students favor, such as viewing favorite videos.

Preferred activity time is not "kicking back" time designed to permit students to chat with each other and do nothing. If students are given the freedom to do nothing, that is most likely what they will do.

**FIGURE 9.1    An Example of a Preferred Activity Time (PAT): Academic Baseball**

**Subject Area**
Math, History, Foreign Language, Science, Vocabulary Development, Spelling, etc.

**Objective**
Test review

**Materials and Preparation**
- The teacher or students prepare questions in four degrees of difficulty: single, double, triple, home run.

- Two baseball diamonds will be needed in order to use a ping pong game format (described below). Mark the bases on the floor.

**Student Grouping**
Two teams.

**The Play**
1. The batter is asked by the pitcher to pick the level of difficulty for the question (single, double, triple, or home run).

2. The pitcher selects and asks a question from the single, double, triple, or home run stack. If, however, the teacher is "pitcher" and does not have stacks of questions already prepared, the teacher just asks the questions "off the top of her head."

3. If the student answers correctly, the student walks to the appropriate base and other runners advance the same number of bases.

4. If the question is answered incorrectly, a "flyball" is called, and the question goes to a player of the team that is "in the field."

   - When the teacher says "flyball," she should wait before calling on a student so that everyone in the field must dig for the answer.

   - If the player in the field answers the question correctly, the flyball has been caught and the batter is out.

   - If the outfielder misses the question, the flyball has been dropped, and the batter goes to first base on an error. All runners advance one base on an error.

5. When using the ping pong game format, the questions alternate between teams. So, the second question goes to the team that was in the field (i.e., playing defense) during the previous question. The ping pong format guarantees that both teams get to bat an equal number of times, that everybody plays all of the time and that both teams are continually engaged in scoring runs.

6. The "ping pong" format does away with innings. In order to make outs meaningful, the final score is computed as *runs minus outs.*

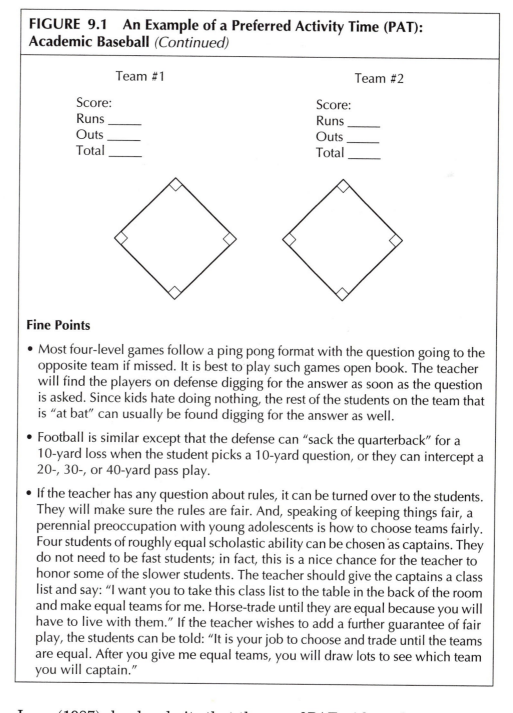

**FIGURE 9.1    An Example of a Preferred Activity Time (PAT): Academic Baseball** *(Continued)*

Team #1                                    Team #2

Score:                                     Score:
Runs _____                                 Runs _____
Outs _____                                 Outs _____
Total _____                                Total _____

**Fine Points**

- Most four-level games follow a ping pong format with the question going to the opposite team if missed. It is best to play such games open book. The teacher will find the players on defense digging for the answer as soon as the question is asked. Since kids hate doing nothing, the rest of the students on the team that is "at bat" can usually be found digging for the answer as well.

- Football is similar except that the defense can "sack the quarterback" for a 10-yard loss when the student picks a 10-yard question, or they can intercept a 20-, 30-, or 40-yard pass play.

- If the teacher has any question about rules, it can be turned over to the students. They will make sure the rules are fair. And, speaking of keeping things fair, a perennial preoccupation with young adolescents is how to choose teams fairly. Four students of roughly equal scholastic ability can be chosen as captains. They do not need to be fast students; in fact, this is a nice chance for the teacher to honor some of the slower students. The teacher should give the captains a class list and say: "I want you to take this class list to the table in the back of the room and make equal teams for me. Horse-trade until they are equal because you will have to live with them." If the teacher wishes to add a further guarantee of fair play, the students can be told: "It is your job to choose and trade until the teams are equal. After you give me equal teams, you will draw lots to see which team you will captain."

Jones (1987) clearly admits that the use of PAT with students is really a "shell game." Such activities as a popcorn party would be permitted as a PAT, but would be considered a poor or weak use of PAT. Under Jones's definition, PATs are fun activities that hold high interest for students but have embedded in them a routine of drill and practice, or even content review of the subject matter. In short, they are process activities involving elements of learning. Watching a video about a book the students will read this semester is a motivating, high-interest activity that the teacher simply turned into a PAT. The book *Positive Class-room Discipline* (Jones, 1987) contains a host of starter games to get teachers going at all age levels. Suggested PATs involve:

1. Team competitions: games with line-ups (e.g., classroom game of baseball, requiring knowledge of the material being taught)

2. Team competitions: games without line-ups (e.g., classroom base-ball, volleyball, or College Bowl, which modifies the game so there is no line-up)

3. Team competition with complex work (e.g., math teams and cut-throat)

4. Path games (e.g., spelling, typing, Bingo)

5. Enrichment activities (e.g., permitting the students to break from the tradition and try advanced applications of the subject area)

6. Fun and games (e.g., simple party time, which the teacher will rely on the least as the students gradually learn to use the academically mixed games above)

Students might see such games as "not cool." Teachers should per-mit feedback from students in choosing and modifying the activities for their own interest. Historically, games with rules are passed down from one generation of students to another. They normally are not taught by adults, but are strictly dependent on the student culture. Because of television, mall arcades, and the general marketing of leisure activities, these traditional games are being lost and not passed down by students today. The commercial games, such as Nintendo or its sibling Game Boy, are isolated activities; therefore, children are losing out on the very valuable social interaction that traditional games have long taught them.

## Scheduling Reinforcers

The awarding of reinforcers—either edible, tangible, or PATs—is time consuming and administratively cumbersome. Most teachers may ini-tially feel it is important to work toward positive behavior, but in prac-tice this has not been easy to accomplish through a hit-or-miss form of giving reinforcers. A suggested schedule (see Figure 9.2) would involve that type 1 edibles be used heavily the first week, then dropped or faded, moving to type 2 tangibles, and then in the last weeks type 3 PATs are mostly used. Generally, the teacher follows this schedule over a six-week period (see the explanation of Mars Days in Chapter 13).

The suggested scheduling assures that the reinforcers in the incen-tive system of edibles and tangibles will gradually fade. Once the stu-dents have developed normal classroom habits, the Rights and Responsibilities Game will be stopped—but not the PAT. The PAT should continue throughout the year, with normal classroom teaching

| FIGURE 9.2 | Suggested Schedule for Awarding Reinforcers Over a Six-Week Period | | | | |
|---|---|---|---|---|---|
| Week | Monday | Tuesday | Wednesday | Thursday | Friday |
| 1 | edible<br>edible<br>edible | edible<br>edible<br>tangible | edible<br>tangible<br>tangible | edible<br>tangible<br>tangible | tangible<br>tangible<br>PAT |
| 2 | edible<br>edible<br>edible | edible<br>tangible<br>tangible | tangible<br>tangible<br>PAT | _____<br>tangible<br>tangible | tangible<br>_____<br>PAT |
| 3 | edible<br>tangible<br>tangible | _____<br>tangible<br>tangible | tangible<br>_____<br>PAT | _____<br>PAT | tangible<br>_____<br>PAT |
| 4 | tangible<br>_____<br>PAT | _____<br>_____<br>_____ | tangible<br>_____<br>PAT | _____<br>_____<br>_____ | _____<br>_____<br>PAT |
| 5 | PAT<br>_____<br>PAT | _____<br>PAT | _____<br>_____ | PAT<br>_____ | _____<br>PAT |
| 6 | _____<br>_____<br>PAT | _____<br>_____ | _____<br>_____<br>PAT | _____<br>_____ | _____<br>_____<br>PAT |

and learning becoming more fun and game-like until the learning and the having fun begin to blend into one activity for the students.

## Scoring and the Score Card

A Rights and Responsibilities Score Card should be mounted on the wall at the front of the classroom within easy reach of the teacher (see Figure 9.3). A team scores a point in one of three ways: misbehavior by a member of another team, bonus points to all teams, and bonus points for the student who needs encouragement.

*Mr. Martin is teaching a language arts lesson, when it becomes apparent that Casey and Steve are not paying attention. The boys are off task and are talking so loudly that they are disturbing their neighbors and disrupting Mr. Martin's lesson. While maintaining his rhythm and continuity of his lesson, Mr. Martin walks to one side of the chalkboard, where a mounted score chart represents the five study groups by number. The teacher places a check mark under groups 1, 3, 4, and 5, but does not*

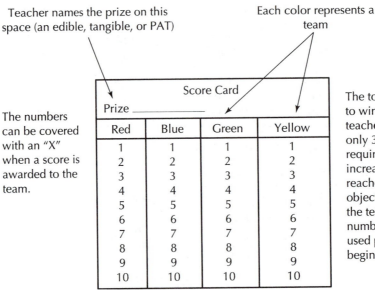

FIGURE 9.3 Score Card

Teacher names the prize on this space (an edible, tangible, or PAT)

Each color represents a team

The numbers can be covered with an "X" when a score is awarded to the team.

The total number needed to win will be set by the teacher. First, perhaps only 3 points will be required, slowly increasing until 10 is reached. When the objective is less than 10, the teacher will "X" out numbers that will not be used prior to the game beginning.

*put a mark under group 2—of which Casey and Steve are members. The boys look up to see what is happening, and realize that they have caused the other four classroom groups to score a point. They quickly return to the lesson, and Mr. Martin has lost no time or momentum.*

This scoring of points on the mounted score card is done in a low-profile manner without saying a word. The teacher goes to the Score Card and awards a point to each of the other four teams, and returns quickly to teaching. Notice in the vignette that no reprimand is made to the misbehaving students. If need be, the teacher may make eye contact and square off with the misbehaving students to cue or body-telegraph to them that they were the ones causing others to lose points. More likely, however, fellow students will signal or cue them about their behavior.

## Body-Telegraphing

Through nonverbal body actions (kinesics), the teacher communicates to the observing students that he or she "means business." Bonus points are awarded by the teacher to all teams if no misbehavior occurs during a specific time interval, announced as a verbal contract with the class beforehand. The teacher gradually fades this bonus reward by lengthening the time period.

## Bonus Points for the Student Needing Encouragement

At times, there will be one or two very difficult students whose behavior disrupts the incentive system, and the team members get so unhappy with them that they do not want or refuse to have such a student on their team. This student has been described as the "best bad kid" in the classroom or in the school (see Section V for further actions in dealing with this discouraged student). To prevent the class from making this student the outside aggressor, the teacher begins a bonus-awarding process by establishing a contract with the class and the misbehaving student, agreeing that if he or she can maintain positive behavior for a short period of time (a timer can be set for this interval), all teams will win points.

At first, this time interval is small, such as 5 or 10 minutes, making sure that the difficult student and, in turn, the entire class is able to win. The teacher awards points for all teams so that if the difficult student succeeds, the entire class may applaud the student in a further reward for his actions. Then the Bonus Points Contract is restarted with a slightly longer interval. The time interval for bonus points continues to increase until it no longer is needed and the difficult student can behave in such an appropriate manner that he or she can be a positive team member. This misbehaving student does not get some independent-individual reward, but he or she helps all teams get reinforced.

A second variation in working with this "best bad kid" is to give the student his or her own personal score card. Each time the student maintains good behavior for a specific time interval, the teacher punches the personal score card with a hole punch. Once the difficult student has reached the same number of holes as the number on his or her personal card, all teams cheer the student and all teams win a point. This second variation works well for out-of-classroom or open-field activities such as on the field or in the cafeteria.

The difficult student is then given a new personal score card, with a higher number or an increased time interval, to challenge the student to increase his or her time on task and his or her self-control. This type of social dynamic prevents the misbehaving student from being rejected by his peers or from gaining status by his misbehavior, making him or her the "best bad kid." The classmates celebrate and reward the student for his or her ability to grow and become more cooperative.

## A Word about Winning

Because of the nature of early adolescence, too much activity that involves intense competition should be avoided (Kohn, 1986). However, U.S. society seems to put a great deal of stress on the importance of competition. Competition is a part of our lives and has its place. The key to whether its use is destructive or healthy to our young adolescents lies in how, and to what degree, it is employed. Historically, schools have used competition that rewards one individual as "King" or "Queen" of the Christmas Ball, or one team of students winning over large groups of other students. This competition, where few can win, makes the majority of the students "losers." If one is chosen as the most attractive, it makes the rest feel unattractive and suggests inadequacy. This contradicts the general philosophy inherent in the Rules and Responsibilities Game. Teachers want all students to be winners, to work as teams and as a class so that everyone is successful.

Games of competition are found in most cultures, but there are cultures that, through their games, teach cooperation rather than "destroying" or beating the other for the benefit or glory of a small group or an individual. Early Eskimo games were played in such a manner that the game continued until all members of the group succeeded or "won." Then, with great cathartic release, all members cheered their success. This cooperative gaming is also seen in the movement called New Games, where games selected from other cultures are played for the purpose of cooperation and the success of all participants—no individual or small minority beats others. So, the teacher's approach in refereeing the Rights and Responsibilities Game is not to get caught up in winning and the destructive form of competition, but to play the game so that all teams can and do win and receive awards. This is especially important in the first few weeks of Mars Days (the first six weeks of school; see Chapter 13). The teacher should deliberately work in such a manner by liberally dispensing points or lessening the time period for getting points. This enables all teams to have many early experiences of winning and getting the rewards, before any team has to experience not getting a reward.

## Out-of-Classroom Supervision

During these first six weeks of school, the so-called Mars Days, the Rights and Responsibilities Game is played by not only the classroom teacher but also the special-area teachers in such subjects as art, music, physical education, media, or exploratory wheel classes. It can also involve all school personnel, including administrators, bus drivers, and cafeteria supervisors. The special-area teacher who has a defined classroom may organize his or her classroom so that the students can identify where their team or group will sit, according to color, number, or whatever group distinction plan the academic teachers are using. If interdisciplinary team organization is not used in a particular middle school, different grouping may be used in different classes. However, the Rights and Responsibilities Game is most effective if the teams or groups are consistent throughout the classes. The special-area teacher also has a score card and will play the Rights and Responsibilities Game just like the classroom teacher, issuing his or her own rewards.

In this way, there is continuity between the special-area and classroom teachers, and the special-area teachers can send notes back to the classroom teacher telling which teams have "won" points for the classroom teacher to record for "team success at special area."

During open-field supervision such as in the cafeteria, if the open-field supervisor gives a student a desist (see Section II) and the student fails to comply, the supervisor sends to the classroom a pink card with the student's name and transgression. At a predetermined time, the classroom teacher will announce the student's name and transgression, and score points for the other teams. The teacher may also choose to do a plus/delta meeting with this misbehaving student or his or her team, with the open-field supervisor in attendance.

## Plus/Delta Meetings

Historically, misbehaving students would find themselves knee to knee or face to face with the teacher, receiving reprimands and criticism regarding their negative behavior and threats of punishment if they failed to desist. By contrast, Relationship-Listening forms of interaction—discussion of problems, finding answers, counseling, mediation, and "talking out" misbehavior, conducted between or among teacher and student(s) or between student and student—are the ultimate goal of the Rights and Responsibilities Game. The control of students through rewards is only a short-term powerful process for class control and to teach rights and responsibilities to both the misbehaving and the well-behaving students. Plus/delta meetings are held repeatedly and consistently with the misbehaving student, with a team that needs to deal with one of its misbehaving team members, or with the entire class. They are used throughout the Rights and Responsibilities Game. After the first six weeks of school, the rewards are faded and the games disappear, but plus/delta meetings continue throughout the remainder of the school year to help the teacher maintain positive behavior and to gain more mature behavior from the students.

The teacher holds a plus/delta meeting to discuss a topic that involves some incident of social conflict repeatedly occurring within the classroom: "Steve, let's talk about the fight in the cafeteria" *(Step 1: Defining the Problem)*. The teacher then leads the students through the Six Steps to Problem Solving *(Step 2: Generating Solutions; Step 3: Evaluating Solutions,* and so on). The Six Steps to Problem Solving provides a structure for helping students think out problems and come up with creative solutions. (See Chapter 8 for a full explanation of the techniques and procedures for carrying out the Six Steps to Problem Solving and a plus/delta meeting.)

## Contracting

The failure to obtain a reward (edible, tangible, or PAT), either by the individual well-behaving team member or by the misbehaving student, is a serious matter because the negative action may destroy the motivation of all the students involved. It is critical to make sure that all students in the Rights and Responsibilities Game get plenty of rewards during the early stages of the six-week schedule.

The awarding of an edible, although a very powerful reinforcer, is quickly consumed and normally quickly forgotten by most students. Thus, the loss of such reward is generally easier for the student to handle emotionally. But the loss of a tangible can be a more serious action, and the loss of a PAT is the most serious. In our earlier example, Steve caused his group to lose points. Once this occurs, tension will build within Steve's team and team members will begin to feel "put upon" by Steve's misbehavior. The first plus/delta team meeting, under the guidance of the teacher, is now held to deal with this tension. Participants define the problem, generate solutions, and go through the complete Six Steps to Problem Solving. When they get to *Step 4: Deciding on the Solution*, the teacher now turns this into a verbal contract and, later, a written contract. Here is an example:

> ***Teacher:*** *"Team, we have now decided on a solution to this problem so that your team will not lose. Do we all agree?"*
> ***Team:*** *"Yes!"*
> ***Teacher:*** *"Do we now have a contract?"*
> ***Team:*** *"Yes!"*
> ***Teacher:*** *"Now, I need to shake your hands (the teacher does so with each team member) to seal this agreement. (The teacher approaches the misbehaving student.) Steve, do we now have an agreement, a contract, that when [so and so] occurs, you will do [so and so]?"*
> ***Steve:*** *"Yes."*
> ***Teacher:*** *(shakes Steve's hand) "Now that we have a contract, and we have all agreed, I will give you today's reward, even though your team lost."*

Now if the misbehaving student or the team loses again and again, the tension builds within the group and a second plus/delta meeting is held in a similar manner. But this time, after the contract is agreed upon and hands have been shaken, all well-behaving team members will receive the reward, but the misbehaving student will not. We caution against depriving the well-behaving team members of a reward, with this one exception: If the team fails to discuss the problem and is not willing to work together, the entire team might be deprived of an edible or even a tangible, but never a PAT. Well-behaving children will consider it extremely unfair to be deprived of a "big ticket" reward such as a PAT just because they happen to be on the same team as a very difficult peer, and you will soon have very unhappy parents knocking at your classroom door to complain.

Now, if the misbehaving student has failed to receive the reward, the teacher holds a one-to-one meeting with the misbehaving student following the procedures given in Table 9.1. The one-on-one personal counseling and advisement session always takes a problem-solving attitude and approach. It escalates through the Teacher Behavior Continuum and the Three Faces of Discipline.

## SUMMARY

The Rights and Responsibilities Game, built on the developmental need of middle grade students to compete in a games-with-rules structure, is used as a behavioral incentive system. It is used first to help the teacher gain classroom control, then to teach the misbehaving student how to

| TABLE 9.1 | One-on-One Meeting Techniques | |
|---|---|---|
| **TBC** | **TECHNIQUES** | **EXAMPLES** |
| *Relationship-Listening Face* | | |
| Looking | Proxemics | Teacher and misbehaving student are seated on chairs in a knee-to-knee position; teacher makes eye contact. |
| Naming | Active listening | "Wow! You have had a disappointing morning, and have lost a reward. You must feel disappointed." |
| | Door openers | "Rod, help me understand what is happening with you." |
| | I-messages | "When students take other's property (behavior), this disrupts the class (effect) and that is disturbing (feeling), and stops me from teaching." |
| *Confronting-Contracting Face* | | |
| Questioning | "What-how" questions | "Rod, what did you do? What was the rule? What will happen if you continue to act like this?" |
| | (or, if need be) | "Rod, here is what you did____. The rule is____." |
| | Contracting | "You and I need to work this out! How will you change?" (shaking hands or a contract signed) |
| | Logical consequences | "If the contract is broken, this consequence will happen ____." |
| *Rules and Consequences Face* | | |
| Commanding | Assertive command | "Rod (say name, make eye contact), when this happens, I want you to do so and so" (tell what to do, not what not to do). |
| | Promise a consequence | "If this occurs again, then this will happen." |
| Acting | Transporting | Backup system begins. |

move to more productive behaviors, and finally to teach the well-behaving student how to defend his or her rights. The process begins with reinforcers involving external control, which are faded through scheduling to permit the student to gain self-control. The tension caused by team membership and the loss of points because of a member's misbehavior is used in plus/delta meetings to solve problems and teach the misbehaving student his or her interdependence with others. Through the entire process of the incentive system, the teacher's actions are positive and devoid of punishment or reprimands. The tension created by team competition creates the context for the teacher to teach new social skills and positive ways of behavior for the misbehaving student.

The classroom incentive system can, through the Rights and Responsibilities Game, help the students acquire new behaviors, maintain already learned behaviors, and increase the rate of their work activities. The motivation for doing such actions must be built on this developmental interest—that is, group membership and identity, rules, "gaming," and competition for rewards that are real or symbolic.

## REFERENCES

Bennett, B. J. (1997). Middle level discipline and young adolescents: Making the connection. In J. L. Irvin (Ed.), *What Current Research Says to the Middle Level Practitioner* (pp. 73–85). Columbus, OH: National Middle School Association.

Brooks-Gunn, J., & Reiter, E. O. (1990). The role of pubertal processes. In S. S. Feldman & G. R. Elliott, (Eds.), *At the Threshold: The Developing Adolescent* (pp. 16–53). Cambridge, MA: Harvard University Press.

Elkind, D. (1984). *All Grown Up and No Place to Go.* Reading, MA: Addison-Wesley.

Jones, F. H. (1987). *Positive Classroom Discipline.* New York: McGraw-Hill.

Kohlberg, L. A. (1964). Development of moral character and moral ideology. In M. L. Hoffman & L. W. Hoffman (Eds.), *Review of Child Development Research* (Vol. 1). (pp. 212–214). New York: Russell Sage Foundation.

Kohn, A. (1986). *No Contest: The Case against Competition.* Boston: Houghton Mifflin.

Kounin, J. (1970). *Discipline and Group Management in Classrooms.* New York: Holt, Rinehart and Winston.

Lipka, R. (1997). Enhancing self-esteem in young adolescents. In J. L. Irvin (Ed.), *What Current Research Says to the Middle Level Practitioner* (pp. 31–39). Columbus, OH: National Middle School Association.

Lipka, R., & Irvin, J. (1986). Positive self-esteem and learning in early adolescence. *Middle School Journal, 28* (1), 52–53.

Maehr, M. L., & Midgley, C. (1996). *Transforming School Cultures.* Boulder, CO: Westview Press.

Milgram, J. (1992). A portrait of diversity: The middle level student. In J. L. Irvin (Ed.), *Transforming Middle Level Education: Perspectives and Possibilities* (pp. 16–27). Boston: Allyn and Bacon.

Piaget, J. (1965). *Moral Judgment of the Child.* (Marjorie Gabain, Trans.). New York: Free Press.

# The Encouragement System

Discipline systems provide the tools necessary for the classroom teacher to organize the room in order to reduce the potential for behavioral outbursts and to provide incentives for the students to perform well and behave properly. Inevitably, however, there is one particular student (or perhaps more) who has endured so much negative input that he or she has grown frustrated and discouraged. This type of student needs something special to be encouraged to participate in the learning environment and to become a fully functioning member of the class. The encouragement system offers an array of techniques for the teacher to use in drawing that one discouraged student out of his or her shell and into the broader world of classroom life.

# 10

# Finding Acceptance

*Since the child is a social being, his strongest motivation is the desire to belong. His security or lack of it depends upon his feeling of belonging with the group. This is his basic requirement. Everything he does is aimed at finding his place. From infancy on, he is very busy exploring methods of being a part of his family group [later the school group].*

*From his observations and his successes, he draws conclusions—not found in words, but definite knowingness—"Ah! This is how I can belong. This is how I can have significance." ... The desire to belong is his basic goal while the method he devises for attaining his basic goal becomes his immediate goal. (Dreikurs, 1968, p. 32)*

Why is it that some middle school students are so disruptive that they prevent teachers from teaching and their students from learning? The explanation for their destructive behavior is that they are discouraged and they feel left out of a group.

*It is the first day of school at the beginning of a new year, and Mr. Lansing is casually observing the new group of eighth-graders entering his room for the first time. He finds nothing particularly distinctive about this new group, until Michael appears. This student is dressed in faded blue jeans that are covered with patches bearing the logo of a popular motorcycle company. Even more noticeable are two patches running across the seat of his pants bearing the words "Screw You" on one hip pocket and "Life Sucks" on the other. The rest of Michael's attire includes a T-shirt and a western-style hat pulled down over his eyes. To see while walking, he has to lead with his chin and look out over his nose.*

*Mr. Lansing gradually loses sight of Michael as he visually skims over the remaining faces in the classroom. Suddenly, he hears one girl scream and another student laugh, and then the classroom quiets. Everyone's attention focuses on Michael, who is slouched down in his seat with his hat pulled over his face. The students glance from the teacher to Michael and back to the teacher. Seeing that neither Mr. Lansing nor Michael is going to make any further move, the class members return to their chatting. A few minutes later, Mr. Lansing begins reading through the class roster, calling each student's name and receiving in return a proper acknowledgment such as "I'm here." When he calls out "Michael Flemming," there is no response. He repeats it a second time to no response, but all eyes turn toward Michael. The teacher asks, "Isn't Michael Flemming here?" Michael replies, "Yo, chill, man!" The teacher states, "You're Michael?" Michael gives the slightest "yes" nod of his head.*

*Mr. Lansing ignores Michael's lack of a solid response, finishes calling the roll, and finally introduces himself and the content of the course. He turns his back to the class and begins to write on the chalkboard. Before he can finish, he hears the same girlish scream, but this time with such intensity that it is clear something more serious is occurring. The girl seated in front of Michael suddenly jumps out of her seat and runs from the classroom. As she passes, it is apparent that Michael has unfastened her bra.*

As the year progresses Mr. Lansing will discover that Michael is a student who will be a continuous and serious discipline problem, costing Mr. Lansing considerable classroom teaching time and stress throughout the school year. Michael Flemming's behavior may be viewed as goal directed. One central goal for students (as well as adults) is to find social acceptance and recognition. When a student is unsuccessful in obtaining social acceptance and recognition (sometimes as early as his or her infancy and toddler years at home), a pattern of misbehavior begins. Once such a child has entered the school during the elementary years, he or she begins to attempt to find acceptance and recognition among peers through the use of similar negative behaviors. As the child reaches early adolescence and middle school, the increasing need for peer approval only enhances his or her use of these negative behaviors. The child now begins to understand, and fairly accurately evaluate, his or her strengths and limitations within the context of the peer culture and school. If poor patterns of getting acknowledgment and recognition were used in the home, the child will attempt to use similar misbehavior patterns in the new school setting.

Michael's behavior is that of a discouraged student who has not found positive ways of gaining acceptance and who has developed a pattern of behavior designed to get acknowledgment and recognition—even if negative. Subconsciously, students such as Michael are essentially saying, "If I cannot get recognition for being the best 'good' kid, I will get recognition for being the best 'bad' kid. This will make me someone—others will see and know me as being special." Thus, Michael's misbehavior is a result of being discouraged, possibly very early in life, in not finding full social acceptance. Out of this feeling of discouragement, he has acquired the motivation and behavior to compensate for this nonacceptance. If a student like Michael cannot find acknowledgment and acceptance, he will subconsciously begin to work from four "mis-motivations": attention getting, power, feelings of revenge, and helplessness.

## MIS-MOTIVATIONS

The first mis-motivation of the discouraged student is to attempt to get *attention* by any manner. This will begin with a series of disruptions that stop the class from working, stop the teacher from teaching, and draw all the attention to the student. When the teacher reprimands and insists that the student stop, he or she will smile sheepishly and stop the disruption at that moment—but before long, the attention-getting student is again doing something disruptive to draw attention. This need for excessive attention through repetitive disruptions seems to "nickel and dime" the teacher into submission, who feels clearly annoyed by the student's actions and toward him or her.

The second mis-motivation of the discouraged student is the quest for *power*. The student will engage in a host of classroom disruptions, but when asked to stop, will challenge the power and authority of the teacher overtly, by defiance or passively appearing to not acknowledge the authority figure and continuing with the misbehavior. The response to a request to stop is, "Let's see you make me!" The strongest and most extreme forms of threats and punishments can be used, but the power-seeking student is not fearful of any sanctions and appears to love the center stage that these punishments give him or her. The teacher's feeling toward this misbehaving student is one of feeling beaten. The power-seeking student will challenge a teacher for power, take any punishment, and appear to delight in it.

The third mis-motivation for the discouraged student is a feeling of *revenge*. The revengeful student will do physical or psychological damage to the teacher, fellow classmates, or the school and school building, and appear to take delight in hurting others. It is almost as if the revengeful student is saying, "I have been hurt by the world of others and I am going to get even!" Such a student is sometimes called the "hit-back-first kid." This means that the revengeful student, when first engaging in social activity with others, immediately concludes that the other person will not only reject him but will do him harm. Therefore, before such outcome can occur, he will hurt the other person first. A teacher will have clear feelings of being hurt by this student. At times, such students are psychologically skilled at finding sensitive personal characteristics and knowing how to offend or hurt by their actions and comments.

The fourth and final mis-motivation is that of *helplessness*. The student feels so rejected by others that he or she retreats into a passive shell, isolating from others, and wanting not to be seen or acknowledged. It is as if the student is saying, "I know that I am unworthy. Please do not see me or draw attention to me in any way." Such a student will sit as a passive shadow in your classroom, not causing any disruption, and may go unseen because he or she does not cause any discipline difficulties. However, this is the student who is in the most serious difficulty and needs a clear intervention and encouragement. This is most difficult for the teacher, however, because the helpless student is so introverted and nonresponsive that he or she causes feelings of inadequacy in educating or in dealing with them.

So, the behavior of Michael is viewed by saying that he is a discouraged student. Somewhere in his past development, he was unable to find basic acceptance, and has developed destructive patterns of behavior based on one of the four mis-motivations. This view, based on concepts of social membership, also gives added justification for the use of the Rights and Responsibilities Game and team competition used within the incentive system. The incentive team competition gives the student practice at being a member of a group.

Mr. Lansing knows that Michael's motivation is not helplessness, but he may not be sure which of the other mis-motivations Michael may be working from. In dealing with Michael, Mr. Lansing would begin collecting data and observing Michael in school and social settings. One of the central techniques is for the teacher to attempt to analyze how he truly feels toward Michael. Does he, as the teacher, feel annoyed? (If so, the motivation may be attention getting.) Does he feel beaten? (If so, the motivation may be power.) Does he feel hurt by Michael's actions? (If so, it is revenge.) Does he feel inadequate? (If so, it is helplessness.)

## DETERMINING THE NEED

To begin, the teacher must determine which of the four faulty goals is motivating the student. This determination follows a four-step process:

1. The teacher observes and collects information about the student in situations involving peers and family.

2. Once the teacher has gathered information about the student, he or she can then hypothesize which of the underlying goals is held by the student.

3. The teacher can verify this hypothesis by reflecting on what feelings arise within the teacher as a result of the student's behavior.

4. Final verification is achieved by confronting the student with a series of four questions and looking for a recognition reflex by the student.

## Looking

> *Mr. Lansing, immediately faced with 31 pairs of eyes peering at him, becomes uninvolved emotionally from Michael's behavior. He has noted the first impression of rudeness, braggadocio, and flashiness that Michael has created. Mr. Lansing makes a mental note to search for more information by checking school records, talking to former teachers, and possibly making a home visit. For now, though, with limited information, he suspects that Michael's goal may be attention getting, power, or revenge. It certainly is not helplessness!*

It is important to remain calm during the beginning encounter with a student operating under any of the faulty goals, and not give the student what he or she seeks. For example, the worst thing Mr. Lansing could do would be to call out loudly and angrily to Michael. To do so would give Michael the attention he seeks (attention getting), or it would accelerate the battle of who will win out (power), or it would drive him into physically lashing out (revenge).

Mr. Lansing can remain calm because he knows that Michael's behavior is not directed at him personally but is simply Michael's previously learned mode of responding in groups. Of course, a quite human reaction by a teacher would be to explode, but this urge must be held in check. Examining this emotional urge or feeling toward the student will be most helpful in narrowing down and identifying the student's goal.

## Questioning (Clarifying Teacher Feelings)

Now, Mr. Lansing can covertly assess the inner emotions that Michael's behavior has evoked by asking himself four questions related to the goals:

1. Do I feel annoyed? (If so, Mr. Lansing may have reason to suspect attention getting as a goal.)

2. Do I feel beaten or intimidated? (If so, Mr. Lansing may have reason to suspect power as a goal.)

3. Do I feel wronged or hurt? (If so, Mr. Lansing may have reason to suspect revenge as a goal.)

4. Do I feel incapable of reaching the student in any way? (If so, Mr. Lansing may have reason to suspect helplessness as the goal.)

Mr. Lansing analyzes his feelings as annoyed, to say the least, and even slightly intimidated, which suggests that Michael's goal was attention getting or power. If Mr. Lansing had yelled at him, Michael might have responded with, "Chill out, chill man, no need to lose it, just chill!" In other words, if Michael's goal was power, he would have won at that point. He would have "shown up" Mr. Lansing in front of the class, revealing a teacher who becomes easily flustered while he, a 13-year-old student, was more of a man with calm and collected reactions. For the class members, this would be "show time." If, on the other hand, Michael's goal was to get attention, he would have responded in a different way. Mr. Lansing's yells might have caused Michael to put his head down sheepishly and grin to himself. The rest of the class would be observing Michael, and as soon as Mr. Lansing turned away, Michael's head would be back up, face smiling and looking around to make sure that everyone had seen him. In both cases, Mr. Lansing's primary reaction would have done little to prevent numerous future occurrences. Mr. Lansing knows he cannot play into the student's scheme and is ready now to take specific action. He makes a guess that Michael's primary goal is to gain attention.

## Commanding

The previous reflective thinking and covert behaviors of looking and questioning were primarily done to gather information, to narrow down and identify the student's possible goal, and to make a tentative plan for action. A teacher trained in the *Three Faces of Discipline* approach would take only a split second from the time he first witnesses the girl running out of the classroom to the moment he begins action toward Michael.

Having identified attention getting as Michael's underlying goal, Mr. Lansing acts in a way that deprives Michael of the attention related to his misbehavior. Because of the public nature of the results of Michael's misbehavior, Mr. Lansing is forced to drop the limit-setting system and move to the backup system.

> *Mr. Lansing turns to the girl and quietly tells her to come back in the classroom when she is ready and to take another seat away from Michael. He then turns to the class and states, "Class, I would like to introduce you to some of the special science equipment you will be using this year. In a few minutes, I would like you to break up into groups of four people and gather around the tables at the back of the room. When you get settled, open to the first page of your manual, where you will find pictures of the various kinds of equipment. As a group, see if you can first learn the equipment names, then I will join each group briefly to demonstrate how to use some of the more dangerous equipment, such as the Bunsen burner." As the students quietly move to their groups, Mr. Lansing turns to Michael and says, "Oh, Michael Flemming, your behavior has told me that you are not ready to work with others. I want you to remain in your seat."*

Having tended to the class and taking away the students who could provide Michael an audience, Mr. Lansing gives Michael a command. For now, let's say that Mr. Lansing has employed as a logical consequence the loss of the student's right to engage in an activity as a result of behavior that would be counterproductive to performing that activity. Before Mr. Lansing can conclude definitely that attention getting is Michael's goal and initiate a long-range plan based on that goal identification, the teacher needs further verification. He can achieve this by returning to overt questioning with Michael.

## Questioning (Overt)

*Michael is seated alone, slouched down with his hat over his face for nearly half the period. (This is a further sign that Mr. Lansing has correctly identified Michael's goal. If Michael had wanted power, he would have continued to defy the teacher's rules. If Michael had wanted revenge, he would have physically retaliated against the girl or teacher.)*

*Mr. Lansing eyes Michael slowly getting out of his seat and moving toward the work table. Only one spot is open in the groups of four, and he heads toward that spot. When the trio notices that he is ready to join them, one of the girls at the table (the very one that Michael annoyed) begins to complain and shout, "No, no, you don't! You're not joining our table, turkey." Michael then turns to another nearby group and is greeted with, "You're not coming into our group. There is dangerous stuff here—you'll get us killed!" With a parting shot, "You're all a bunch of jerks," Michael returns to his desk. Mr. Lansing moves toward him* (closing space), *takes a seat nearby* (proximity-near), *and, in a voice that cannot be heard by anyone else, begins to question Michael.*

*Mr. Lansing:* *"Do you know why you acted like you did this morning?"* (confronting).

*Michael:* *(simply shrugs his shoulders)*

*Mr. Lansing:* *"I have some ideas. Would you like to know?"*

*Michael:* *(nods yes)*

*Mr. Lansing:* *"Could you want special attention?"* (verifying).

*Michael:* *(For the first time, his eyes look directly at Mr. Lansing, and he gives a slight smile)* (recognition reflex).

During a discussion in a calm setting, it is proposed that the teacher do as Mr. Lansing has done. Ask the student if he or she is interested in knowing why he or she behaves that way. If the student does not resist, ask one of four questions. Here are the central questions related to each mis-motivation:

1. Could it be that you want special attention?          *(Attention)*

2. Could it be that you want your own way
   and hope to be the boss?          *(Power)*

3. Could it be that you want to hurt others
   as much as you feel hurt by them?                    *(Revenge)*

4. Could it be that you want to be left alone?          *(Helplessness)*

After asking each of these questions, look for behavioral verification. If the student smiles, laughs, looks up suddenly, moves his or her shoulders, or shows other signs of response to the implied goal, then conclusive evidence is rendered that the hypothesis is correct and actions can proceed. Formulate a plan and return to appropriate commanding.

Now that Michael has given the recognition reflex, Mr. Lansing can be confident that attention is Michael's goal. Mr. Lansing's task now becomes one of finding ways for Michael to receive attention through constructive social behavior. In other words, he needs to give Michael the attention that the boy craves. Following are descriptions for treatment for each of the four goals, with a corresponding prescriptive chart for teachers.

## ATTENTION

A student who seeks attention should not receive it when he or she acts out. To give attention to the student for inappropriate behavior would be playing into the student's plan and would not help the student learn how to behave productively in the group. Instead, the teacher might use some of the techniques shown here.

---

### NONSOCIALLY ADAPTIVE STUDENTS: ATTENTION GETTING

**Student's Motivation**
Attention Getting

**Behavior Characteristics**
Repetitively does actions to make him or her the center of attention. When asked to stop, will comply but will start again later.

**Teacher's Feelings**
Annoyed

**Techniques with the Attention-Getting Student**
*Minimize the Attention*

- Ignore the behavior.

- Give "The Eye." (Look straight at the student until he stops.)

- Stand and move physically close by. (Move into the personal space.)

- Mention the student's name. (Called "low-profile desist" to make the student aware of his behavior but not disrupt the thought process of the other class members.)

---

**NONSOCIALLY ADAPTIVE STUDENTS: ATTENTION GETTING**
*(Continued)*

- Send a secret signal. (Wink or make a similar humorous nonverbal signal the student understands that says, "I see you and I recognize you," but continue your teaching.)

- Give written notice. (Have previously made and stored in your lesson plan book small notes with a desist message, humorous if possible, and simply slip it to the student so there is no break in the continuity of your teaching.)

- Give an I-message. (A statement containing the teacher's reference to himself or herself as I, and then the student's behavior, effect on the teacher, his or her feelings, and a request for the student to desist.)

*Legitimize the Behavior*

- Make a lesson out of the behavior. (The math teacher makes spitball throwing permissible by making it a part of a lesson, with the students counting distances, graphing each person's throw, and teaching probability concepts related to hitting a target with the spitballs.)

- Extend the behavior to its most extreme form. (A student making spitballs now must make 500. A student who is constantly out of his seat now must stand for the entire period.)

- Have the whole class join in the behavior. (When the student does some annoying behavior, such as tapping pencils or burping, the entire class is asked to do so, stealing attention from the attention-getting misbehaving student.)

- Use a diminishing quota. (Make a contract that the student can do the attention-getting behavior but 25 percent fewer times in the class period. Put a check on the board for each time he may do it, and while continuing to teach, keep erasing the checks until he runs out of his allotted quota. Continue every day from this point on, dropping the permitted number of times until the behavior becomes zero.)

- Play a musical sound.

- Lower your voice to a whisper.

- Change your voice. (Pretend a silly accent.)

- Talk to the wall. (Tell the wall that so-and-so is doing something specifically to get attention and you wish he or she would stop. This steals the attention from the attention-starved student.)

- Use one-liners. (These are jokes, maybe about the teacher himself, that do not ridicule or make fun of students.)

*(Continued)*

---

**NONSOCIALLY ADAPTIVE STUDENTS: ATTENTION GETTING**
*(Continued)*

- Cease teaching temporarily. (Simply stop and say nothing until the attention-getting student stops. Students will stop and look at him but not in a supportive way.)

*Distract the Student*

- Ask a direct question.

- Ask a favor.

- Change the activity.

*Notice Appropriate Behavior*

- Thank the student.

*Move the Student*

- Change the student's seat.

- Send the student to the thinking chair. (This chair is located at the back of the room out of the view of other students.)

*Source:* Adapted from *Cooperative Discipline: A Teacher's Guide to Cooperative Discipline* by Linda Albert, pp. 31–44 © 1989 American Guidance Service, Inc., 4201 Woodland Road, Circle Pines, MN 55014-1796. Adapted and published here with the permission of publisher. All rights reserved.

---

## POWER

A student who wishes to possess power should not be able to engage the teacher in a struggle. The teacher who falls for this "bait" and gets pulled into the battle is merely continuing the excitement and challenge for the student. The student becomes increasingly bolder and pleased with trying to test the teacher. The teacher should attempt to remove the issue of power altogether and force the student to look for some other goal for behaving.

## REVENGE

In this case, the teacher is dealing with a more difficult task. A student who feels hurt and wishes to retaliate must be handled in a caring, affectionate manner. It is probable that this student appears unloving and uncaring, and is very hard to "warm up to." But this is exactly what the student needs (to feel cared for). Techniques that are helpful with students who seek power and/or revenge are shown here.

---

## NONSOCIALLY ADAPTIVE STUDENTS: POWER AND REVENGE

| Student's Motivation | Behavior Characteristics | Teacher's Feelings |
|---|---|---|
| Power | Repetitively does behavior to make him or her the center of attention. When asked to stop, he becomes defiant and escalates the negative behavior and challenges the adult. | Annoyed |
| Revenge | Hurts others physically or psychologically. | Hurt |

### Techniques with the Power and Revengeful Student
*Make a Graceful Exit*

- Acknowledge the student's power (You may actually say, "You can beat me on this—I have no wish to take you on!")

*Remove the Audience*

- Table the matter. (State that you will not deal with this now, but at a later date, decided by you. You can then calm down and assert your power in a different context on your ground.)

- Make a date. (Tell the student when you wish to deal with him—time and place.)

- Agree with the student. (Revengeful student: "You're an ugly bitch!" Teacher: "Well, I probably wouldn't win a beauty contest.")

- Change the subject.

*Use Time Out*

- Time out in the classroom.

- Time out in another classroom.

- Time out in the office.

- Time out in the home.

*Set the Consequence*

- Loss or delay of activity.

- Loss or delay of using objects or equipment.

- Loss or delay of access to school areas.

- Denied interactions with other students.

*(Continued)*

---

### NONSOCIALLY ADAPTIVE STUDENTS: POWER AND REVENGE
*(Continued)*

- Required interactions with school personnel.

- Required interaction with parents.

- Required interaction with police.

- Restitution: Repair or replacement of objects.

*Source:* Adapted from *Cooperative Discipline: A Teacher's Guide to Cooperative Discipline* by Linda Albert, pp. 31–44 © 1989 American Guidance Service, Inc., 4201 Woodland Road, Circle Pines, MN 55014-1796. Adapted and published here with the permission of publisher. All rights reserved.

---

## HELPLESSNESS

The student who shows inadequacy or helplessness is the most discouraged. He or she has lost all initiative for ever trying to belong to the group. The teacher must exercise great patience and attempt to show the student that he or she is capable. Some practices that might assist a helpless student are discussed here.

---

### NONSOCIALLY ADAPTIVE STUDENTS: HELPLESSNESS
### (AVOIDANCE OF FAILURE)

| **Student's Motivation** | **Behavior Characteristics** | **Teacher's Feelings** |
|---|---|---|
| Helplessness | Wishes not to be seen; passive and lethargic. Inadequate, rejects social contact; refuses to comply or try most educational demands. | Incapable |

**Techniques with the Helpless (Avoidance-of-Failure) Student**

*Modify Instructional Methods*

- Use concrete learning materials and computer-assisted instruction.

- Teach one step at a time.

- Provide tutoring.

- Extra help from teachers.

- Remediation programs.

- Adult volunteers.

- Peer tutoring.

- Learning centers.

---

### NONSOCIALLY ADAPTIVE STUDENTS: HELPLESSNESS (AVOIDANCE OF FAILURE) *(Continued)*

*Teach Positive Self-Talk*

- Post positive classroom signs. (Posted in the classroom are signs such as "I can do it!" or "With a little effort, I'll succeed.")

- Require two "put-ups" for every put-down. (Make a rule that for every negative statement that the student says out loud, he or she must say two positive statements.)

- Encourage positive self-talk before beginning tasks. (When a task is given, require the discouraged student to make two positive "I can" statements into a tape recorder.)

*Make Mistakes Okay*

- Talk about mistakes.

- Equate mistakes with effort.

- Minimize the effect of making mistakes.

*Build Confidence*

- Focus on improvement.

- Notice contributions.

- Build on strengths.

- Show faith in students.

- Acknowledge the difficulty of a task.

- Set time limits on tasks.

*Source:* Adapted from *Cooperative Discipline: A Teacher's Guide to Cooperative Discipline* by Linda Albert, pp. 31–44 © 1989 American Guidance Service, Inc., 4201 Woodland Road, Circle Pines, MN 55014-1796. Adapted and published here with the permission of publisher. All rights reserved.

---

Returning now to our vignette:

*Michael is obviously interested in Mr. Lansing's suggestion that he (Michael) is seeking attention, but he jars Mr. Lansing back to the immediate situation with a sarcastic, "Well, that sounds cool, but there's one big problem. I can't do all these things without equipment, and no one wants me in their group. What do you suggest? Maybe you'll buy me my own table?"*

*Mr. Lansing, as a teacher, knows that he must capitalize on using the group as a model to help Michael adjust. Mr. Lansing informs Michael that at the end of class today, and on every Friday, there will be a short class meeting—a plus/delta meeting—to discuss problems that are of concern to the members of the class. He adds that Michael could bring up his problem at that time and see what he and the class might work out.*

The *Three Faces of Discipline* orientation is that schools and classrooms, as part of a democratic society, need to be models or laboratories for that society. In other words, students need to practice democratic principles in school to learn how to contribute later to society as a whole. The central process for carrying out this modeling of democracy is the use of the class meeting, which Mr. Lansing refers to as the plus/delta meeting. Regular meetings should be held to discuss everyday occurrences as well as long-range policies.

Voting should be avoided, as it has a tendency to alienate the minority. Instead, decisions should be made through arriving at a consensus of all members. When any people agree with a decision, peer pressure tends to influence the one or two "holdouts" and thus makes the decision unanimous. (We see this at political party conventions. After a hard battle among several candidates, one individual finally emerges.) Let's see how Mr. Lansing capitalizes on the group process.

*Mr. Lansing calls the students back to their seats and tells them that, in his classes, he always has a class meeting on Fridays for the last 20 minutes of the period or during advisory time. However, since this is the first week of a new school year and they have a lot of problems to work out, they will have a meeting every day this week, beginning today. The class is then encouraged to begin an open general discussion. One or two students bring up different problems pertaining to locker assignments, how they are going to be graded, and the length of the lines in the cafeteria.*

*Finally, Michael raises his hand, and everyone turns to look at him. "I have no equipment and I'm in no group." The girl he previously embarrassed shouts, "Serves you right." Mr. Lansing interjects, "What Michael has done is in the past. What can we do about his not having a group to join?" The class begins in earnest to discuss the issue. Most students express the feeling that if Michael has no equipment, he cannot pass the activity and that would be unfair. Some students ask members of the trio if they would let Michael into their group. Again, the girl who had been embarrassed states, "No way! He will bug us and keep us from our work. He is dangerous!" However, the other two members of the group say they would be willing to work with him on a trial basis. Finally, after much discussion, it is decided that the girl will change places with a student in another group and Michael would now have three people with whom he can work at the science table. Michael appears greatly relieved to hear this decision.*

## CONSEQUENCES

Up to this point, everything seems to have been resolved. But what happens if Michael continues to misbehave? What recourse does the teacher or class have? To answer these questions, we need to look at logical consequences.

### Reinforcement

Although some approaches to discipline rely on the use of punishment, negative reinforcement, praise, or positive reinforcement, some experts substitute natural/logical consequences and the process of encouragement. Each of these will be explained as it applies to Michael.

### Natural/Logical Consequences

If Michael should create a commotion after becoming accepted in the group, he could be disciplined as a result of some of the following logical consequences:

1. Have the group of three decide what should be done with Michael.

2. Have Michael work alone and have him use the laboratory equipment on his own time (at lunch, before or after school).

3. Bring Michael's misbehavior back to the entire class in a classroom meeting to decide on future consequences.

Specifically, for Michael, this means:

1. If Michael has been causing a disturbance by poking students with a pencil, take away all of his pencils and tell Michael that whenever he needs to write, he'll have to come to the teacher's desk to ask for a pencil.

2. If Michael has been constantly moving out of his chair and distracting others, tell Michael that he does not seem to need a chair and take it away from him. Let him stand until he requests to have it back and promises to stay in it.

A *natural consequence* is defined as that which happens as a result of one's behavior. If a student is rushing to be first in the lunch line and falls, this is called a natural consequence. On the other hand, if a student is rushing and pushing others in order to be the first in the lunch line and is removed by a teacher or administrator to a place at the end of the line, then this would be identified as a *logical consequence*.

In other words, a natural consequence is an inevitable occurrence that happens by itself, whereas a logical consequence is arranged but directly related to the preceding behavior. The *Three Faces of Discipline* position is that, in a democratic classroom, students must be responsible for how they behave. There is no room for autocratic punishment that further alienates and discourages a student. Extensive punishment serves as a force to drive a student toward the goal of revenge. Punishment is not seen as being logically related to a student's behavior inflicted as a reaction to personal dissatisfaction felt by the teacher. Punishment says to the student, "You had better behave or I (the teacher) will make life miserable for you." If the student does "knuckle under," it is because of the power of the teacher and not because the student has learned how to be a productive member of the group. If one accepts the *Three Faces of Discipline* definition of human behavior as a purposeful attempt to belong, then one understands that a teacher who uses punishment blocks a student's purpose. Punishment plays back into the student's misdirected goals. It gives attention, enhances the power struggle, stimulates further revenge, and keeps the helpless student in his or her place.

Additionally, many of today's students are not easily coerced by the use of authoritarian power. Not only does punishment thwart a student's ambition but it simply does not work. Sending a student home with a note, keeping him or her after school, paddling, scolding, ridiculing, or standing the student in a corner are all forms of physical or psychological punishment. The teacher's actions are aimed at hurting the student or making him or her feel bad. Punishment is the teacher's vengeance for committing a crime. On the other hand, students who clean up the mess they created, who are put at the end of the line for shoving, who miss a special activity because of tardiness with their assigned work, or who are barred from using certain materials until they choose to use them properly are all actually involved in the effects of logical consequences. Logical consequences are not always easy to tailor to every disruptive action. However, it is the teacher's task to arrange the situation that follows the disruption in a way that the student can see a relationship between the consequences and his or her behavior.

Finally, it is important to note the differences in a teacher's attitude and manner in the application of logical consequences as opposed to the act of punishment. Two teachers might arrive at the same solution for a problem caused by a student's behavior, but one will be an example of logical consequences and the other will be an example of punishment. For example, during a quiet work time, Alysha continually pokes Nigel with a pencil. One teacher, Mr. Matter-of-Fact, tells the girl, "Alysha, if you do that again, you are showing that you cannot control your pencil, and I will need to take it from you. You will be able to finish your work here in the classroom after school." The other teacher, "Mr. How-Dare-You," says, "Alysha, I have told you a thousand times not to do that. Can't you understand anything? If I catch you once more, I'll take all your pencils away and you'll stay after school. Maybe being alone is the only way that you can work!" Mr. Matter-of-Fact has calmly told the student to use the pencil correctly or give it up. Mr. How-Dare-You acts as though he has been personally affected and that Alysha's misbehavior is a direct challenge to his authority. He tries to hammer her down by scolding, questioning her competence, and challenging her. The same outcome has occurred—the student has had the pencil confiscated—but Mr. Matter-of-Fact has used logical consequences and Mr. How-Dare-You has applied punishment.

## The Process of Encouragement

At the same time that the class and Mr. Lansing are applying logical consequences to Michael's behavior, Mr. Lansing is also using the encouragement process. Mr. Lansing asks Michael to keep inventory of all playground equipment. Mr. Lansing also makes a mental note to greet Michael warmly each day.

The encouragement process is an attitude taken with a misbehaving student that results in a climate of respect and optimism. One must remember that a student whose goal is attention feels stifled by authority and may retreat to the even more destructive power seeking. When that goal is "beaten down" by an overbearing, punitive teacher, the student may then resort to the goal of revenge to retaliate. When revenge is crushed by ever more coercive means, a teacher may finally have the most pathetic result—a student who has simply given up and has internalized the goal of helplessness. This lowering of goals is the result of a student becoming further discouraged. Not only does the student retreat further back into gloom and despair, but so does the teacher. The vicious cycle compounds the problem.

The role of the teacher is to stop this dissipation of hope by using encouragement. This is accomplished by teacher actions such as:

- Emphasize improvement rather than perfect product.

- Criticize the student's actions, but not the student (i.e., "I like you but I don't like to hear you shouting").

- Keep the student in a group with other students who are willing to help. Determine those peers who are most accepting and tolerant of the student in question. Seat the student with them and arrange for him or her to work with them in groups. Find a companion or friend for the student.

- Refrain from having the student compete against others. Do not compare the student to others ("Why can't you behave like Walter?") or constantly single out or praise others who outperform the youngster.

- Deemphasize grades; try to grade the student on effort and growth, not rank in relation to others.

- Avoid contests for the best-behaved student or citizen of the week, where the student has little chance of winning.

Praise as a way of promoting positive reinforcement is generally not a desirable method. Encouragement is much broader than behavior modification's use of verbal praise or material/situation rewards as conditioning to achieve appropriate behavior. More than three and one-half decades ago, Dinkmeyer and Dreikurs (1963) wrote, "Unfortunately, even the well meaning and sincere educator may often fail to convey much needed encouragement if he tries to express his approval through praise.... Praise may have a discouraging effect in the long run, since the student may depend on it constantly and never be quite sure whether he will merit another expression of special approval and get it" (p. 68).

Dinkmeyer and Dreikurs, on whose work this encouragement system is based, did not say that praise should be totally avoided, but rather that too much praise makes a student dependent on the teacher. The student who is "won over" by the teacher to work quietly due to the teacher's praise ("Oh, look at Hillary! What a fine student to be working so quietly! I am so proud that you are being so quiet") has not learned social behavior. Instead of learning how to act out of consideration for others, the student is learning how to act for purposes of receiving the teacher's special compliments and dispensation. In other words, the student behaves well, but for all the wrong reasons. If the teacher is removed from the scene, the student's behavior will deteriorate. The student needs to internalize the correct motivation for being well behaved (acting as a productive member of the group) for it to be lasting.

In addition, the student who sees himself or herself as a failure and is motivated by revenge or helplessness will tend to disbelieve the authenticity of the teacher's words. A student who refuses to work and gives up on carrying out any order may have reason to speculate on why the teacher makes such an effort to praise him or her ("Oh, Sam, look what a good job you did! You make me so pleased when you enter the room quietly!" "Margie, it's great the way you answered that question!"). The student will, in effect, believe that the teacher is overcompensating and that he or she is being singled out because he or she is indeed inferior. The student may think: Why make such a big deal about entering the room or answering a simple question? The teacher must think I'm a real loser. Thus, the result will be the opposite of what the teacher intended (a further sign that reaffirms the student's sense of inferiority). There is a fundamental difference between the act of reward and the act of encouragement. Few realize that, at times, success can be very discouraging. The student may conclude that, although success was achieved once, it could not happen again. The student's recent "success" may become a threat to his or her future ability to succeed. Worse, such an event often conveys to the student the assumption (actually shared by most of his or her teachers and fellow students) that he or she is worthwhile only when he or she is successful.

Praise or other forms of reward seem to heighten a student's anxiety always to have to "measure up." It puts constraints on a student who feels such pressure. He or she feels comfortable only when being successful. The discomfort with being unsuccessful further discourages a student from feelings of being accepted and of being an acceptable person. He or she feels accepted only when successful, but not when something less than success occurs as a result of efforts expended. The student who needs to learn to be a member of a group must learn to accept his or her individual self as being a person capable of both success and failure but who, despite outcomes, is still worthy of being loved and accepted by others.

A student who is always dependent on being rewarded for what he or she does is in a bind when it comes to taking a risk. The individual who is learning how to belong must be encouraged to try new ways of behaving. The student who learns that it is safe and rewarding to be meek and passive will not easily venture into the unknown by being assertive and active. He or she will not venture into untried areas. This is the danger of having "fail-proof" programs or "praise-laden" teachers.

The teacher must not stress the concept of success, but instead promote a climate of always accepting the student as worthwhile. This happens when a teacher uses encouragement rather than reinforcement as praise. Following are two contrasting lists that give examples of praise versus encouragement. Praise focuses on the teacher being pleased by the student and on the student achieving a completed product. Conversely, encouragement focuses on the student and on the process of the student trying.

## Praise

"I (teacher) like what you have done."

"Great job! What a smart person you are."

"You get a star (token, free time) for doing that."

## Encouragement

"You're trying harder."

"You must be happy with (playing that game, being with others)."

"It must be a good feeling to know you're doing well."

"You have every reason to be proud."

## Acting and Isolation

Forms of teacher intervention such as spanking or shaking a student must be avoided. Such treatment is seen as a form of punishment that would drive a student further away from social cooperation. Discomfort experienced as a natural consequence (without the possibility of serious harm) may be allowed. Some examples of this might be the student who rushes to be first in line and in his or her haste falls and is bruised, or the student who, after repeatedly provoking the class gerbil, is bitten. On the other hand, there are some natural consequences that can follow when a student precariously tilts back in the chair, or when a "90-pound weakling" begins to taunt and enrage a 250-pound high school football tackle. These could be dangerous consequences, and the teacher would be wise to prevent them from occurring. It is important to note that a teacher should carefully judge the natural consequence before deciding to act or not to act in a given situation.

Isolation, through various forms of time out, must also be used judiciously by the teacher. The *Three Faces of Discipline* advocates the use of isolation only as a logical consequence. Michael was isolated temporarily by Mr. Lansing when his behavior was immediately disruptive of others. However, Michael was given the opportunity to rejoin the group once he decided that he wished to belong.

It is evident that if being part of a group is the ultimate goal for all individuals, then each person needs to learn to relate successfully to others. A student learns such relationships only by practicing appropriate behaviors with others; he or she does not learn cooperation by being lectured to or having to sit alone. For these reasons, instead of relying on isolation, the teacher is required to look constantly for ways to encourage attachments between the offending student and other members of the class.

## Encouragement and the Outside Aggressor

Let's look in on another classroom.

*In art class, the students are allowed to select their own seats among the many tables in the room. Five girls have been sitting together at a round table for four weeks so far. Amy, a pleasant new student at the school, has been sitting by herself but has started to become friendly with some of the girls at the "in" table. After class, Marcia, one of the girls at the table, tells Amy to make sure to get to art class early tomorrow and to grab a seat at the round table. She confides that she and three others will also be early so they can all sit together. The next day, Amy and the four girls are already seated by the time Julie, a past member, walks in. She seems startled and walks up to Amy and says, "Pardon me, but you're in my seat!" Amy isn't too sure what to say and looks around at the other girls who are smiling at her. Marcia looks up at Julie and says, "We've invited Amy to join us. I'm sure you can find somewhere else to sit where you'll fit in." Stunned, Julie walks away.*

*During art class that same day, the teacher is placing paints before Julie when one pot accidentally tips and spills, making a small yellow paint mark on Julie's blouse. Julie shouts at her teacher, "Look what you did, you damn stupid old cow!" The entire class quiets while "the gang" giggles and laughs at Julie.*

The incident with Julie and "the gang" shows clearly that Julie has lost her past friends and companions and is now being socially isolated. The *Three Faces of Discipline* position is that Julie's acting out (the verbal aggression, "you old cow") is a result of built-up revengeful feelings being directed at an innocent party: the teacher.

All misbehavior by children in your classroom—whether attention-getting power acts, revengeful acts, or passive behavior—is seen by the *Three Faces of Discipline* as a failure to find social acceptance. However, rarely does one get such a clear observation as in the Julie incident to actually verify this position. Instead, one typically sees a repetitive host of misbehaviors and aggressive actions that on the surface do not appear to be related to immediate behavior by other children. For example, a student hits other students without any provocation. Children's first feelings of acceptance come out of the home setting with parents and siblings. If they felt they were rejected in early family interaction, they assume that they will be rejected in a classroom situation and will set out with negative actions to prove that others do not like them.

The less skilled teacher might bring "the gang" aside and verbally reprimand and lecture them for their actions, applying large doses of guilt for their behavior. Such actions might unknowingly make members of "the gang" even more hostile to Julie, and now they will be revengeful toward her in more subtle ways that the teacher will not see or detect. Instead, Julie needs to acquire social skills that will enable her to find acceptance.

The Julie incident is another example of the phenomenon of the outside aggressor, first introduced in Chapter 5. The teacher may employ a number of techniques to be proactive in helping children acquire social skills to overcome this potentially significant problem. Reaction to the outside aggressor is an expectable, normal behavior among students. The teacher's role, of course, is to develop ways through which students can learn to be social in a more healthy manner and to help children like Julie find belonging and acquire social skills. This can be done through beneficial use of social engineering.

## Social Engineering

*After the "we don't want you in our group" incident, but before any outburst such as the "you old cow" verbal aggression could occur, the art teacher, Mrs. Anderson, calls Julie to the table. She has seen Julie being made the outside aggressor and summons her in a voice loud enough for "the gang" to hear. She states, "Julie, we are going to make the centerpiece for the holiday pageant, and I am going to let you be the chairperson of this project. You may choose helpers to work with you!" Every member of the class is eager to be on this committee. Julie chooses six nearby students. Members of "the gang" see what is happening. Their facial expressions show that their excitement has been deflated, and they begin to wander over to the art table and look on as this new project is being organized. They loiter about, and then gradually plead in a whining voice, "Mrs. Anderson, can we be on the committee, too?" The teacher responds, "I don't know. I am not the chairperson of this project—Julie is! You will have to ask her." The gang approaches Julie and asks, "Can we join your committee?" Julie hesitates for a few seconds, then smiles and says yes. The teacher hovers nearby, watching all the committee members working on the art arrangement, her presence helping Julie to maintain her power. Later, when the pageant programs are printed, Julie's name is listed as the chair of this committee, and she has her photograph taken while working on the project for the school newspaper. During a subsequent class discussion, Mrs. Anderson will encourage other students to express their joy at being a part of the project and working under Julie's leadership* (encouragement).

In the use of social engineering, the teacher considers a student who is acting out or misbehaving and views that student as being powerless, lacking the skill to find social belonging. The teacher deliberately "engineers" or sets up activities whereby students such as Julie are empowered and helps them enjoy the experience of successfully working within a group. The teacher deliberately points out to classmates, genuinely, how the student has given and contributed to making the classroom a happy and accepting place.

Thus, positive experiences are deliberately engineered for misbehaving students. After the centerpiece experience, you may question Julie with Confronting-Contracting "What?" questions, such as, "Julie, what did you do as committee chair? What worked for you as you worked with friends? What did not? What will you do next time when you want friends?" Notice that you do not tell Julie how well she did, or make any value judgments, or offer a prescription for her in further interactions. Through your questions and counseling of students who are having social difficulty, you want them to become reflective after social experiences, to become aware of their own behavior, to evaluate their success, and to come up with ideas of how they may be even more effective the next time.

## Friendship Charts (Sociograms)

Since the *Three Faces of Discipline* theory places membership and belonging as the primary motivator, teachers may wish to study the social makeup of the class with the use of a friendship chart (sociogram; see Figure 10.1). This may be done by asking the students to state preferences for other members of the class in response to such questions as: Who would you like to sit beside? Who would you like to work with on an art project or math problems? Which student would you most like to visit at home? Which boys or girls do you like least? Based on the results, the teacher constructs a diagram similar to Figure 10.1.

Even the best designed social engineering plan cannot be expected to eliminate all problems associated with students who are at risk of becoming outside aggressors. A close look at the problem student's classmates and school personnel will reveal that after a period of time, this student has become the outside aggressor in the classroom. He or she gets blamed by all students and staff for all accidents and negative occurrences. Others, including teachers, do not want this student at their table or sitting near them at social events. Most everyone, including adults, has unknowingly begun a process of "shunning" the problem student.

This shunning and unwanted status as the object of the outside aggressor phenomenon now severely complicates the intervention and dynamics of ever helping this student to change. The difficult student

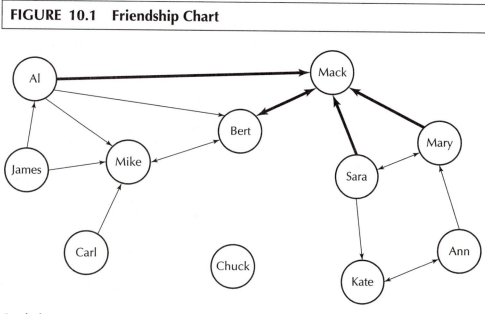

**FIGURE 10.1    Friendship Chart**

*Symbols*

A ⟵————— B:  B chooses A, but A does not mention B

A ⟵————⟶ B:  A and B choose each other

A ▬▬▬▬⟶ B:  A dislikes B

A ◀▬▬▬▬▶ B:  A and B dislike each other

*Explanation*

There is a clique centering around Mike, as leader.

Al is a *fringer* in this group; only James has chosen him.

Carl, James, and Chuck are *isolates*; they have not been chosen by other students.

Mack is a *reject*; two boys and two girls dislike him, and he has no friends.

There are three pairs of mutually chosen friends (Sara and Mary, Kate and Ann, and Mike and Bert).

There are two boys who mutually dislike each other (Bert and Mack).

*Definition of Terms: fringers* may consider themselves a member of a group but are chosen only by one member of the group; *isolates* have no close friends; *rejects* are disliked by others.

has dug a deep social hole that he or she will never be able to climb out of by himself or herself. You must now address a new question: How can you reduce or even eliminate this collective anger and shunning toward the student?

## The Most Wanted

A staff meeting must be called to involve all adults who come into daily contact with a difficult student. At the beginning of this meeting, it might be helpful if members of the group of adults are permitted some time to express their honest feelings toward the student. Staff members who are frightened by their own negative feelings toward the difficult student might receive some reassurance if they hear a skilled and respected teacher state, "I am wondering how you are feeling about Michael Flemming these days. I must confess that at times I find myself getting angry and even frightened by him. At times I don't want him in my class, and at times I am having a hard time liking him." The first step in changing the staff's negative behavior toward a difficult student is to get honest feelings "out on the table."

As already noted, the problem student has dug a deep social hole that he cannot climb out of by himself. Because he feels rejected, he sits about day in and day out, his negative actions evoking further rejection from classmates and adults. The problem student is still in the formative years of development, and these young adolescent years are the most robust years for making an impact on his development that will serve him—or mis-serve him—for the remainder of his life. As the expression goes, "Love begins with love!" The very nature of a teacher's job is to make a lasting contribution to these difficult young people. Almost all adults can recall one significant experience where a teacher befriended and helped them at a difficult point in their lives. A teacher must understand what a lasting impression this can have and how it can produce long-term positive results for a student's well-being.

This is the challenge, and the opportunity, for a teacher dealing with any difficult student. If teachers do not bond with these students, who will? Literally anyone can teach a student who has been well parented, but it is the difficult student who enables teachers to "earn their stripes." Adulthood rarely provides a person willing to take the time to help someone with whom it is difficult to get along.

This help begins with a staff meeting using the Confronting-Contracting procedures to break the pattern of unknowingly shunning the student and making him the outside aggressor. Staff members should express past incidents verbally in which they have moved away from this problem student. Mrs. Anderson confesses, "I am embarrassed to admit it, but one time when I was seated at the table with a group of students, we had one chair remaining at our table. I saw Michael approaching, and—again, I'm embarrassed to admit it—but I grabbed another student and had him take this free seat so that Michael would not be at my table." This outward admission is most important! (The teacher working alone might want to write this out.) Mrs. Anderson's candor may then encourage other staff members to share similar experiences or feelings.

The next question is: What can be done to change? The answer is that for the next two weeks, Mrs. Anderson will put Michael, as her difficult problem student, on the "Most Wanted" list. Unlike a police Most Wanted list, however, this list will single Michael out for special positive behavior. Perhaps you have witnessed the behavior of staff and students when you had a visiting student, maybe from another country. Visitors enjoy special status while spending the day in the classroom.

Everyone rolls out the "red carpet" for them: They are greeted warmly at the door, shown where to be seated, and told how and where things work. Placing the difficult student on a Most Wanted list means treating him as an honored guest throughout a two-week period. When every staff member—even those who do not have him in their group or classes—sees the difficult student passing by, they are to say hello, make eye contact, say the student's name, and make some pleasant verbal overture. The teacher helps him and invites him to be a part of any group activities. During every time period throughout the day for the two weeks, some adult should be helping the student as if he were new to school procedures and practices—a stranger visiting without friends. At any discussion groups involving the entire class, the teacher will point out to classmates any and all positive behavior by the difficult student as statements of encouragement.

Almost as if a whistle has been blown, all adults deliberately change their behavior toward the difficult student. If the teacher does not change, then classmates and the student himself cannot change. The problem student can "climb out" of the deep social hole that imprisoned him by changing the entire social environment in the school. At first, a teacher is likely to feel phony acting in such a manner, but pushing through such feelings and a commitment to perform these "motor actions" eventually helps the student. A campaign of welcoming the student day in and day out can have a real impact to change a problem student's behavior and help him gain a feeling of acceptance. By contrast, if social engineering techniques (described previously) are initiated but the school climate (the actions of the other adults and classmates) still shuns the difficult student as an object of outside aggression, it will be unlikely that progress can be made.

At the end of the two-week period of the Most Wanted program, another staff meeting must be held. This will be a follow-up meeting to evaluate the success or lack of success of the welcoming process. The remainder of the staff meeting should follow the Six Steps to Staffing (described in Chapter 8) in which teachers and staff focus on the student's problem behaviors and address what actions can be taken by each of them individually to deal with misbehavior. Also, it is given that the welcoming and accepting attitude toward the difficult student should and must continue, even if not in such a ritualistic manner.

## The Encouragement Plan

An Encouragement Planning Form (Figure 10.2) is provided to guide the teacher through the planning process for establishing a clear plan to encourage one particular student. Each step requires the teacher to take some action, then write the results on the form, thus using the concepts of mis-motivation, questions that the teacher would ask herself, thinking through actions for social acceptance, and other concepts previously described.

| **FIGURE 10.2 Encouragement Planning Form** | |
|---|---|
| Name of Student | Date |
| Step (a) Observe and describe the student's behavior: | Step (b) Ask oneself, "Do I feel…" |
| 1. | |
| | (check one)___annoyed?    ___beaten? ___incapable? |
| 2. | |
| | (check one)___annoyed?    ___beaten? ___incapable? |
| 3. | |
| | (check one)___annoyed?    ___beaten? ___incapable? |
| Steps (c) Confront the student (write your verbal statements): | |
| | |
| Step (d) Verify the goal ("Could it be that you want: special attention, to be the boss, to hurt others, to be left alone?") | What is the student's goal?: |
| Step (e) Make a plan | |
| | |
| | |
| | |
| | |
| Step (f) Use the classroom group ("How could a class meeting/discussion enlist peers to help?") | |
| | |
| | |
| | |
| | |
| Step (g) State natural/logical consequences to be used. | Step (h) State encouragement strategy. |
| 1. | 1. |
| | |
| | |
| | |
| 2. | 2. |
| | |
| | |

| | |
|---|---|
| **FIGURE 10.2    Encouragement Planning Form** *(Continued)* | |
| | |
| 3. | 3. |
| | |
| | |
| | |
| Step (i) Describe social engineering strategies. | Describe a Most Wanted strategy. |
| | |
| | |
| | |
| | |
| | |
| | |
| | |
| | |

## SUMMARY

The central position of the *Three Faces of Discipline* model is that students need to find acceptance or membership with others. The Rights and Responsibilities Game serves as a start-of-the-year school process to deliberately structure this gaming activity to teach all students ways to gain group membership. The encouragement system is a process of focusing on the one or two very difficult students who the incentive system fails to help. The teacher now views the student as needing encouragement. The Teacher Behavior Continuum (Figure 10.3) summarizes the steps that teachers may use to help such students. These steps begin with observing and gathering data on the student, then determining the goal that motivates the misbehaving student. Finally, the teacher sets out a plan to help meet this goal in a socially acceptable manner.

**FIGURE 10.3  Teacher Behavior Continuum and Encouragement System**

| Looking | Naming | Questioning | Commanding | Modeling | Reinforcement | Encouragement |
|---|---|---|---|---|---|---|
| **Step (a)** Observe and collect information about the student • with peers • with family • with other teachers | | **Step (b)** Ask oneself "Do I feel..." (1) "annoyed?" (Attention getting) (2) "beaten?" (Power) (3) "incapable?" (Helplessness) | **Step (e)** Make a plan according to the verified goal. | **Step (f)** Use the classroom as an example of democratic living. Allow classmates to discuss and propose ways to help the student. | **Step (g)** State natural/logical consequences. • Do not punish. • Arrange outcome as immediately related to student misbehavior. | **Step (i)** Describe social engineering strategies and a Most Wanted strategy. |
| | | **Step (c)** Confronting "Do you want to know why you are behaving like this?" | | | **Step (h)** State encouragement strategy. • Recognize student's attempts to improve, not the end product ("You are trying...") • Avoid teacher praise ("I like what you have done...") | |
| | | **Step (d)** Verifying "Could it be that you want... • special attention?" • to be the boss?" • to hurt others?" • to be left alone?" | | | | |

## REFERENCE

Dinkmeyer, D., & Dreikurs, R. (1963). *Encouraging Children to Learn: The Encouragement Process*. Englewood Cliffs, NJ: Prentice-Hall.

## SUGGESTED READINGS

Albert, L. (1989). *A Teacher's Guide to Cooperative Discipline: How to Manage Your Classroom and Promote Self-Esteem*. Circle Pines, MN: American Guidance Service.

Dinkmeyer, D., & McKay, G. D. (1976). *Systematic Training for Effective Parenting (STEP)*. Circle Pines, MN: American Guidance Service.

Dinkmeyer, D., & McKay, G. D. (1981). *Padres Eficaces con Entrenamiento Sistematico (PECES)*. Circle Pines, MN: American Guidance Service.

Dinkmeyer, D., & McKay, G. D. (1983). *Systematic Training for Effective Parenting of Teens (STEP/Teen)*. Circle Pines, MN: American Guidance Service.

Dreikurs, R. (1964). *Children: The Challenge*. New York: Hawthorne Books.

Dreikurs, R. (1968). *Psychology in the Classroom: A Manual for Teachers* (2nd ed.). New York: Harper and Row.

Dreikurs, R. (1972). *Discipline without Tears: What to Do with Children Who Misbehave*. New York: Hawthorne Books.

Dreikurs, R., & Loren, G. (1968). *Logical Consequences*. New York: Meredith Press.

# The Management System

Discipline is not affected only by what goes on within the classroom; it is also affected by the classroom itself. How the room is set up and how the teacher makes classroom resources available to students will have a profound impact on the kind of discipline that will be necessary, and effective, with the students who will spend their school year within that room. When teams of teachers work together on a similar design and classroom procedures, students benefit by operating within a predictable structure.

The key method of eliminating many discipline problems is understanding and skillfully using the technology of management of (1) the design of classroom objects, furniture, and materials; (2) the establishment and teaching of rules; and (3) the method and techniques for beginning the school year and orienting the students to integrate all of the systems previously learned.

In short, a very direct correlation exists between the effective use of skilled management techniques and the prevention of many of the typical discipline incidents that disrupt the school day and year. The management system provides these techniques.

# 11

# Design of the Classroom

*The scene is a round table at which a group of five sixth-grade boys and girls are seated. This group is working on a geography unit in which they are to make a model of Africa. The teacher places eight large markers and a collection of art paper and materials in the middle of the table for the students to use. A marker rolls across the table and falls to the floor, and four of the five students pursue it. They are now out of their chairs and underneath the table, scrambling on hands and knees to find the runaway marker. Two of the students find it at the same time and now fight over it. A third student hits his head on the underside of the table as he forgets where he is and tries to stand. The fourth student is still crawling on hands and knees, until he gets his fingers stepped on by a passing classmate. The crawler grabs the ankle of the passing classmate causing the walking student to tumble onto the group's table, sending most of the remaining supplies flying to the floor. The teacher is immediately drawn to this group, and as a result, one-third of the students have their hands raised, wanting the teacher's attention and complaining that they do not have the needed materials.*

Chaos, conflict, and total class disruption are seen here, and major discipline problems are on their way! Whose fault is this? The fault lies with a lack of understanding of the concept of classroom.

In a direct instruction classroom, students typically are bolted to a desk and chair for long periods of time and must ask permission before they may get up and move about or do any other task. Such a regimented classroom can be organized with little care for classroom concepts. But in a case where 20 or more students are freely moving about in a fairly limited space with a host of learning centers or groups and a wide variety of equipment, this space and materials must be planned with scientific precision.

Consider any space where large numbers of people gather for specific purpose, and you will find that the space uses a concept of design that either facilitates this activity in a smooth and safe manner (a grocery store, hospital, cafeteria) or hinders the activity to the point that it can cause injuries (construction work on city streets or even a sixth-grade classroom). At the elementary school level, teachers have to deal with special area classrooms, such as art and music, as well as for special group activities in regular classrooms. At the middle and high school levels, teachers also have to deal with industrial arts classrooms, home economics classrooms, a band room, science labs, a gymnasium, and grouping arrangements in the regular classrooms—each of which is a complicated and demanding space with a wide variety of materials, furniture, and equipment.

It is imperative that the teacher who wishes to create a supportive classroom, with a minimal amount of the kind of conflict seen in the preceding marker example, actually creates a paper floor plan/map of the classroom area, as demonstrated in Figures 11.1 and 11.2. It is suggested that at the end of each day for the first 10 days a new classroom design is used (at the beginning of the school year or after the classroom has been rearranged), the teacher should mark the floor map with small check marks, indicating where some difficulty has occurred (such as the marker incident).

## SCIENTIFICALLY DESIGNED CLASSROOM: DOUBLE E CLASSROOM (FIGURE 11.1)

1. Desks/chairs are clustered into four obvious groupings—double E arrangement (teams: red, blue, green, yellow).

2. The teacher's desk is placed to the side of the room and is not a barrier between the teacher and students. The desk is close to the door, permitting the teacher to take messages delivered at the door. Also, when seated at the desk, the teacher can easily see off-task behavior. (A back-of-the-room desk, located where F table is positioned, is even better for this supervision.)

3. The pencil sharpener and waste paper basket are placed near the door.

4. The chalkboard is located at the front of the room, and the assignment board is located to the right.

5. The teacher's power position (C) is established as a position to obtain student attention.

6. Open space in front of the teacher permits the teacher to move quickly in front of every student with a minimum of steps (proximity: far, near, intimate).

FIGURE 11.1    Double E Classroom

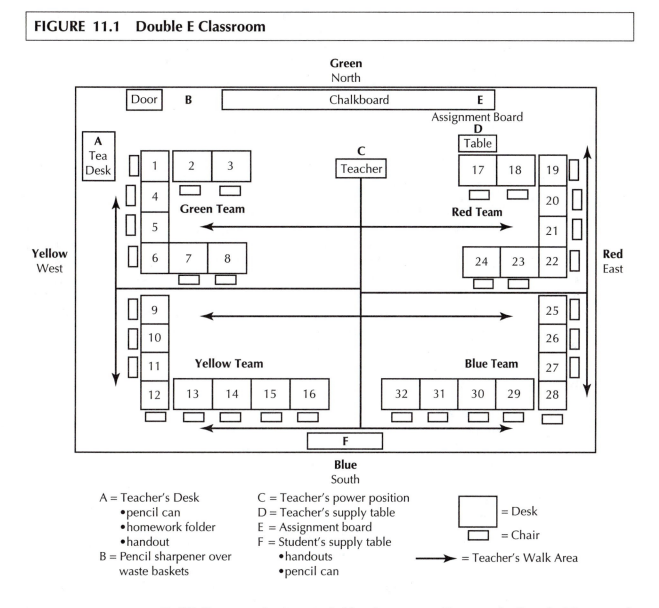

7. Walls are designated North–green, East–red, South–blue, and West–yellow, which can be used to create a student's sense of directionality in the classroom and assist in storage of materials.

## Concepts and Principles versus Techniques

Not every teacher will want to copy the technique exactly; for example, not every teacher has to have the classroom in a Double E. However, the concepts and principles should be used to guide the teacher to create a classroom arrangement and techniques that are in keeping with the *Three Faces of Discipline* framework.

1. Establish an X, Y, Z pattern on the desks of the students. Generally, X should be a high-achieving student, Y a middle-achieving student,

and Z a low-achieving student. (*Note:* Some teachers also choose to have an alternating boy-girl arrangement.)

2. Misbehaving students should be placed at desks 8, 16, 32, and 24.

3. Well-behaving and dependable students are placed at desks 6, 10, 11, 12, and 13, and at 22, 26, 27, 28, and 29.

4. During the first six weeks of the school year or a new semester, the teacher should feel free to repeatedly change students' desks so a skilled and effective cluster of students is obtained. Or using cooperative learning may necessitate different student grouping.

5. Pseudo-mature students or similar students who need excessive attention may be most effectively seated at desks 14, 15, 30, and 31. They are in direct facial position to the teacher, thus receiving *Looking* from the teacher, but the back-row position permits the teacher to determine the distance (proxemics) she or he will give or withhold with these students. Never place such students in desks 1, 4, 19, or 20 because they will repeatedly act out to get the teacher's Looking and the teacher will be drawn off to the extreme right or left.

## Floor Mapping

Drawing a schematic map of the classroom to provide the best design for the classroom space is called *floor mapping*. Many city traffic departments maintain a bulletin board map of the city streets, and place pins on the map to show where accidents occur. After a short period of time, it is evident that a handful of intersections accounts for an overwhelming percentage of accidents. *The solution?* Physically alter the troublesome intersections by using an understanding of traffic flow to prevent accidents from happening, thereby saving the considerable costs of accident damage and perhaps saving lives.

The teacher will be surprised to discover that the same process will occur on his or her classroom map. The students may literally be falling over the equipment or one another. The check marks, indicating points of conflict and difficulty, will begin to cluster at key spots on the classroom map, perhaps near a certain science station, supply cupboard, or water source. *The solution?* Alter the space by moving equipment and materials around with the concepts described here, thereby eliminating large numbers of incidents that call for disciplinary action or require the teacher to "put out a fire" (as with the rolling marker).

The arrangement of furniture and equipment within the classroom space establishes a structure that will control proximity or physical closeness of teacher to student and student to student, and, if improperly designed, can actually prevent the teacher from seeing the students who need his or her visual and personal investment (TBC's *Looking*). What follows is a description of a scientifically designed classroom arrangement that, in seconds, allows desks to be moved to create all three spheres of relationships.

Classroom space in most elementary, middle, and high schools generally supports a limited number of basic classroom teaching and learning activities: (1) lecture or direct group instruction (one-to-all relationship); (2) small group direct instruction (one-to-group relationship); (3) independent student group work (may involve one-to-one); and (4) independent work (may involve one-to-one helping).

Many middle schools operate in classrooms that are arranged in groups to facilitate cooperative learning. The classroom design suggested in Figure 11.1 lends itself well to such an arrangement. However, some middle school and most high school classrooms are set up for lecturing and direct instruction, with six rows containing six desks and chairs all facing the chalkboard, with the teacher's desk in front, a waste paper basket and a pencil sharpener near the door, and one prominently located bulletin board. What educational architect designed this classroom? Jones (1987), a leading discipline expert, would say it was the janitor. This room arrangement of furniture permits the janitor to move without stopping to run a dry mop from the door, up and down the rows and out the door again, leaving the floor "clean." The pencil sharpener and waste basket can be reached from the doorway and emptied quickly. But the furniture arrangement in rows forces a one-to-all (teacher to students) relationship and communicates coldness and distance that can make the students feel as if they are nothing more than numbers who will be herded into their stall-like seats, force-fed a diet of academic content, and herded to the next feeding carrel when the bell rings.

So, how can the classroom teacher arrange the desks and chairs so that direct instruction (such as a lecture) may occur with as much intimacy as possible? The answer lies with the construct of spatial proximity (proximity far, proximity near, and proximity intimate) as well as eye contact. Intimacy is expressed at an eye-to-eye nonverbal level from the first moments of life; an infant meets her parent eye to eye and face to face and later through "peek-a-boo"—deliberately engineered play in which the parent's eyes are "lost" and then joyfully "found" again. The traditional arrangement of desks in a row inhibits the teacher's freedom to move physically close to students. This prevents the TBC's *Looking* while the teacher is lecturing, blocking the teacher's visual investment in her students. The construct of the double E configuration is recommended whenever possible.

Using Figure 11.1 as a guide, desks and chairs can be arranged in the E and reverse E patterns. Once the desks are properly arranged, these directions can be followed:

1. *Floor (visual) prompts:* Using a permanent marker (or tape), draw circles on the floor around the feet of desks 1, 12, 28, and 19. These marks will serve as visual prompts for the students as to where the desks should be located, thus providing anchor desks for other students to use in arranging their rows. Small symbols may be placed on the wall in eight key locations to serve as visual prompts for desk alignment, permitting most students to look front and back or left

and right to find two or three alignment points to know if their desks are in line. If possible, the teacher may have lines painted in a double E arrangement on the floor so that the front legs of each desk can be placed on the line prompt.

2. *Teacher's desk:* The teacher's desk (letter A) is never placed in the front of the room because one wants the students and their desks to be as close as possible to the front chalkboard and to the teacher (at letter C). Placing the desk in front of the room would create a barrier between the teacher and the students. The desk located near the door and off to the side provides easy access for the teacher. Placed on top of the desk would be a pencil can (extra old pencils to be borrowed by students) and a homework folder (students will always know where to place their written work as they arrive and depart past this desk). Students will also be taught to pass by this table to look for and pick up any handouts.

3. *Waste can / Sharpener:* At the B location will be a pencil sharpener and a waste basket underneath it. Students moving in and out of the room will repeatedly pass these two items and can use them quickly—and the janitor will love it.

4. *Assignment board:* One end of the chalkboard is always dedicated to an Assignment Board (E). The students will be able to depend on finding their current assignments in writing here, listed in descending order of priority by the teacher.

5. *Storage:* A small table (D) placed before desk 17 will serve as a storage place for items the teacher needs to have nearby while teaching. This is not a space to be shared by students.

6. *Table F:* A table of flat surface holds any materials that the teacher displays and wishes the students to inspect.

7. *Seat assignment:* After sufficient time, the teacher will be able to identify those students who are going to be discipline problems and those who will be very well behaved with a strong, dependable academic ability. The problem students will be placed in desks 3, 8, 16, 32, 24, and 17. This will keep these difficult students in the proximity-near position, only a few steps from the teacher, in the teacher's power position (C). Students who are very well behaved and have strong academic ability will be seated at desks 11, 12, 13, 29, 28, and 27. These desks will be in proximity-far, so the teacher will want to have very independent and trustworthy students in these seats.

8. *Adding desks:* The map (Figure 11.1) shows seating for 32 students, but more than this number can be added by placing them in this order:
   - Desks 33 and 34 are placed between seats 6 and 7, pushing seats 7 and 8 deep into the middle of the room.
   - Desks 35 and 36 are placed between seats 22 and 23, pushing seats 23 and 24 deeper into the middle of the room.

- If still more desks must be placed into this arrangement, remove table F and create a row of desks centered in the back of the room and directly facing the teacher.

9. *Pathways:* Notice that the arrow lines show the teacher's walking area, permitting him or her to "work the crowd" and see all students without being embedded in furniture. Notice the openings between seats 9 and 6, 22 and 25, and 16 and 32; these permit the teacher to move behind the students and camp out from behind.

**Classroom Mapping Activity (Figure 11.2)**

1. Cut out silhouettes of furniture.

2. Draw classroom walls on grid paper (1 square = 1 foot).

3. Draw in or color with markers to show rugs or permanent items such as doors, windows, water fountains, shelving, and so on.

4. Arrange silhouetted furniture in a classroom design:
   a. Permit quick proximity to all students.
   b. Allow for effective transitions between groups of students.
   c. Determine, based on the map, the degree of openness-closeness.

5. During the first weeks of school or the semester, place a small check mark on the map where a discipline difficulty has occurred. These checks will cluster, indicating that you may need to move the seating of certain students or change the space with regard to "control of error."

## THREE SPHERES OF RELATIONSHIP

A classroom that brings together students and a teacher involves degrees of relationships, and it is the quality of those relationships that will enable students to feel welcomed and accepted. Adults who are put in charge in institutional settings (nurses in hospitals, guards in prisons, teachers in schools) or businesses (airline counter attendants, store check-out personnel), when under day-in and day-out stress, may begin to show institutional behavior. They begin to deal with the public in a mechanical manner, showing curt speech, flat expressionless behavior, and an unthinking administration of the rules. They exhibit little consideration of the needs of the individual with whom they are dealing and communicate no warmth. This same attitude can be seen in the behavior of some teachers in the elementary, middle, and high school classrooms, especially if the classroom is imbalanced with too many students, lacks adequate help for the teacher, and lacks equipment and classroom material.

The airline counter attendant is burned out because he has to manage too many passengers. A snowstorm has grounded five flights and he must deal with literally hundreds of angry passengers—the situation is

**FIGURE 11.2  Classroom Mapping**

obviously out of balance. Teachers working in an imbalanced classroom (too many students, not enough equipment or materials) can begin to become burned out and take on institutional behavior. Students may spend eight hours a day traveling to and from school and in classrooms, and they feel the need for significant emotional investment by administration and teachers. To go days, weeks, or months being cared for or taught by adults and teachers who are depressive and burned out can have a real and lasting destructive effect on groups of students. The three spheres of relationship construct can be used to determine how to best use time with students.

---

### SPHERES OF RELATIONSHIP

| | | |
|---|---|---|
| One to One | A teacher interacts with one student (knee to knee); a private meeting. | The student receives near to total emotional attention from the teacher and may dominate conversation. |
| One to Group | A teacher interacts with a small group of 4 to 8 students. | The student feels more emotional connectedness with the teacher and peers, but needs to share conversation with peers. |
| One to All | A teacher speaks or teaches to the total group of students. | The student feels little emotional contact (a spatial distance) with teacher, and must generally inhibit the desire to talk and instead must simply listen. |

---

Viewed in reverse order, the *one-to-all sphere* is a lecture format where the students must sit passively, refrain from communicating, and listen to the teacher speak.

The *one-to-group sphere* occurs where the teacher is seated together with a group of four to eight students and there is conversation among all members of the group. An example of this would be when the teacher is working with a cooperative group of students at a science table. More warmth is felt among this smaller group, but the students do have to share the teacher's warmth and attention with their table mates—one teacher to a group of up to eight students.

The *one-to-one sphere* is the time when the teacher and student are totally invested in one another, screening out others. The student can receive total warmth and attention from the teacher and is free to dominate the conversation. Such Relationship-Listening techniques as active listening, door openers, and acknowledgments can be very helpful in communicating with students during this one-to-one sphere of relationship, and to a lesser extent with a group of students in the one-to-group sphere.

The anger and excessive need for attention that many students feel today is a result of the institutional behavior they see as emotionless and lacking in caring. They may have first felt this in group daycare as a very young child, and seen a continuation from a host of elementary school teachers—and perhaps even from busy parents who have not given them attention and time at home. The dramatic increase in discipline problems reflects the large number of students wanting a relationship and social interaction with adults. If it does not come to them through positive behavior, they become discipline problems and get it in the negative form. These students are saying by their behavior, "Please see me!"

Every student should get sufficient personal time with a teacher. In staff meetings and during teacher planning time, the three spheres construct can be used in planning the student's day to assure that every student will have a relationship with the teacher in each of the three spheres. The double E classroom arrangement demonstrates how the teacher may physically have students move in to and out of groups with little confusions or discipline activities. Most discipline incidents occur during transitions, and a clear understanding of how to make these movements will eliminate much of this difficulty.

## Making a Group of Two

The students transition into groups of two by simply turning toward their partner, following basic combinations. The partners are:

*Group: North–East*
(Red Team)        1 and 4        5 and 6        7 and 8        2 and 3

*Group: South–East*
(Blue Team)       9 and 10      11 and 12     13 and 14     15 and 16

*Group: North–West*
(Green Team)     17 and 18     19 and 20     21 and 22     23 and 24

*Group: South–West*
(Yellow Team)    25 and 26     27 and 28     29 and 30     31 and 32

Notice that the students located in desks 12 and 28 present a problem. Should they be seated facing north toward the chalkboard, or east and west so they will be seated beside their partner for group work without needing to continually move? The answer depends on which location enables these two students to see the chalkboard best (alternatively, the teacher may simply elect to give them a choice).

## Making a Group of Four or Eight

The double E desk arrangement also permits quick movement into group work that might involve four or eight students in a group (see Figure 11.3). For example, this can be done by having desk 2 pull back and put the front of that desk against the back of desk 4; repeat the process with desk 3 joining desk 1, desk 8 joining desk 5, and desk 7 joining desk 6. This creates an easy group of eight. To have groups of four, simply force a space between desks 4 and 5, and create two groups of four with desks 4, 1, 2, and 3 sliding north in the classroom. This can be done in like manner with the remaining three large groups. Numbers 9, 10, 11, and 12 should swing to join the stationary 13, 14, 15, and 16, and in like fashion, desks 25, 26, 27, and 28 swing to their counterparts 32, 31, 30, and 29. It is important to teach the students which desks move and which stay in place during changes.

## Making a Group of Three

A group of three (see Figure 11.4) can also be formed from the basic E arrangement, but usually is done by keeping all desks in place and having one student carry his or her chair and place it behind the chairs

---

**FIGURE 11.3    A Group of Four and Eight Arrangment**

FIGURE 11.4    A Group of Three Arrangement

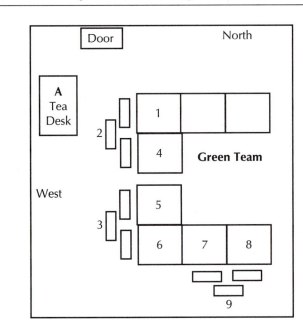

of two other students, centered between the two receiving chairs and desks. The teacher will need to clearly identify which students are to move and which pair is to receive a third member. This may be done as follows:

*Green and Yellow Team*
Student moving chair behind pair

| 3 | 2 | 11 | 10 | 9 |
|---|---|----|----|---|

Pair receiving student above

| 5 and 6 | 1 and 4 | 14 and 15 | 12and 13 | 7 and 8 |
|---------|---------|-----------|----------|---------|

*Red and Blue Team*
Student moving chair behind pair

| 17 | 18 | 27 | 26 | 25 |
|----|----|----|----|----|

Pair receiving student above

| 21 and 22 | 19 and 20 | 31 and 32 | 30 and 29 | 24 and 23 |
|-----------|-----------|-----------|-----------|-----------|

Numbers 32 and 16 are still without partners, so 32 moves his seat to number 16, thus forming a pair; if three people are required for the activity, the teacher joins this pair.

If the desk and chair is a single piece of furniture that cannot be moved as simply (or quietly), the following combinations can be used quickly:

*Green and Yellow Team*
Student moving desk-chair combination

| 1 | 8 | 7 | 13 | 12 |

Pair stationary and receiving student above

| 2 and | 4 and | 6 and | 10 and | 14 and |
| 3 | 5 | 9 both | 11 | 15 |
| | | moving | | |

*Red and Blue Team*
Student moving desk-chair combination

| 19 | 24 | 23 | 29 | 28 |

Pair stationary and receiving student above

| 17 and | 20 and | 22 and | 26 and | 31 and |
| 18 | 21 | 25 both | 27 | 30 |
| | | moving | | |

Numbers 32 and 16 are still without partners, so 32 moves his seat to number 16, thus forming a pair; if three people are required for the activity, the teacher joins the pair. In the description of the movements from the basic double E arrangement, we have used an arbitrary class size of 32 students for purposes of example. Each teacher's class size will vary dramatically, so it is important to understand the smooth organized movements between the pairs and groups of 3, 4, and 8, and make minor adjustment to the preceding movements to accommodate the particular number of students involved.

This double E basic lecture classroom is a well-engineered design and has these advantages:

1. The teacher is not behind any barriers and can move quickly from her power position in order to use proximity-near or intimate and eye contact. During instruction, students will be able to feel the presence and greater intimacy from the teacher because the teacher will actually come to them and make eye contact.

2. With the simplest command, the teacher can have each member of a pair turn and face each other or move to groups of 3, 4, and 8 to immediately begin working as a team and just as quickly return to a lecture arrangement. This feature is especially useful in middle schools that employ cooperative learning groups in classrooms, but also, at times, include full group instruction.

3. Misbehaving students are in the closest proximity to the teacher at all times, permitting the teacher to use eye contact and be close to the student's comfort bubble. Misbehaving students generally need this attention and feeling of closeness.

4. Students can use the visual prompts (marks) on the floor and walls of the room and can centrally place their desks without repeated directions or nagging from the teacher.

5. Students can obtain handouts and turn in assignments in a predictable manner and as a matter of routine.

6. The assignment board always communicates to the students what work they should be doing as seatwork and in what order. As soon as they walk through the door, they will begin the first item as a matter of routine at every class period. If the students work quickly, there is always a catch-all general assignment at the bottom of the assignment list (such as reading a library book) (see Figure 11.5).

7. The seating arrangement creates four spatially clustered teams (Northeast, which we will label the Red Team, Southeast as the Blue Team, Northwest as the Green, and Southwest as Yellow) that can be used as competitive teams as a part of the incentive system (explained previously).

---

**FIGURE 11.5   North-Green Wall**

Motor rules will need to be taught for using the trash can, pencil sharpener, light switch, chalkboard, and assignment board.

The bulletin board may be covered with the color coordination of the room wall (in this case, with a north wall, it would be green).

Light Switch

Chalkboard

Bulletin Board

Green Paper

Wastepaper can

Teacher's Power Position

Calendar

Through teaching students attending behaviors, the teacher would create a spot to stand that would get the class's attention — "the power point."

The assignment board would always contain the first two assignments; the third would be a general assignment such as "When done with the first two assignments, read a book!"

8. When students are taking a test and need to be seated so they are not tempted to look at another student's paper, every odd-numbered desk can be pulled backward one desk length and every even-numbered desk pushed forward one desk length. In a matter of seconds the students can be in, and out, of a test seating arrangement, moved by the teacher's simple verbal prompt: "Testing positions."

9. The double E seating arrangement permits total group discussion because, with the exception of just eight students (2, 3, 7, 8, 17, 18, 24, and 23), every student can see anyone who is talking, and with a slight turn of the head most of the eight can see a high percentage of their classmates.

## Motor (or Spatial) Rules

Automatic motor actions suggested by the room or zone in which the student is located (such as throwing paper in the trash when done with it, closing the door behind you, or putting things away when done) are called *motor rules*. The double E basic desk arrangement does almost everything the teacher needs. It supports a lecture format or direct group instruction (a one-to-all relationship), small group direct instruction (one-to-group—with two, four, or eight members), and independent student group work (may involve one-to-one). It also provides the open walkways that permit the teacher to get immediately to a student (may involve one-to-one helping).

A concept of classroom means engineering the basic furniture and equipment in the classroom to serve a predetermined function. When the teacher has developed a clear understanding of the desk arrangement, the students can be taught key classroom verbal prompts during the first days of school. Within seconds, a classroom full of students can be positioned for a new form of teaching and learning.

## CLASSROOM TRANSITIONS

Except for fire drills (which are practiced in advance), teachers are advised never to issue a command for the entire group to perform in one mass action—an entire gym class, an auditorium of 1,000 students, or a classroom of 32. The aggressive student will bolt for the door, knocking over others and possibly even causing injury. In addition, the teacher can never be sure that his or her prompt command is understood by everyone, when forgetting is symptomatic with students. Therefore, it is best to view any classroom group, for purposes of making any transition, through the concept of transitional threes. One-fourth of the group is requested to move first; the teacher and other students watch this group to see if these students are performing the correct actions. Then a second group—involving approximately one-half of the class—is asked to move, before the final one-fourth is asked to clean and organize the area before making the transition.

*The seventh-grade teacher has all 32 students seated at their desks in a double E configuration. Having completed a directive lesson, he now needs all the students to move to the science tables at the back of the room. With the help of students, he has previously prepared each of these tables with beakers, delicate instruments, and a host of similar sensitive materials. If he commands, "Class, move to the lab tables," there will be a mass exit from the desks, with students pushing to be seated with friends. This, of course, carries a likelihood that something will get broken or someone will get injured.*

*Instead, the teacher follows the concept of transitional threes, dismissing one-fourth of the class first. "Class, in just a few minutes I will dismiss you in groups to move to the back tables to carry out your science experiments. You will remember that what you are to do and in what order is written here on the Assignment Board. Follow these directions, please. Now, don't move until I tell you, but Blue Team will move first. Remember, I have already assigned you a spot at the science tables. Remember that on these tables are delicate items, so I want you to move slowly and safely to your seat and wait until everyone is seated at their places before you begin. Mark, I see you turning on the Bunsen burners. The rule is to wait until everyone is seated. Would you please return to your classroom seat." Having sent one-quarter of the students as the first group, the teacher observes to see if they are modeling the proper behavior. If they are not, the teacher reteaches the rule or may take other corrective actions (such as sending Mark back to his classroom seat).*

*At this time, the teacher is assured that everyone has seen the rules properly carried out by the first group and now feels comfortable with dismissing the second, larger group consisting of about half the class. "Would the Red and Yellow Teams move carefully to the lab tables, now. Finally, I would like the Green Team to erase the board, pick up any waste papers laying on the floor, arrange the desks, and then move to your science positions." Finally, the teacher says, "Mark, you may now take your spot at the science table."*

When the class moves out of a special zone, the last group to be dismissed is responsible for ordering and cleaning up that space before moving on. For example, in physical education class, the final group may be asked to pick up the bases, bats, balls, and any other equipment and carry the items to the storage area.

*The teacher checks his watch and sees that there is only five minutes left before the students must leave for the school assembly in the auditorium. Because everyone is working and visually and sensorily invested in the table activity, he does not broadcast across the entire class by shouting, "OK, now every-one listen up—here is what I want you to do." Such broadcast-ing-shouting will produce a number of negative effects. For one, the teacher would be modeling shouting in the classroom, encouraging the students to follow this example. Second, since the students are engrossed in their work, only a few will really hear the instruction and will take forever to give proper atten-tion. Instead, the teacher moves into each group and gives the announcement as preparatory to a transition. "Students in this group, you have three minutes to finish up and get ready to return to your seats. See the steps for cleaning up that I have written on the chalkboard—all of these steps need to be accom-plished. When I see your group done cleaning, I will dismiss you to your classroom seats."*

*Getting out the door when the bell rings is a powerful incentive for students. The directions as given use that incen-tive to create a contingency contract. "Do this (clean up) and you will get this reward (able to depart)." On the chalkboard are the verbal prompts for guiding the students through the steps of cleaning up, thus taking the burden off the teacher or requiring the teacher to nag. The teacher now works the crowd, watching for how the students are cleaning up, tutoring if nec-essary, and waiting until three-fourths of the students are ready. Seeing that three-quarters are now ready, the teacher dismisses one table first (group one), then dismisses all but the last table (group two), and then asks this last table to order and clean whatever items need to be taken care of. Students are now in their classroom seats when the bell rings.*

*Again, the teacher will use the concept of transitional threes. This routine of dismissal will be rotated with each of the four teams having a chance to go first, but always moving out as three separate groups—the concept of transitional threes in action.*

A number of summary points need to be made about handling tran-sitions. The students need to know where they are going and what action they will perform once they get there. It is necessary to teach this to them before the transition begins and to have a verbal prompt, such as the list of steps on the chalkboard. There could also have been activity cards placed on each table for that group to follow, particularly if each group will be doing different work. The teacher dismisses in three groups, monitoring behavior. Finally, the teacher is now free to work the crowd.

At first glance, this may seem a bit too structured. But remember, many of today's children are growing up with a lack of home structure to teach behavior concerning how to work with regard to time, rules of behavior, and care of property. After the principles of classroom man-agement and management technology are learned, a teacher can partially relax some of the structure because the steps have been learned as habits and the students can exhibit self-control. By the third day of class and thereafter, when the dismissal bell rings, no student stands to go running out the classroom door; instead, all students wait and know the structure of how dismissal will unfold. The world for them is predictable, understandable, and secure. Jones (1987) proclaimed, "Either the teacher sets the classroom agenda or the students will set the agenda!" (p. 46).

## Verbal Prompts

When people live together in a closed space, over time they develop an "in"-group language to the point where one member might give a verbal statement (a prompt) and all members, having shared past experiences, understand that a host of future actions will occur. For example, a group of friends is traveling in the fall in the Northeast, and at every rest stop they see a huge display of fresh red apples for sale. Later, when one member feels a need for a rest stop, he simply gives the verbal prompt, "Apple time." Everyone laughs and knows exactly what that passenger wants to do. However, a stranger having recently joined that "in" group may not understand. These short abbreviated verbal prompts save the group time and effort. Rather than saying three paragraphs to explain what is wanted and what will happen next, one member simply utters one word or phrase ("Apple time") and everyone understands. This type of group familiarity must quickly be developed in the first minutes of each semester with a new group of students. Thus, we have the concept of Mars Days (described in Chapter 13), where we pretend that these students have just come from another planet, and we teach the abbreviated verbal prompts to facilitate good transitions.

## Group Transition Prompts

- *Order and clean:* This prompt is given by the teacher at the beginning of each class and is the last prompt before students depart, getting all students to slightly move their desks by using the floor and wall prompts.

- *Testing positions:* Moving odd-numbered desks back one length and even-numbered desks forward so the students will not be tempted to look on classmates' papers.

- *Pair groups:* Odd- and even-numbered partners will turn to face each other and work together.

- *Groups of three:* One-third of the students will move their chairs behind a preassigned pair.

- *Groups of eight:* Certain students will move their desks against a counterpart's desk to form eight-desk clusters.

- *Groups of four:* Groups of four should only be reached after the students first move to groups of eight, with a second prompt moving them to have the group separate to fours.

## Directionality (Materials)

Orienting oneself in space, even classroom space, involves directionality. In arranging space for purposes of having a *concept of classroom,* the teacher can use the directions of north, south, east, and west. We have now organized desks and chairs, formed students into groups of twos, threes, fours, and eights, and have shown how to make transitions between spaces. Now it is time to gain control of materials. Materials are a specific problem in classroom management because they have to be kept in some order to access them when needed. They have to be stored for their care and safety while at the same time 30 or more students are taking them from storage, using them, and hopefully returning them for future use. This materials management problem is solved by the concept of directionality and the concept of storage (left to right, top to bottom).

Simply put, any student using any material that is not fixed to the wall or floor knows what to do if the teachers says, "Please put this item away." The student should (1) turn and walk to the wall where the item is stored and (2) be able to place the item on shelving or in the drawer where it is stored. Every student should be able to do this with every item every time—a quality system.

---

### COLOR CUEING

A systematic method of marking instructional materials with colored marks so that the students can readily identify the object and its proper shelf or storage location.

---

## Visual Prompts

When visiting the restrooms at Happy Harry's Crab House, one must choose between two doors, Gulls and Buoys. How do we know which door to choose, other than deciphering the cute verbal signs? The answer is symbolic visual prompt, through the symbol of a man or woman placed at eye level on the outside of the bathroom door. Hundreds of visual prompts positively control our behavior. A symbol of a cigarette inside a red circle with a crossing red slash tells us that smoking is not permitted in that area; a blue sign with a white wheelchair emblem tells us that the parking space is reserved for drivers who are disabled.

Teachers can use a similar visual prompt system, in the form of color coding, to control students' behavior positively when they use materials in the classroom (see Figure 11.6). Some classrooms have scores of reference books, dozens of hand tools with a host of related pieces, a huge collection of equipment, and a wide variety of supplies. Large numbers of today's students come to school without an orderliness or structure in the objects they use and live with at home, and you are now asking 30 of them to do this at school. Needless to say, this can be a major challenge. The solution is to teach students to use color prompts and symbolic visual prompts to help make sure each article finds its proper storage location.

First, through the spatial concept of directionality, arbitrarily declare the north wall to use all green prompts, the south wall to use blue prompts, the east wall for red, and the west wall for yellow. Use construction paper, tape, wallpaper boarders, or any other solidly colored item with these four colors, placing them on the appropriate walls in a decorative manner so it becomes obvious that each wall has its own specific color. Once this has been established, every material or the container used to bring items out from storage will be marked with a colored prompt, corresponding to the color of the wall on which it is stored. Once these items have been used by the student and are ready to be put away, the student needs only to look at it and think, "Oh, yellow!" and can stand and turn to the west (yellow) wall and know that these items belong somewhere on that wall (see Figure 11.7).

The next step in the materials return and storage is to place the item in the predesignated location for that item. Materials can be stored on or near a wall in a number of ways:

**FIGURE 11.6   Visual Prompts: Color/Number/Symbol/Word**

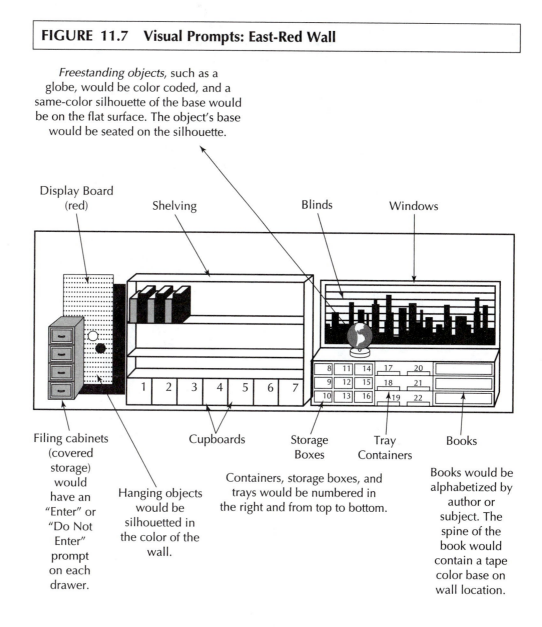

**FIGURE 11.7    Visual Prompts: East-Red Wall**

*Freestanding objects,* such as a globe, would be color coded, and a same-color silhouette of the base would be on the flat surface. The object's base would be seated on the silhouette.

Display Board (red)    Shelving    Blinds    Windows

Filing cabinets (covered storage) would have an "Enter" or "Do Not Enter" prompt on each drawer.

Hanging objects would be silhouetted in the color of the wall.

Cupboards    Storage Boxes    Tray Containers    Books

Containers, storage boxes, and trays would be numbered in the right and from top to bottom.

Books would be alphabetized by author or subject. The spine of the book would contain a tape color base on wall location.

- Hung from hooks, nails, or velcro
- Self-standing on the floor or flat on a shelf
- Stored on shelves within containers
- Stored in drawers, blocked by a visual barrier
- Stored on shelves behind doors, blocked by a visual barrier

## Hung Items

Most everyone has seen the industrial arts teacher's display of hand tools. A hole is drilled through the tool's handle for the purpose of hanging it on a nail or hook; the item is placed against the wall and a silhouette drawn around it so that when the tool is taken away, a symbolic prompt for a hammer is then painted to match the color of the wall on which the hammer will be stored. Each of the hanging items must be marked with the same color by using such marking devices as paint, plastic tape, or even small dabs of fingernail polish. Now, when Jeff the carpenter needs a hammer, large yardstick, and similar items, he will know where to find them and—more important for a host of reasons, safety being the biggest one—he will now be able to turn to the correct wall, find the symbol prompt, and hang the item back on the wall. This silhouetted symbol prompt can be used in a similar manner for all other classrooms with similar wall displays of equipment.

## Free-Standing Items

A globe used for geography lessons may be stored at the south-blue wall, either standing freely on the floor or on the flat surface of a shelf. The teacher locates the globe at a logical predetermined location and uses the base of the globe to paint a silhouette in the wall's color. Unfortunately, the base produces a common round silhouette that would not immediately identify the globe as the source of the shape. Therefore, the teacher cuts out a picture of a globe from a school supply catalogue and glues this to the center of the circle (symbolic prompts) and might actually write in block letters the word globe. To keep the paper letters or picture from being accidentally torn off through wear, the teacher covers it with clear epoxy paint. A similar process is used for all free-standing items that will be stored on flat surfaces or shelves. Each of these free-standing items is also marked with the color of the storage wall on which it is housed.

## Containers on Shelves

Many types of items come in large quantities that would be impossible to color-code individually, while others are expendable (i.e., color construction paper) and must be kept together and housed in storage containers. In such a case, the container itself is marked with the wall color and the color prompt is placed where the container is to be stored.

## Drawer Storage

Drawer storage presents two problems. First, when the drawer is closed, the student is unable to see what is inside. This can be solved by cutting a picture from a supply catalogue and gluing it to the outside of the drawer (visual prompt), including the object's written name (verbal prompt). Do not depend on name only. Second, if small items (paperclips, pencils, rubber bands, etc.) get scattered about, it can be quite frustrating just "scratching" through the mess trying to locate them. Inside the drawer, all small items should therefore be stored in small cardboard boxes, each with the name of the item written in block letters. Covers should be torn off these boxes so the items can be seen and not be covered by a second barrier. This way, if you are looking for a rubber band and find the drawer with its symbol, only to open it and find an empty box with the words rubber band written inside, you can stop your search, knowing that there are none available. That may be frustrating, but it would be even more frustrating to search for another 10 minutes, never to locate one, and still not know if you have searched in the right location. As a further visual prompt for students, you may also place the visual prompt of touch or don't touch (see Figure 11.8) on the outside of the drawer.

### Storage behind Doors

Often, items are stored behind closed doors, thus creating a barrier as to what is to be found inside. This is especially a problem when it comes time to put away items that belong behind these doors. To solve this problem, use visual prompts (picture of the items) and verbal prompts (item names). Once the doors are open, treat the shelf storage just like any other shelf organization with the use of prompts.

## Storage and Display

Manipulative objects stored in containers or on shelves need to be arranged in such a manner that students can predictably retrieve them and return them. The materials are placed on the shelves in a left-to-right and top-to-bottom organization. The first materials located in the container on the top left shelf would be the ones with the least academic or physical challenge. Moving to the right on the same shelf, the containers would contain increasingly difficult materials, dropping to the shelf below and repeating the same left-to-right arrangement based on difficulty or complexity. For example, if the teacher is arranging geometric puzzles on the shelf in an eighth-grade classroom, the puzzle placed in the first left position would be the least complicated, and easiest to solve, and the puzzles would become more complicated as you move further to the right. The puzzles would continue in difficulty onto the second shelf in the same manner from left to right. The most difficult manipulatives would always be found in the right corner of the bottom shelf.

---

**FIGURE 11.8    Visual Prompts**

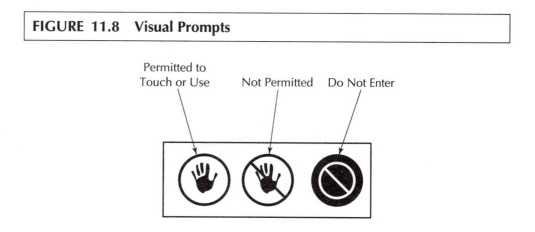

## Control of Error

Returning to the earlier example of the disruption caused by the rolling marker and the sixth-grade students in geography class, the scene can be changed to a more orderly classroom, where the teacher has taken the markers and cemented the marker caps upside-down in an empty, cleaned tuna can. The markers can then be placed back into the cemented caps and placed on the table for the students to use, providing a number of benefits. The students may take out, use, and replace the markers, always knowing where they belong. In addition, storing the markers in fixed caps prevents them from rolling off the table. And, since the markers are now always stored facing down, gravity will keep the tips moist for quick use by the students. There is now less likelihood that the markers will be laying about on a table or in a box, accidentally marking the table or drying out in the open air. The teacher in this classroom has deliberately engineered into the activity and materials the invaluable concept of control and error (see Figure 11.9). The students are less likely to make a mistake or have a problem using the material, and the teacher has prevented potential discipline situations

---

**FIGURE 11.9   Control of Error**

such as those created by having students scrambling on hands and knees under the table and across the floor chasing a runaway marker.

Every space and all materials must be evaluated to determine if they can be creatively engineered, using the concept of control of error, so that students may be free to use materials with little concern for breakage or for the kinds of accidents that may disrupt daily classroom activities. Educational games with many pieces that tend to get lost can be stored and used on small cafeteria trays. Smocks for painting or messy science experiments, plastic eye shields for hammering at the carpentry table—all these provide control of error.

---

### CONTROL OF ERROR

Arranging and putting together materials in a manner that minimizes the chances that students will break, spill, or have accidents while using them.

---

## Bulletin Boards

The best bulletin boards are those that teach; students, therefore, should participate in creating the bulletin boards. Student projects based on the subject matter can be designed so that the final products make good displays on bulletin boards. Never use bulletin boards or wall space to display students' work, which would allow a comparison revealing best to worst students. This is humiliating to the student who has done poorly and uncomfortable to the insecure young adolescent who has done well and might be "put down" for this by peers. Local and national teacher conferences regularly feature educational materials such as teacher "hint" books. Try to find ones that demonstrate a wide array of bulletin board designs. If all else fails, buy the art teacher lunch and see if you can convince him or her to use your classroom space to display seasonal art projects normally done in the art class.

## Posting Class Rules

Posting four to six class rules—positive statements saying what to do rather than what not to do—is a very common practice. These rules are most effective if they are consistent with rules in other classes on the team, if the team concept is being used, or with the schoolwide rules. An example would be:

Rule 1: Bring all needed materials to class.

Rule 2: Be in your seat and ready to begin work when the bell rings.

Rule 3: Respect and be polite to all people.

Rule 4: Do not talk or leave your desk when someone else is talking.

Rule 5: Respect other people's property.

Rule 6: Obey all school rules. (Emmer, Evertson, Sanford, Clements, & Worsham, 1984).

Tradition and discipline models such as Assertive Discipline say that these four to six rules should be permanently posted on the bulletin board. The wisdom of this practice can be questioned for a number of reasons:

1. After 10 days, the students visually saturate on the list and really stop paying attention to it, rendering it ineffective as a verbal prompt. Therefore, the list should be used during the first three weeks of school, or during Mars Days, and then take it down. Put it up again when Mars Days are employed—normally after long holidays, when good spring weather "springs," or any time you feel that these rules are not being obeyed and need to be retaught using this list as a verbal prompt.

2. Rules have to be taught through the process of Say, Show, and Check or Do (see Chapter 12), and once they are learned as habit, the posted list is of very little value.

3. The list of the four to six rules appears as the teacher's holy written commandments, and, if posted permanently, can seem repressive. In addition, the list will begin to weather and yellow and become esthetically offensive to look at day in and day out.

## Pets and Plants

Both pets and plants can add interest to a classroom, but they are meaningful to students only if they care for the creatures themselves. If pets and plants are the teacher's hobby and students are not permitted to look after them, they will see these fascinating items as your possessions, and the pets or plants will be ignored. Mount a record-keeping chart near the plant or pet and require the caregiver to record the amount of water and food given so that the living items are cared for properly.

## Audiovisual and Similar Equipment

During the first six weeks of a new school year (Mars Days), when using a new piece of audiovisual equipment for instructional purposes for the first time, teach one of the four teams how to use the equipment. Conduct this "training" as you are working with the equipment so you do not lose time doing so, and continue the processes until all groups are trained. From that point on, give two members of the groups responsibility among all groups and all students.

## Care of the Windows and Blinds

At about 10 A.M. during the fall and spring months, the sun streams into your classroom, making a blinding glare on the chalkboard and overheating the classroom. Place the care of windows and blinds on a Student Job List, and teach and assign the yellow and blue teams (nearest to the windows) to care for the windows and blinds. Teach them to watch for certain daily patterns and take appropriate actions to eliminate the problem.

## Turning Lights On and Off

When using the concept of transitional threes, teach the last group when departing the room to turn off the classroom lights and teach the first group when arriving to turn them back on.

## Teacher's Desk, Filing Cabinets, and Bookcases

The second-best location for the teacher's desk, if it cannot be placed as shown in Figure 11.1, is at the back of the room and near the west wall. When seated, the teacher can visually scan the students. In fact, if a teacher repeatedly catches the eyes of a student while the class is doing seatwork, it may be a sign that some students are off task and "something is going on." It is wise for a teacher to decide whether the top and inside of the desk belongs only to him or her or whether the top is to be shared with the students (picking up handouts and depositing homework); the inside space should only be accessed by the teacher. During the first days of the semester, students need to know the rules regarding the use of the top and inside of the teacher's desk, as well as filing cabinets, bookcases, and similar storage areas.

## Storage of Hand-Carried Items

Some students are packrats, carrying excessive items that take up too much desk space and surrounding floor space. They may have to carry these items in a backpack or gym bag. Desktops should be free for students to work on, and aisles clear so teachers can work the crowd. Instructing students to leave their backpacks in their lockers and to bring only what they need for class assists in keeping the aisles clear and discourages excessive items. Caution the students against bringing excessive items that are not needed for your instruction. When they are brought despite warnings, the offending student can be sent back to his or her locker to deposit these items. Then, as a logical consequence, keep the student after the bell rings, to work for two minutes before he or she is permitted to leave. (Remember, getting out of the door as soon as possible is a real incentive for most students).

Teachers may also choose to place a large open storage box at the back of the classroom, put a small box of sticky labels nearby, and permit the student to stick a label with his or her name on the item and place the item in the box. Simply point to the item and point to the box (visual prompt)—the student will understand. Put a disclaimer on this box, stating that the teacher is not responsible for these items if they are stolen. Teach this procedure during the first days of the semester.

## Pencil Sharpening

The rule regarding pencil sharpening is the teacher's preference. If a teacher is annoyed by the grinding sound of the sharpener or suspect the students are playing games with "going to the sharpener" to pass a friend a note, pencil-sharpening rules can be taught the very first day of school. As a back-up position, some teachers find a supply of grungy old broken pencils and put them in a pencil can for students to borrow. Jones (1987) suggested that if you do not have grungy pencils, actually break up some good ones so they are not appealing.

Have two cans, one marked "in" and one marked "out." When a student's pencil breaks, he puts his "pointless" good pencil in the "in" can and takes a grungy one from the "out" can. At the end of the period, the student can return the teacher's pencil and retrieve his own. For a student who does not have a pencil, some teachers require that the student actually take off one shoe and place it on the table by the "in" can. When the student has returned the teacher's pencil, he can retrieve his shoe. No pencils "walk" off this way and the "shoe leaving" becomes a disincentive as the student feels rather awkward hopping around the classroom.

## Paper Headings

Students should be taught to use a uniform heading, common to all teachers on a team or in the school. A good example would be:

| | |
|---|---|
| Last Name, First: | Date: |
| Subject: | Teacher's Title (Mr. Mrs. Ms. Dr.) and Last Name: |

A large model of this heading is written on display paper and posted above or on the chalkboard, and taught to all students during the first days of a new semester. During the first two weeks, the students are repeatedly reminded about the heading; at the end of the second week, the model is taken down and the verbal prompting stops. On the third week, with red pencil, the teacher circles all papers missing any parts of the heading (fading to a visual prompt) as a practice reminder. The teacher then announces at the beginning on the fourth week and from then on, the students will lose one point for lacking a completed heading (a disincentive). If this one point makes a difference between a higher or lower grade, or a B or B+, the student always receives the better grade. This way, the student is not downgraded and punished through the use of grades because of behavior rather than through a demonstration of knowledge in academics. This heading will permit the teacher to easily alphabetize the papers so scores can be recorded in the grade book.

## SUMMARY

Many constructs and concepts exist to help the teacher design a classroom balanced with appropriate materials and methods for their proper arrangement. But the steam that makes this classroom engine run remains the teacher. Making use of the balanced classroom, she or he now has the freedom to create a ballet of teacher movement, supervising this space by her or his presence and ability to look on. The teacher plans for ways that every young student may get a share of her or his emotional investment and skilled help. The blend of space, objects, teacher presence, and emotional investment "speak" clearly to students, telling them that they are safe, secure, and wanted in this classroom environment.

## REFERENCES

Emmer, E. T., Evertson, C. M., Sanford, J. P., Clements, B. S., & Worsham, M. W. (1984). *Classroom Management for Secondary Teachers.* Englewood Cliffs, NJ: Prentice-Hall.

Jones, F. H. (1987). *Positive Classroom Discipline.* New York: McGraw-Hill.

# 12

## Rules and Authority

The first minute of the first hour of the first day of the school year has arrived. An experienced teacher starting the final year before retirement or a first-year teacher facing the very first classroom alone, without the help of a supervisor, experiences the same feelings of anxiety. The feeling is not unlike standing on the side of a swimming pool ready to dive in, and realizing that there will be a shock to the body system—it may be pleasant or it may be unpleasant. The journey is about to begin.

The dynamic interaction between teacher and students that occurs on this first day will lay the foundation for interactions for the remainder of the year (Brophy & Good, 1974). So, somewhere deep in the back of your mind a voice repeats the old warning, "Don't smile until Christmas!" However, a clear understanding of the *Three Faces of Discipline* techniques gives new insights into the first day's dynamics and provides procedures, practices, and guidelines for preventing this first "dive" into the new school year from being an unpleasant belly-flop. Instead, it can help make the new school year a pleasant and productive experience.

## RULES ARE SITUATIONAL AND SPATIALLY BOUND

Daily activities are filled with disciplined behavior. People enter a restaurant, are seated, place their order, eat, pay, and depart. People enter a church or synagogue, are seated, listen, sing, pray, and depart. People arrive at a weekend football game, are seated, perhaps eat and drink, cheer, and depart. In each of these situations, the sequence and range of behavior is highly productive and socially accepted. In each case, the person plays a role (customer, worshiper, fan) and there are well-defined rules for the behavior involved in playing these roles (Smilansky & Shefatya, 1990). But what if we mix these behaviors? What if after the minister's sermon a worshiper screams out, "Go Saints!" demands a beer and popcorn with his communion wafer, and gives the minister a tip as he leaves? This clearly would be seen as inappropriate,

248

undisciplined behavior, and nearby worshipers would probably wish to see the offender given the name of a very good psychiatrist.

Each of these behaviors can be completely socially acceptable. What has made them unacceptable is their spatial context—that is, their occurrence in a church with its well-defined parameters of behavior. Acceptable behavior, then, is spatially bound. People obey or follow rules because they have learned a repertoire of motor rules and use them appropriately, based on the spatial context cues, or prompts, that have been modeled for or taught to them by authority figures. This is especially true for classrooms, where both teachers and students play roles governed by rules that give structure for "how to behave."

The difficulty for all students in the first minutes and hours of the first day of class is that they do not know the rules (Kounin, 1970). New sixth-graders (or whichever grade the particular middle school serves first) may be completely unfamiliar with a middle school environment, or the students may not have learned the rules. As a result, they may attempt to use "home" or "street" behaviors and play roles that the teacher might find unacceptable for "school behavior." Older students have been in many classrooms with many teachers and the rules have varied dramatically. They are asking the core question: What will the rules be for this classroom and this particular teacher? They want to know the structure of how this school, this classroom, this teacher will work. The student on the first day of class is like a visitor to a foreign country, wanting to know how to act in this new classroom culture.

## RULES ARE TAUGHT FORMALLY OR INFORMALLY

> *It is 20 minutes into the first day of classroom activity, and the class has been asked to fill out information cards. John's pencil point has broken and needs to be sharpened. He cannot complete the required task and wonders what to do. He bravely gets out of his seat and takes five steps toward the pencil sharpener. The teacher intercepts him with a stern, "Where are you going, young man? Sit down! You do not get out of your seat without my permission!" All eyes bounce back and forth between John and the new teacher. The tension in the room mounts.*

John has informally learned his first rule. The teacher has not explained the classroom rules regarding use of the pencil sharpener, and experienced students subconsciously now recognize that this teacher is going to play the game of "Gotcha" or "Minefield." Only the teacher will know the rules of what is permitted, and the students will have to guess and test their behavior to see what will be permitted and what will be punished. For these students, then, the classroom is like a minefield; they will never know where to place their feet safely. This unpleasant game will be played for many weeks until finally the students have tested and learned all the rules. However, many "mines" will have to be stepped on to expose all the rules, and the students understandably are left "shell shocked," tense, and angry.

## MOTOR RULES

*Carol has just finished eating her lunch in the school cafeteria. She stands, picks up her tray, and begins to walk to the disposal window. Suddenly, she stops, whirls around, and returns to her seat. She positions herself at the back side of her chair and, with a controlled use of her lower body, pushes the chair under the table and out of the aisle. Carol is well disciplined and will be highly prized and praised by her teachers.*

Carol has also demonstrated the use of a motor rule (Piaget, 1965). To be well disciplined at church, at a football game, in a restaurant, or in a classroom means simply knowing and using—almost unconsciously or automatically—a host of motor rules that are socially acceptable for the spatial context.

When students come into the classroom on that first day of school, they simply are entering a new world or culture shaped by the teacher's concepts of what is right or wrong. In some classrooms, students are permitted to sharpen their pencils at any time; in other classrooms, it is a major offense. What is called for in the first hours and days of the new year is not the teacher keeping the values and rules a secret from the students, forcing them to play the game of "Gotcha" or "Minefield" to learn the rules informally. Instead, the teacher must make these motor rules clear to each student and teach them in an overt, formal manner. To state it clearly, the host of motor rules for each classroom must be taught directly to the students by the teacher. Once the students learn the motor rules, they understand where all the "mines" are placed that might cause them to get into trouble, and they are confident they can avoid them. In other words, they feel safe knowing the rules.

### Teaching Motor Rules

Perhaps as a result of the wide acceptance of Lee Canter's Assertive Discipline (Canter, 1992) practices, a common practice in many classrooms is for four to six rules to be written on the chalkboard. As well intended as they may be, such rules as "Raise you hand before speaking out" and "Be courteous to others" are not enough and may not even be understood by students if they are simply taught through a process of "talk." It is highly unlikely that teachers will get the motor actions or motor rules that they desire merely from "talking" their rules. This is like trying to tell yourself where your car is parked in a multilevel parking garage. The teaching of motor rules requires a three-step teaching process— Say, Show, and Check or Do (Englemann, 1980)—that requires motor enactment or motor modeling of the rule so that it becomes second nature, such as pushing in the chair after eating in the cafeteria. As you teach motor rules, your instruction progresses through three steps as shown here.

---

### THE THREE-STEP LESSON

| | | |
|---|---|---|
| Step 1 | Say | The teacher verbally labels or encodes the object or process being taught. |
| Step 2 | Show | The teacher models by displaying the object, or having a student act out the process. |
| Step 3 | Check or Do | The teacher requires a student or students to physically demonstrate the ability to choose the correct procedure from among a series of options. The teacher always ends the lesson by demonstrating the correct example. |

---

## Step 1: Say

*"Students, if you need to use the pencil sharpener, please do it when you first come into the room. The sharpener is placed on the inside of the door. Because of the noise it makes, I do not want the pencil sharpener to be used while I am talking or while you are working. If an emergency occurs and you cannot do your work because your pencil is broken, I have placed a can of sharpened pencils on my desk. You may get up, put your broken pencil in the can, and take one of mine. At the end of the period, return my pencil and retrieve yours—and try to do it without distracting others."*

## Step 2: Show

Once the students are told what the rules are, you move to Step 2—show or demonstrate the motor rules.

*"Now, let me show you what I mean. Pretend that you are all taking a quiz, and I am writing tomorrow's assignments on the chalkboard. John, let's say your pencil breaks; would you now get up and show us what actions you would take?" (John, through behavioral rehearsal, demonstrates the motor action correctly.)*

## Step 3: Check or Do

You now show the students the negation, or the opposite behavior that you disapprove of, and then end by again modeling the correct way to perform the proposed actions. You ask the low-level question to get a unison response from the entire class to have them evaluate the motor response.

> *"Now, did John take the proper actions, class?"*
>
> *The students respond, "Yes."*
>
> *"Now, just for fun, let's do it again, John, and this time you show us what is not the rule. Go to the pencil sharpener and really make some noise as you sharpen your pencil during class." (John models the negation, breaking the rule. The class laughs at his behavior, and you join in with your laughter.) "Class, was that the correct behavior?"*
>
> *The class responds, "No!" and they all laugh again.*
>
> *"Now, Robert, you show us again what you are to do if you break your pencil point and need a pencil to do your work." (Robert performs the correct actions desired.) "Was Robert correct, class?"*
>
> *The class responds, "Yes."*

For older students, you might have to use a sense of humor to carry out this teaching of motor rules through the three-step process, but you still clearly communicate the desired behavior. You will also monitor the rule closely (Kounin, 1970) the first two or three weeks, to stop any rule breaking that has been learned as a habit. If need be, the rule is retaught through another process of Say, Show, and Check or Do. You need to teach the many motor rules of the classroom environment and practices, and you need to do it in the first minutes, days, and weeks at the beginning of each school year or semester. In schools where grade levels are grouped as teams, the team should agree on the rules, reinforced in each class, and taught during the advisor/advisee time. This way, the skills can be broken up between the team teachers so that more can be covered at one time.

## What Should the Classroom Motor Rules Be?

The establishment of motor rules in the classroom and the demand for students to desist their rule breaking is a projection of a teacher's own values (Spitz, 1957). Within each of us, as teachers, are varying degrees of need for control, perhaps derived from our earliest training by adults such as parents and teachers. For instance, when an adult is eating at a table with a 2-year-old child who throws mashed potatoes across the table, the adult immediately intervenes—hopefully in a kind and gentle manner—to get the child to desist, clearly setting a limit by saying "No." All requests to desist are a form of saying "No" to a student's behavior. All our "Nos" are a projection of our values. Therefore, a teacher's values will determine whether students will be required to raise their hands before they speak out or to get permission to leave their seats to sharpen a pencil. For students, particularly at the beginning of the school year, it generally is not of high importance what a teacher says "No" to, but it is important that they know what these "Nos" are. Once the students are aware of the "Nos," teacher behavior becomes orderly and predictable and they are not frightened of unpredictable responses. Why is it that some teachers are hard-nosed with very strict rules, while others allow considerable autonomy by students—similar to the custodial and humanistic pupil control ideologies discussed in Chapter 1—yet both types can be respected and loved by students and maintain effective discipline? It is because students know these teachers by their orderly and predictable use of limits or desists ("Nos").

What about the teachers who maintain poor discipline and in turn receive little or no respect from students? These are the "loosie-goosie" teachers who one day communicate an acceptance of great freedom and use minimal motor rules, and the very next day "slam-dunk" the students by surprising them with a desist and a demand to obey a rule that they never heard of before (Canter, 1992). The students will say, "We can never tell where he's coming from!" They mean that this "wishy-washy" teacher's desist requests for behavior through motor rules are disorderly and unpredictable. This puts the students living in the classroom version of a minefield, where the teacher periodically and unpredictably drops "bombs" on them. What is even more deadly is that once the students in this "wishy-washy" teacher's classroom feel they know where the mines are, the next day the mines are moved. (The rule suddenly is not enforced, or is enforced differently, and the students never know why.)

At the practical level, motor rules will cluster under the large headings (Canter, 1992) of walls and objects, rituals, transitions, and student groupings (these techniques are detailed in books on cooperative learning [Evertson, Emmer, Clements, Sanford, & Worsham, 1984]):

1. *Teaching the rules for walls and objects:* The teacher begins at the doorway and teaches the motor rules for all objects on the walls, or furniture and equipment positioned against the wall. (For example, *light switches:* Are students permitted to turn lights off and on? *filing cabinets:* Are students permitted to open, use, and explore their contents? *windows:* Are students permitted to raise or lower windows and window blinds? *materials:* What may students do with classroom books and other random materials? Are they permitted to take objects from the teacher's desk, or to go into the teacher's desk drawers?)

2. *Teaching the rules for student rituals:* The teacher tells the students how to perform routine actions, such as raising their hands, signaling that they wish to leave their seat or leave the room, putting a standardized heading on papers, and the like.

3. *Teaching the rules for movement or transitions:* The teacher explains procedures for periods between activities, such as arriving on time, departing, moving from desks to special-area tables, fire drills, handing in and passing out materials, and so on.

4. *Teaching the rules for the grouping of children:* The teacher explains how students are to work when assigned to groups, including each student's responsibility to the group.

These procedures, which are designed to become motor rules, may seem on the surface to be overly controlling. However, it is imperative for the students' well-being, as well as for that of the teacher, to think out how much autonomy students will be granted in each particular classroom and under what circumstances. You can then communicate what you need and expect of students by teaching the motor rules through the three-step process. The worksheet found at the end of this chapter (Figure 12.1) titled Materials/Prompts/Motor Rules, may be used by the teacher before school begins to determine in writing just what the rules will be regarding various classroom materials and objects. The worksheet also requires the teacher to apply the previously learned principles related to directionality (color coding of walls) and visual prompts. The worksheet, with its list of rules, would then be used to teach motor rules on the first day of the school year.

## ESTABLISHING TEACHER AUTHORITY AND LEADERSHIP

Even when motor rules are taught, they do not become truly valid to a classroom full of students until they are tested (Johnson, Johnson, & Holubec, 1986). The students wonder, "Ha! He told us these rules, but does he really mean it? Will he back up his word?" In the erratic classroom of the wishy-washy teacher, there is a void of established authority and leadership. All productive groups require leadership and authority. Closely watch the children's sandlot games and you will see peer leaders emerge from the group to toss the coin to see who goes first; teams are formed with all yielding authority and leadership to one individual for the temporary life of the game (Herron & Sutton-Smith, 1971). Normally, in games, the other team becomes the "person or people to exclude" (Isaacs, 1968), and being a member of a team brings acceptance and belonging because each player has an opposing team of "enemies" to "hate."

Similar actions happen in classrooms. When a teacher fails to establish himself or herself as a leader, a powerful personality (usually one student) will become assertive to fill the void, much to the teacher's detriment. The teacher completely loses control. In fact, when groups of students become uncontrollable, they normally make the classroom teacher the "outside aggressor" (see Chapter 10). Once the teacher loses control in the first few days of school, it probably will be next to impossible to regain control by reestablishing his or her authority or leadership. This is why Jones (1987) would say, "Pay in pennies now or pay in dollars later in remediation" (p. 26). This means, of course, time should be taken immediately to establish a classroom management system, and less time in the long run to stop and to deal with discipline incidents.

Watching sandlot games again, when a new set of peers comes together to play, the players heatedly argue the rules for many minutes before the games begin. Once the rules are agreed on, they become spatially context bound: "These are the stickball rules for our street, our neighborhood, or our playground!" These rules reflect their definition of reality for that space. When they are joined by a new player from "outside the neighborhood" who might have played with a different set of rules, play stops and the rules again are debated until everyone—especially the new player—is in agreement that "these are the rules." This need to preestablish rules and create a sense of fairness reflects the school-age child's budding sense of moral development (Spitz, 1957) and social understanding. These developmental needs will be brought into the "game of school" or the "game of classroom."

The common denominator or social dynamic that is central for establishing teacher authority and leadership is a clash (Berne, 1964). This occurs when a student violates a rule, accidentally or deliberately, to test the rule's validity and the teacher as the leader. Daily positive and productive educational experiences with students are the building blocks for a good teacher, and their positive resolution provide the cement that binds these building blocks of relationships together.

The clashes between husband and wife, between friends, between parent and child, and between teacher and student are all pivotal points in social relationships. Critical to maintaining a relationship is one person's use of power to raise an issue, and the use of minimum power to get a change in the other's behavior while still maintaining the second person's dignity. In contrast, the excessive use of power and "slam-dunking" the other person destroys the other's self-worth and destroys the relationship. The careful use of power in setting limits and expressing a desist will be a critical element in successful discipline.

It is the third week of class. The students have been taught the motor rules, and classroom procedures and activities are running smoothly. Just as things seem to be going so well, here comes John, and it is clear to you and all the class that he has broken an established rule. John is testing the validity of the rules and the skill of the teacher. This is the clash! A desist request must be initiated and the manner of skill with which it is executed will provide the cement—the information about the teacher—that will bind the class behind authority and produce a quality relationship between teacher and students. If this challenge is poorly handled, everyone in the class—not just misbehaving John—will fear being slam-dunked or punished unfairly in the future, and therefore will protect themselves by withholding their affection and cooperation.

Poorly handling the desist request is likely to turn the teacher into the class outside aggressor. In Transactional Analysis (Berne, 1964) terms, the comment, "Where are you going, young man? Sit down! You do not get out of your seat without my permission!" is clearly a *parent* statement full of demeaning guilt that communicates the student's unworthiness. This use of *guilt induction* is a psychologically destructive process that strikes the student directly in the conscience, flooding the child with guilt that will soon turn to anger. An *adult* statement, in Transactional Analysis terms, would permit the teacher to be assertive and initiate a desist request in such a manner that it addresses the reality problem at hand and is free of guilt. An example would be, "I need you to stay in your seat during tests so other students will not be distracted."

*Adult*-based techniques can initiate a skilled desist request in a way that cements the relationship. The central motivation for most students is the desire for belonging (Dreikurs & Cassel, 1972), the wish to be valued and accepted by teacher and peers. For the young adolescents, acceptance by peers is more valued than the teacher's acceptance. The risk in asserting a desist request is that it may be loaded with guilt that communicates nonvaluing or nonrespect for the student as an individual. When it is done in front of peers, it threatens the student's prestige among those peers.

## POWER AND DEGREES OF DESIST CONTROL

Teacher techniques can be placed along a continuum of degrees of power and control, and through the *Three Faces of Discipline* construct, can be placed under the broad headings of Relationship-Listening, Confronting-Contracting, and Rules and Consequences. With this power continuum in mind, it is suggested that a desist request with minimum intrusion is first applied, as with the Relationship-Listening attitude and techniques. If this fails to be effective, a move to increased power or intrusion using Confronting-Contracting procedures becomes appropriate, and then finally to maximum control with Rules and Consequences desist techniques.

## ATTENDING BEHAVIORS

The teacher complains, "These students just will not listen!" This may be true for large numbers of students who are raised on large diets of television and in environments that do not require close attention. If this complaint is accepted as valid, the job then becomes one of teaching these students attending behaviors. This is done through the use of teaching techniques called prompts and fading. For example, the teacher wants the class to become quiet so that directions may be given, so she proceeds as follows.

## PROMPTS

1. "Clang, Clang, Clang." (The teacher uses a bell or whistle, blinks the lights, hits a note on the piano, etc., as an aversive stimulus [auditory prompt] that will get the student's attention.)

2. "Class!" (The teacher gives a verbal prompt by labeling who he or she is addressing.)

3. "Stop!" (The teacher gives a verbal prompt as a command.)

4. "Look at me!" (Second command; the teacher points to his or her eyes as a visual prompt.)

5. The teacher scores a point (reinforcer) on the Incentive System's Score Board for all teams that comply (see Chapter 9).

6. The teacher "squares off" (see Chapter 3).

7. The teacher repeats steps 1, 2, 3, 4, 5, and 6 three times (complete three cycles).

## FADING

The teacher continues to "square off" and wait. These nonverbal prompts signal the students that their attention is wanted, but the teacher will gradually fade this out:

| Request | Teacher Actions |
|---|---|
| First | Does three cycles of steps 1–6 above. |
| Second | Does only two cycles of steps 1–6. |
| Third | Does one cycle of steps 1–6. |
| Fourth | Does two "Clangs" and steps 2–6. |
| Fifth | Does one "Clang" and steps 2–6. |
| Sixth | Fades (stops doing) "Clang" but does steps 2–6. |
| Seventh | Fades (stops doing) step 2, and begins with steps 3–6. |
| Eighth | Fades step 3, and begins with steps 4–6. |
| Ninth | Fades step 4, and begins with step 5 and does step 6. |
| Tenth | Fades step 5, and then squares off and waits. |

From this point on, the teacher needs only to square off at the power position in the classroom, which is shown on the classroom map of Figure 11.1. This is the repeated location at which the teacher regularly stands to begin nearly all activities or to get the attention of the entire class before directions are given. The teaching of attending behaviors begins with aversive stimuli and involves "training" the students, but with the fading techniques, the teacher gradually leads the students to respond to his or her language and physical presence. Attending to others' language progresses from simply training, as might be done with animals, to the human process of communication through language that teaches the listening skills necessary for the teacher to instruct and for the students to comprehend and attend.

## SUMMARY

Returning to the sea of faces of the new group of students on the first minute of the first hour of the first day of the school year, students are eager to understand what "Nos" the teacher uses and the motor rules wanted in the spatial context of the classroom. Rules, of course, are broken soon after they are made, and a desist or limit-setting request must follow. A range of power in limit setting, from minimal to quite assertive demands, for appropriate behavior and action exists, and the teacher may wear one of the three "faces." The more genuine and relaxed you can be in using desists and the power inherent in them, the more skilled you will become as a teacher and disciplinarian.

# REFERENCES

Berne, E. (1964). *Games People Play: The Psychology of Human Relations.* New York: Grove Press.

Brophy, J., & Good, T. L. (1974). *Teacher-Student Relationships: Causes and Consequences.* New York: Holt, Rinehart and Winston.

Canter, L. (1992). *Assertive Discipline: Positive Behavior Management for Today's Classroom.* Santa Monica, CA: Lee Canter & Associates.

Driekurs, R., & Cassel, P. (1972). *Discipline without Tears.* New York: Hawthorn Books.

Engelmann, S. (1980). *Direct Instruction.* Englewood Cliffs, NJ: Educational Technology Publications.

Evertson, C. M., Emmer, E. E., Sanford, J. P., Clements, B. S., & Worsham, M. W. (1984). *Classroom Management for Secondary Teachers.* Englewood Cliffs, NJ: Prentice-Hall.

Herron, R. E., & Sutton-Smith, B. (1971). *Child's Play.* New York: John Wiley and Sons.

Isaacs, S. (1968). *Social Development.* New York: McGraw-Hill.

Johnson, D. W., Johnson, R. T., & Holubec, E. J. (1986). *Circles of Learning: Cooperation in the Classroom.* Edina, MN: Interaction Book Company.

Jones, F. H. (1987). *Positive Classroom Discipline.* New York: McGraw-Hill.

Kounin, J. S. (1970). *Discipline and Group Management in Classrooms.* New York: Holt, Rinehart and Winston.

Piaget, J. (1965). *The Moral Judgment of the Child.* (Marjorie Gabain, trans.). New York: Free Press.

Smilansky, S., & Shefatya, L. (1990). *Facilitating Play: A Medium for Promoting Cognitive, Socio-Emotional and Academic Development in Young Children.* Gaithersburg, MD: Psychosocial & Educational Publications.

Spitz, R. (1957). *No and Yes.* New York: International Universities Press.

Willoughby-Herb, S., & Neisworth, J. T. (1983). *HICOMP Curriculum.* Columbus, OH: Charles E. Merrill.

Wolfgang, C. H., & Wolfgang, M. E. (1992). *School for Young Children: Developmentally Appropriate Practices.* Boston: Allyn and Bacon.

**FIGURE 12.1  Materials/Prompts/Motor Rules**

| | Materials | Visual Prompt (number silhouette) | Check Column Indicating the Wall on Which the Materials Are Located | | | | Interior Items | Motor Rules |
|---|---|---|---|---|---|---|---|---|
| | | | North (green) | East (red) | South (blue) | West (yellow) | | |
| 1. | **Door** | | | | | | | |
| | a. Hallway passes | | | | | | | |
| 2. | **Light Switch** | | | | | | | |
| 3. | **Pencil Sharpener** | | | | | | | |
| 4. | **Trash Can** | | | | | | | |
| 5. | **Chalkboard (chalk, erasers)** | | | | | | | |
| 6. | **Filing Cabinets** | | | | | | | |
| | a. Cabinet #1 (name): | | | | | | | |
| | b. Cabinet #2 (name): | | | | | | | |

*(Continued)*

FIGURE 12.1 Materials/Prompts/Motor Rules *(Continued)*

| Materials | Visual Prompt (number silhouette) | Check Column Indicating the Wall on Which the Materials Are Located | | | | Interior Items | Motor Rules |
|---|---|---|---|---|---|---|---|
| | | North (green) | East (red) | South (blue) | West (yellow) | | |
| c. Cabinet #3 (name) | | | | | | | |
| 7. Teacher's Desk/Chair | | | | | | | |
| a. Teacher's grade/lesson plan books | | | | | | | |
| b. Teacher's purse/briefcase or similar property | | | | | | | |
| c. Drawers | | | | | | | |
| d. Top items (assignment boxes, pencils, etc.) | | | | | | | |
| e. Item #1 (name): | | | | | | | |
| f. Item #2 (name): | | | | | | | |
| g. Item #3 (name): | | | | | | | |
| h. Item #4 (name): | | | | | | | |

| | | | | | | |
|---|---|---|---|---|---|---|
| **8.** | **Shelved Materials** | | | | | |
| | a. Open shelves | | | | | |
| | (1) Free-standing items (microscope, globe, etc.) | | | | | |
| | (2) In containers | | | | | |
| | (3) On trays | | | | | |
| | (4) Stacked (such as puzzles) | | | | | |
| | b. Closed (doored) shelves | | | | | |
| | (1) Free-standing items (microscope, globe, etc.) | | | | | |
| | (2) In containers | | | | | |
| | (3) On trays | | | | | |
| | (4) Stacked (such as puzzles) | | | | | |
| **9.** | **Windows** | | | | | |

(Continued)

**FIGURE 12.1   Materials/Prompts/Motor Rules** *(Continued)*

| Materials | Visual Prompt (number silhouette) | Check Column Indicating the Wall on Which the Materials Are Located | | | | Interior Items | Motor Rules |
|---|---|---|---|---|---|---|---|
| | | *North (green)* | *East (red)* | *South (blue)* | *West (yellow)* | | |
| a. Blinds/curtains | | | | | | | |
| 10. **Water Fountain** | | | | | | | |
| 11. **Sink** | | | | | | | |
| a. Towels | | | | | | | |
| b. Soap | | | | | | | |
| c. Trash can | | | | | | | |
| 12. **Restroom** | | | | | | | |
| a. Toilet | | | | | | | |

| | | | | | | |
|---|---|---|---|---|---|---|
| b. Tissue | | | | | | |
| c. Sink | | | | | | |
| d. Towels | | | | | | |
| e. Soap | | | | | | |
| f. Trash can | | | | | | |
| g. Other (name): | | | | | | |
| 13. **Exhibits** | | | | | | |
| a. Flora | | | | | | |
| (1) Name: | | | | | | |
| (2) Name: | | | | | | |
| (3) Name: | | | | | | |
| b. Livestock (rabbits, fish, hamster, etc.) | | | | | | |
| (1) Name: | | | | | | |

*(Continued)*

**FIGURE 12.1** Materials/Prompts/Motor Rules (*Continued*)

| Materials | Visual Prompt (number silhouette) | Check Column Indicating the Wall on Which the Materials Are Located | | | | Interior Items | Motor Rules |
|---|---|---|---|---|---|---|---|
| | | North (green) | East (red) | South (blue) | West (yellow) | | |
| (2) Name: | | | | | | | |
| (3) Name: | | | | | | | |
| c. Other | | | | | | | |
| (1) Name | | | | | | | |
| (2) Name | | | | | | | |
| (3) Name | | | | | | | |
| 14. **Display Tables** | | | | | | | |
| a. Name: | | | | | | | |
| b. Name: | | | | | | | |
| c. Name: | | | | | | | |

| | | | | | | | | | | | | |
|---|---|---|---|---|---|---|---|---|---|---|---|---|
| 15. | **Student Coat Racks** | | | | | | | | | | | |
| 16. | **Student Storage Bins (Wall)** | | | | | | | | | | | |
| 17. | **Student Desk** | | | | | | | | | | | |
| | a. Desk surface use | ■ | | | | | | | | | | |
| | b. Desk storage | | | | | | | | | | | |
| | (1) Book arrangement | | | | | | | | | | | |
| | (2) Loose paper | | | | | | | | | | | |
| | (3) Pencil/erasers | | | | | | | | | | | |
| | (4) Loose items | | | | | | | | | | | |
| | (5) Personal items | | | | | | | | | | | |
| | c. Notebook organizer | | | | | | | | | | | |
| | d. Chairs (carrying of) | ■ | | | | | | | | | | |
| 18. | **Audio-visual Equipment (Permanent)** | | | | | | | | | | | |

*(Continued)*

265

**FIGURE 12.1  Materials/Prompts/Motor Rules** *(Continued)*

| Materials | Visual Prompt (number silhouette) | Check Column Indicating the Wall on Which the Materials Are Located | | | | Interior Items | Motor Rules |
|---|---|---|---|---|---|---|---|
| | | North (green) | East (red) | South (blue) | West (yellow) | | |
| a. Name: | | | | | | | |
| b. Name: | | | | | | | |
| c. Name: | | | | | | | |
| 19. **Apparatus/Equipment** | | | | | | | |
| a. Computer | | | | | | | |
| (1) Keyboard use/care | | | | | | | |
| (2) Diskette storage/care | | | | | | | |
| (3) CD-ROM use/care | | | | | | | |
| (4) Desk storage/care | | | | | | | |
| (5) Mouse storage/care | | | | | | | |

| (6) Printer storage/care | | | | | | | | | | | |
|---|---|---|---|---|---|---|---|---|---|---|---|
| b. Name | | | | | | | | | | | |
| (1) | | | | | | | | | | | |
| (2) | | | | | | | | | | | |
| (3) | | | | | | | | | | | |
| (4) | | | | | | | | | | | |
| c. Name: | | | | | | | | | | | |
| (1) | | | | | | | | | | | |
| (2) | | | | | | | | | | | |
| (3) | | | | | | | | | | | |
| (4) | | | | | | | | | | | |
| (5) | | | | | | | | | | | |

# 13

## The First Days of School
### Teaching the Basics of Good Classroom Discipline

Spatial location communicates a specific set of motor rules and behavior. Well-socialized people generally respond appropriately. In a movie theater, people act with certain defined motor rules; at a football game, they act in an entirely different way.

A great number of today's students are growing up without being taught a sensitivity to spatial rules in their home setting. Teachers may remark: "Where do these kids come from—they don't know how to act! Are they from Mars?" Well, compared to the way the teachers were raised and taught value systems, students may just as well come from Mars, considering the dramatic gap between the teachers' values and those of the students. The mission of the quality school is now clear: Students must be taught to be socially sensitive to expected and "proper" social behavior based on where they are and the social context of the moment. Developing this awareness is a skill, and once students learn it, they will be ready for the life experiences of a working world filled with rule-based environments. We start this all-important educational process by declaring Mars Days.

If a student had come to a classroom from a foreign land, or another planet, you would not expect him or her to know your habits, routines, and cultural dos and don'ts. Similarly, even though they have had several years of classroom experiences, you cannot expect many of today's students to know how to behave. This initiation is especially important as students transition into a middle school. It may be best to consider them as having just stepped off a spaceship from Mars. In dealing with these "Martians," they cannot be expected to know anything about how the middle school classroom works. Declare Mars Days (1) during the first six days of a new school year or semester, (2) when a large number of new students enter the school or classroom and will not know the routine, (3) after a long holiday break that has kept the students away from the school and school routines, and/or (4) when classroom behavior generally begins to deteriorate and too many discipline incidents erupt. Too many accidents, especially in the hallways or cafeteria, would also signal a need to declare a schoolwide Mars Days.

## ORIENTATION DAYS

The following schedule works best if it is coordinated between teachers within a team or grade level. The schedule in Figure 13.1 (found at the end of the chapter) has been designed so that the Mars Days instruction is shared by teachers and divided by subject taught. Participants include the language arts, social studies, math, and science teachers, referred to as the *core* teachers. However, since not all middle schools have identical grade-level structures, the schedule shown in Figure 13.1 may need to be adapted to your particular school site.

During the first six weeks of the school year (labeled Mars Days), the classroom should follow a schedule similar to the one seen in Figure 13.1. On the first day (presumably Monday), each core teacher assigns seats based on the numbering system described in Chapter 11. If elective or special area teachers are included in the Mars Days activities, they would also assign seats if their subject area is conducive to having assigned seating. Next, the core teachers teach the Rights and Responsibilities Game (see Chapter 9) during their first class period with students and then review it in the class periods remaining in the first day as part of their incentive system. Next, the math and science teachers will teach the motor rules. These motor rules will need to be divided between these two core teachers to avoid redundancy. The language arts and social studies teachers will teach the transitional prompts using the three-step concept for making transitions (see Chapter 12) while conducting any transition within the classroom—such as moving to groups or departing the classroom. Again, these transitional prompts will need to be divided between these two core teachers. At the end of each class period, the language arts and social studies teachers should award a Type 1 reinforcer (edible) as a part of the Rights and Responsibilities Game. Once this has been accomplished, a new "game" begins.

During the second day (Tuesday), each of the core teachers should introduce the Assignment Board (see Chapter 11) and how it is to be used, giving the class one or two easy assignments. Next, the math and science teachers conduct another lesson on motor rules, but this time divide only half of the previous day's list of rules between the two core teachers, focusing on the rules you know are more difficult for the students to use and remember. At the end of each class period, the math and science teachers should reward a Type 2 reinforcer (tangible) as a part of the Rights and Responsibilities Game. The language arts and social studies teachers should continue teaching, and reviewing, the transitional prompts. The elective or special area teachers should begin to reinforce the motor rules and transitional prompts, and use the Rights and Responsibilities Game.

Beginning the third day (Wednesday), each core teacher should hold a plus/delta classroom meeting during the last 20 minutes of the class period, encouraging the students to discuss openly what went well during the first half of the day. Place a summary statement under a "plus" column on the chalkboard. Students should also be encouraged to tell what they did not like or any problems they faced, with these listed under a "delta" column. (Delta is the mathematical or scientific notation for a problem that needs a solution or a change that needs to occur—hence the name plus/delta discussion.) This is an honest discussion and the teacher must be prepared to hear criticism about his or her own actions, be willing to list this on the board, and then invite the students to come up with solutions as to how to make classroom change, thus moving the problems in the delta column into positives on the plus side.

Most of the items on the Orientation Week (Mars Days) chart (Figure 13.1) will now be self-explanatory. What is important to see as you progress through the six weeks is that items are faded with time. Reinforcers change from time-consuming Type 1 and 2 reinforcers to the use of Type 3 preferred activity time (PAT). Later, preferred activity time can be relegated to Fridays. Rules are taught less and less frequently until they fade out as well.

## SUMMARY

A program of orienting students into the new classroom setting, the concept of Mars Days, is typically conducted over a period of six weeks. For most middle school classrooms, this time period will be sufficient. However, depending on the age of the students or the number of very difficult children in the class, the teacher's professional judgment may indicate that Mars Days may need to be extended to two weeks, or even longer. (On the rare occasion, the teacher may need to use the Mars Days structure for the entire school year.)

The goal of the Mars Days program is to fade out gradually the need for the Rights and Responsibilities Game with its reinforcers, replacing it with a process through which the students solve difficulties and conflicts—especially discipline problems—through the use of plus/delta meetings. Obtaining the ability to discuss problems through the use of language, within the context of group membership, is the ultimate goal of the *Three Faces of Discipline* philosophy.

## CONCLUDING COMMENTS

Teaching young adolescents, on most days, is a very rewarding experience. Among the developmental tasks of early adolescence is forming self-concept, learning appropriate social skills, and becoming autonomous. Classroom interaction provides a logical forum for the development of these important tasks. The *Three Faces of Discipline* philosophy is to provide a structure for student behavior and to create an environment of caring and consistency for young adolescents. We, the authors, believe these environments maximize student potential and help students make a transition to the self-discipline they will need in their adult lives.

FIGURE 13.1 Orientation Week 1 (Mars Days)

Teacher assigns seating in a boy-girl arrangement, and in teams. Once the teacher knows the students better, seating may be rearranged to balance teams by sex, race, ability, and difficulty of behavior.

Teach the motor rules through a Show, Say, and Check/Do three-step teacher process. Also teach the Rights and Responsibilities Incentive Game.

Teach transitions as a three-step process to in- and out-of-room movements.

| | Monday | Tuesday | Wednesday | Thursday | Friday |
|---|---|---|---|---|---|
| Begin Day | ☐ Assign Seats & Teams (number system) ☐ Teach Rules & Responsibilities Game ☐ Teach Motor Rules (100% of rules) | ☐ Teach Motor Rules (50% of rules) ☐ Review Monday's (+/–) Meeting Results ☐ Teach Assignment Board | ☐ Teach Motor Rules (4 rules only) ☐ Teach and Use Assignment Board | ☐ Use and Monitor Assignment Board ☐ Teach Motor Rules (2 rules only) | ☐ Use and Monitor Assignment Board ☐ Teach Motor Rules (rules as needed) ☐ Award Reinforcer (Type 1) |
| During A.M. | ☐ Teach Transitional Prompts 1. Depart/return from classroom | ☐ Teach Transitional Prompts | ☐ Teach Transitional Prompts | ☐ Teach Transitional Prompts Hold (+/–) Meeting with Losing Team | ☐ Teach Transitional Prompts Hold (+/–) Meeting with Losing Team |
| Just Before Lunch | ☐ Award Reinforcer (Type 1) | ☐ Award Reinforcer (Type 1) | ☐ Award Reinforcer (Type 3) | ☐ Award Reinforcer (Type 2) | ☐ Award Reinforcer (Type 2) |
| Just After Lunch | ☐ Hold (+/–) Meeting | ☐ Hold (+/–) Meeting | | ☐ Hold (+/–) Meeting | |
| During P.M. | | | Hold (+/–) Meeting with Losing Team | Hold (+/–) Meeting with Losing Team | Hold (+/–) Meeting with Losing Team |
| End of Day | ☐ Award Reinforcer (Type 2) ☐ Hold (+/–) Meeting | ☐ Award Reinforcer (Type 2) ☐ Hold (+/–) Meeting ☐ Review and Use Assignment Board | ☐ Award Reinforcer (Type 1) ☐ Hold (+/–) Meeting ☐ Use and Monitor Assignment Board | ☐ Award Reinforcer (Type 3) ☐ Hold (+/–) Meeting ☐ Monitor Assignment Board | ☐ Award Reinforcer (Type 3) ☐ Hold (+/–) Meeting |

Hold a +/– Class Meeting

Teach and begin using the Assignment Board

Award Reinforcer Type 1: Edibles

Award Reinforcer Type 2: Tangible

Award Reinforcer Type 3: PAT

(Continued)

**FIGURE 13.1  Orientation Week 2 (Mars Days)**

| | Monday | Tuesday | Wednesday | Thursday | Friday |
|---|---|---|---|---|---|
| Begin Day | ☐ Reassign Seats & Teams (number system) <br> ☐ Teach Motor Rules (50% of rules) | *(Fade to Reinforcers, Types 2 & 3)* <br> ☐ Teach Motor Rules (4 rules only) <br> ☐ Review Monday's +/– Meeting Results | ☐ Teach Motor Rules (2 rules only) | ☐ Teach Motor Rules (rules as needed) | ☐ Teach Motor Rules (rules as needed) |
| During A.M. | ☐ Teach Transitional Prompts | ☐ Teach Transitional Prompts <br> Hold +/– Meeting with Losing Team | | Hold +/– Meeting with Losing Team | ☐ Teach Transitional Prompts <br> Hold +/– Meeting with Losing Team |
| Just Before Lunch | ☐ Award Reinforcer (Type 1) | ☐ Award Reinforcer (Type 2) | | ☐ Award Reinforcer (Type 3) | |
| Just After Lunch | ☐ Hold +/– Meeting | ☐ Hold +/– Meeting | | ☐ Hold +/– Meeting | |
| During P.M. | ☐ Teach Transitional Prompts | ☐ Teach Transitional Prompts | Hold +/– Meeting with Losing Team–contracting | ☐ Teach Transitional Prompts <br> Hold +/– Meeting with Losing Team–contracting | ☐ Teach Transitional Prompts <br> Hold +/– Meeting with Losing Team–contracting |
| End of Day | ☐ Award Reinforcer (Type 2) <br> ☐ Hold +/– Meeting <br> ☐ Monitor Assignment Board | ☐ Award Reinforcer (Type 2) <br> ☐ Hold +/– Meeting <br> ☐ Monitor Assignment Board | ☐ Award Reinforcer (Type 2) <br> ☐ Hold +/– Meeting <br> ☐ Monitor Assignment Board | ☐ Award Reinforcer (Type 2) <br> ☐ Hold +/– Meeting <br> ☐ Monitor Assignment Board | ☐ Hold +/– Meeting <br> ☐ Award Reinforcer Type 3 |

**FIGURE 13.1   Orientation Week 3 (Mars Days)**

| | Monday | Tuesday | Wednesday | Thursday | Friday |
|---|---|---|---|---|---|
| Begin Day | □ Reassign (elective) Seats & Teams (number system) <br> □ Teach Motor Rules (2 rules only) | (*Fade to Reinforcers, Type 3*) <br> □ Teach Motor Rules (rules as needed) <br> □ Review Monday's +/− Meeting Results | | | □ Teach Motor Rules (rules as needed) |
| During A.M. | | □ Teach Transitional Prompts <br> Hold +/− Meeting with Losing Team | | Hold +/− Meeting with Losing Team | Hold +/− Meeting with Losing Team |
| Just Before Lunch | □ Award Reinforcer (Type 2) | □ Award Reinforcer (Type 3) | | | |
| Just After Lunch | □ Hold +/− Meeting | □ Hold +/− Meeting | | □ Hold +/− Meeting | |
| During P.M. | □ Teach Transitional Prompts | | □ Teach Transitional Prompts <br> Hold +/− Meeting with Losing Team–contracting | Hold +/− Meeting with Losing Team–contracting | □ Teach Transitional Prompts <br> Hold +/− Meeting with Losing Team–contracting |
| End of Day | □ Award Reinforcer (Type 3) <br> □ Hold +/− Meeting <br> □ Monitor Assignment Board | □ Award Reinforcer (Type 3) <br> □ Hold +/− Meeting <br> □ Monitor Assignment Board | □ Hold +/− Meeting <br> □ Award Reinforcer (Type 3) <br> □ Monitor Assignment Board | □ Award Reinforcer (award PAT points) <br> □ Hold +/− Meeting <br> □ Monitor Assignment Board | □ Hold +/− Meeting <br> □ Award Reinforcer (Type 3) |

(Continued)

**FIGURE 13.1  Orientation Week 4 (Mars Days)**

| | Monday | Tuesday | Wednesday | Thursday | Friday |
|---|---|---|---|---|---|
| Begin Day | □Teach Motor Rules (2 rules only) | □Teach Motor Rules (rules as needed) □Review Monday's +/– Meeting Results | □Hold +/– Meeting | | □Teach Motor Rules (rules as needed) |
| During A.M. | | Hold +/– Meeting with Losing Team | | Hold +/– Meeting with Losing Team | Hold +/– Meeting with Losing Team |
| Just Before Lunch | | □Award Reinforcer (Type 3) | | □Award Reinforcer (PAT points) | |
| Just After Lunch | | | | | |
| During P.M. | □Teach Transitional Prompts | | Hold +/– Meeting with Losing Team–contracting | Hold +/– Meeting with Losing Team–contracting | Hold +/– Meeting with Losing Team–contracting |
| End of Day | □Hold +/– Meeting □Award Reinforcer (Type 3) □Monitor Assignment Board | □Award Reinforcer (Type 3) | □Hold +/– Meeting □Award Reinforcer (Type 3) □Monitor Assignment Board | □Award Reinforcer (Type 3) | □Hold +/– Meeting □Award Reinforcer (Type 3) |

**FIGURE 13.1 Orientation Week 5 (Mars Days)**

| | Monday | Tuesday | Wednesday | Thursday | Friday |
|---|---|---|---|---|---|
| Begin Day | ☐ Teach Motor Rules (rules as needed) | | | | ☐ Teach Motor Rules (rules as needed) |
| During A.M. | | Hold +/− Meeting with Losing Team | | Hold +/− Meeting with Losing Team | Hold +/− Meeting with Losing Team |
| Just Before Lunch | | | ☐ Award Reinforcer (PAT points) | | |
| Just After Lunch | | | | | |
| During P.M. | | | Hold +/− Meeting with Losing Team–contracting | Hold +/− Meeting with Losing Team–contracting | Hold +/− Meeting with Losing Team–contracting |
| End of Day | ☐ Hold +/− Meeting ☐ Award Reinforcer (Type 3) ☐ Monitor Assignment Board | ☐ Award Reinforcer (Type 3) | ☐ Hold +/− Meeting ☐ Monitor Assignment Board (for individual students only) | | ☐ Hold +/− Meeting ☐ Award Reinforcer (Type 3) |

(Continued)

**FIGURE 13.1** Orientation Week 6 (Mars Days)

| | Monday | Tuesday | Wednesday | Thursday | Friday |
|---|---|---|---|---|---|
| Begin Day | ☐ Teach Motor Rules (rules as needed) | | | | |
| During A.M. | | Hold +/– Meeting with Losing Team | | Hold +/– Meeting with Losing Team | Hold +/– Meeting with Losing Team |
| Just Before Lunch | | | | | |
| Just After Lunch | | | | | |
| During P.M. | | | Hold +/– Meeting with Losing Team–contracting | Hold +/– Meeting with Losing Team–contracting | Hold +/– Meeting with Losing Team–contracting |
| End of Day | ☐ Hold +/– Meeting ☐ Award Reinforcer (Type 3) ☐ Monitor Assignment Board (for individual students only) | | ☐ Award Reinforcer (Type 3) | | ☐ Hold +/– Meeting ☐ Award Reinforcer (Type 3) |

# Glossary

**Acknowledgments**  A modality behavior, such as making eye contact or nodding your head, to indicate that you are listening to what the student is saying and you are encouraging him or her to continue.

**Active Listening**  The process of mirroring back to a student his or her emotional feelings and the problem being expressed, to the extent that you can understand them.

**Adrenaline "Bleed"**  A state of hyper-alertness where the body is in a partial fight-or-flight state, continually producing adrenaline and causing constant tension.

**Adrenaline Dump**  An emotional state, triggered by some action, causing a fight-or-flight state with a huge rush of adrenaline into the blood stream, resulting in extremely high and sudden levels of tension or stress.

**Body Telegraphing**  Through nonverbal body actions *(kinesics),* you communicate to the observing students your disapproval, or that you "mean business."

**Broken Record**  The process by which, after a student fails to act on your request for a particular behavior, you repeat the command over and over in a controlled manner (as if a "broken record").

**Calming Phase**  After a violent act, the student feels guilty and remorseful, and you approach the child to reestablish friendly relations and dispel negative feelings.

**Camouflage**  You stop and whisper to several students about their work, but when you whisper to a misbehaving student, you deliver a limit-setting statement, thus disguising the confronting behavior from the other students.

**Camping Out from Behind**  A limit-setting technique through which you move behind the off-task student and place an elbow on the student's desk, putting up a wall that blocks out a second misbehaving student, all the while using limit-setting teacher behaviors.

**Camping Out in Front**  A limit-setting technique through which you place your palms on the misbehaving student's desk, indicating that you will stay until the student's behavior changes.

**Check It Out**  You periodically scan the classroom for off-task behavior while at the same time continue to work with students.

**Closing Space**  In limit setting, you escalate the confrontation by moving toward the student and "accepting" the student's challenge.

**Color Cueing**   A systematic method of marking instructional materials with colored marks so that the students can readily identify the object and its proper shelf or storage location.

**Comfort Bubble**   An invisible three-foot circle around the student, in which the student is secure and feels threatened if someone invades this space.

**Confronting**   You respond to misbehavior with a verbal instruction to the student to stop the action.

**Control of Error**   Arranging and putting together materials in a manner that minimizes the chances that students will break, spill, or have accidents while using them.

**Door Openers**   When a student is having difficulty expressing something that is troubling him or her, you use a question (as a "door opener") to invite the student to talk about his or her concerns.

**Escalation/Deescalation of Power**   The gradual movement up and down the TBC through the use of stronger or more demanding teacher behaviors (escalation of power) or a retreat back through this continuum with less intrusive behaviors (deescalation).

**Eye Contact**   You establish eye contact with a misbehaving student and maintain it unwaveringly until the student returns to work.

**"Faces" or Teacher Attitudes**   A metaphor for the concept that a teacher may act toward a misbehaving student in a number of conscious, predetermined ways, and that the teacher's attitude and methods can change (take on a new "face") to match circumstances.

**Fight or Flight**   A primal, unthinking reflex action either to dig in for a fight or to run away, all triggered by frightening or confrontational behavior.

**"Going Brain Stemmed"**   In a heated conflict, the brain downshifts to the reflexive, noncognitive reptilian brain. When this occurs, it suggests that you are out of control and are instead controlled by emotions.

**"Gone Chemical"**   During a confrontational limit-setting process, you become so emotional that adrenaline is heavily released into the body, making you so tense that you cannot think correctly.

**High-Profile Correction**   An intrusive process whereby the teacher stops his or her teaching to spotlight an off-task student, and in turn disrupts the ongoing activities and imposes guilt on the student, making all students feel reprimanded. High-profile correction is highly correlated with poor academic gains and ineffective classroom management (Kounin, 1970).

**I-Message**   A technique of expressing to a student that a behavior is having a negative effect on you. This statement must contain three elements: the student's *behavior,* its *effect* on you, and your *feeling* as a result of the behavior.

**Individualized Discipline Plan (IDP)**   A written plan, created at the end of a staffing process, that details the specific techniques to be utilized in dealing with a difficult student and that identifies those who will be responsible for carrying out the techniques.

**Life-Stance Position**   When a student (or adult) becomes so overwhelmed by a world of frustration and accompanying inner emotional turmoil, he or she may defensively take a passive or aggressive stance, 24 hours a day, toward life experiences and toward classmates and teachers.

**Low Roller**   A student who attempts to play power games with you in subtle ways that do not involve much risk of detection.

**Modeling**   The demonstration by you or a student of a behavior or group of behaviors that you wish a targeted student to imitate.

**Outside Aggressor**   Groups of students—out of fear, rivalry, or dislike—project their hate (their outside aggression) toward a fellow student or teacher who is not a member of the group.

**Private Conferencing**   A meeting, either planned as part of the backup system or spontaneous, held between the student and the teacher to work out either person's problem and how behavior might be changed accordingly.

**Promise of Safety**   When the student has been violent, you repeatedly tell him or her that you are not going to return that violence (hit) and that the child is safe with you.

**Pseudo-Compliance**   When you signal a student to get back to work, the student performs a series of behaviors designed to convince you that the student is complying when in reality he or she is not.

**Quick Vote**   A nonbinding process to gauge support for the list of proposed solutions in evaluating solutions. The solutions are ranked according to those the group likes (+), dislikes (−), or is not sure of (?).

**Restraining Techniques**   Nonviolent methods of holding students so they will not hurt themselves or others.

**Secretary**   One team member appointed by the difficult student's teacher, assigned responsibility for carrying out the writing duties during the staffing process.

**Severity Clause**   If the student's actions threaten to endanger himself or herself or destroy significant property, you are justified in escalating up the continuum to the most intrusive or demanding teacher behaviors of *Acting (Physical Intervention)*.

**"Smiley Face"**   A misbehaving student's attempt to be "innocent" and appeal to the confronting teacher by showing an open-mouth-and-teeth grin (typically the student's eyebrows lift in the middle and the head is cocked to one side).

**Square Off**   When confronting a misbehaving student, you place your feet parallel so they face the student.

**Staffing Agenda**   The established six-step process (stating the problem, generating solutions, evaluating solutions, deciding on a solution, implementing the solution, and reevaluating) that defines team members' roles, the purposes of each step, the amount of time to be used, and the actions needed to be accomplished.

**Supportive Stance**   When a student is about to be violent, you approach to calm him or her down. You face the student at a 45-degree angle and, without gesturing, attempt to communicate that you are not going to physically confront or assault the student.

**Teacher Behavior Continuum**   A systematic process that you may use daily to intervene with the kinds of misbehavior normally seen in most students in classroom settings. The TBC contains a group of five general teacher behaviors (*Looking, Naming, Questioning, Commanding,* and *Acting*) placed on a continuum, suggesting that actions may move from minimum teacher intrusion or power to maximum teacher control.

**Timekeeper**   A team member appointed by the difficult student's teacher, assigned responsibility for monitoring the time and keeping the staffing steps on task.

**Verbal Encoding**   Labeling the student's emotions and feelings, both positive and negative, through the use of your words.

**What-How Questions**   Questioning language that confronts the misbehaving student to reflect on his or her past misbehavior or to reflect on the rules, and to consider how he or she will change.

**With-it-ness**   Your ability to be perceptually aware of what is going on in the classroom.

**Working the Crowd**   While instructing, you walk around the room to make eye contact and be physically close to each student (proxemics) to retain control and compliance.

# Index